MOTION PICTURE PROBLEMS

The Cinema and the League of Nations

By

William Marston Seabury

Former General Counsel to the Motion Picture Board of Trade and the National Association of the Motion Picture Industry. Author of "The Public and the Motion Picture Industry."

The Avondale Press
INCORPORATED

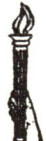

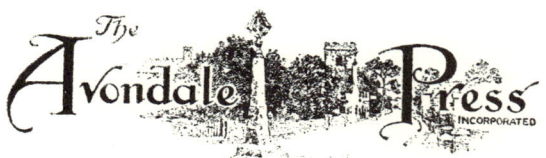

NEW YORK

COPYRIGHT 1929

By

THE
AVONDALE PRESS
INCORPORATED
NEW YORK CITY

---

*Printed in the United States of America
All Rights Reserved*

To

K. E. S.

Foreword

National and international film inspection, of the kind advocated in this work, supplemented with international cooperation of the character recommended, will achieve adequate industrial regulation. International cooperation of the kind described will result in a just reapportionment of the world's trade in this industry. Both inspection and cooperation in the manner outlined are essential to improvement in the educational, moral and cultural quality of motion pictures exhibited everywhere.

MOTION PICTURE PROBLEMS
The Cinema and the League of Nations

PREFACE

The problems presented by the motion picture have quite definitely attained a position of importance which requires that they be examined, solved and permanently treated by competent authority.

The problems primarily are those of the nations and of the people of the world.

They are broadly of two kinds, those which affect public welfare and those of an economic, industrial and commercial nature.

They are of grave governmental concern and they are not merely the problems of one nation. They are the problems of all, and involve international as well as national considerations.

Motion pictures are produced in comparatively few countries and the problems of these producing nations are more intricate than those of non-producing states, yet all nations constitute and are markets for the pictures of producing states, and the public of every nationality is reached through the almost unrestricted and unrestrained dissemination of motion pictures everywhere, and hence, there is a vast common ground and unity of interest in this subject.

All nations would be immeasurably benefited by participation in an international cinema alliance evidenced by a simple accord which should include, among its provisions, a joint request upon the League of Nations to create a cinema committee of the League, to supervise the execution of the proposed accord, to deal with the specific cinema problems committed to it and to treat such problems as are otherwise within the jurisdiction of the League of Nations.

Thus the international problems could be competently examined, solved and treated.

This work presents a discussion of this branch of the subject.

The vast field of national problems must be left for future treatment, but it may prove helpful to complete here, in outline at least, the analysis of the subject and to indicate that while there are marked, even fundamental, differences in national conceptions, in policies and in treatment of the subject, there are nevertheless uniform policies which are applicable to all nations similarly situated, and even methods, which are at fundamental variance with one another, will, when pursued effectively, produce similar or identical results.

In their present stage of development these national problems are governmental rather than industrial, because the cinema industries of the world, outside of America, are now so critically distressed that they are incapable even of self-preservation, under existing economic conditions, without the active and vigorous aid of their several governments.

This aid in the first instance must be legislative or executive in character and the objective must be, first, the protection of the public from undesirable pictures and, second, each branch of each nation's cinema trade must be rehabilitated and resuscitated as the necessities of each may require.

Two types of governmental action are available.

Some nations will choose a form of governmental regulation or control which, as a matter of degree, may place the whole subject in the hands of a single administrative officer with power to formulate appropriate rules for the conduct of one or more branches of the industry, as France has done, or the regulation may extend even to the monopolization or the ownership or operation of distribution, or of one or more of the other branches of the industry, by the State, and this governmental control, wherever it is exerted, will be justified and based upon the ground that the instrumentality in question is in reality a new public utility which ought to be subject to governmental control to the extent to which the conduct of the industry in each State makes that control necessary for the public welfare.

Other nations, such as the United States of America, Great Britain and her Dominions and Colonies, which, as a matter of policy, have heretofore preferred to indulge in as little governmental interference with trade as possible, even though a particular trade may involve, as in this instance, matters affecting public education, morals and culture, may achieve results which will contribute materially to the betterment of the industrial as well as the public welfare aspects of the subject, by the passage of laws which will effect a suppression of all unfair trade practices by means of which the existing monopolization of the world's trade in this industry has been accomplished and is now maintained.

Either method adopted and effectively pursued by a substantial group of nations acting collectively or even separately, will inevitably force or induce, by voluntary agreement with those who now control it, a reapportionment of the world's trade.

The reapportionment of the world's trade in this industry, by voluntary agreement, will prove far more beneficial to the nations and their respective cinema industries, and far less harmful to the industry in America, than the continued pursuit of the efforts to achieve the rehabilitation of the cinema industries of Great Britain, France, Germany and other cinema producing states, by means of nationalistic legislation or drastic executive national decrees.

Already Great Britain has legislated ineffectively on the subject.

Great Britain adopted the German quota system just as Germany abandoned it for more effective methods.

Germany and France both now point the way to a more complete nationalistic success.

Germany has limited the volume of pictures which may be imported into that country within a stated period of time and has vested a considerable degree of discretion in her cinema officials whose duty it is to regulate film imports into Germany.

France has also pursued this course and by executive decree of February 18, 1928, has prohibited the importation and the showing of any pictures in France except under rules and regulations adopted by the Ministry of Public Instruction and Fine Arts, and it has been declared that visas would be granted only after the Minister and an advisory committee of his appointment approved of all pictures offered for importation, not only as to matters of censorship, but also as to the extent to which opportunities for the reciprocal exhibition of French pictures are accorded to French producers in the countries from which the pictures offered for importation into France may come.

Thus the importation and showing of motion pictures in France is now under governmental and political control, and the motion picture is now recognized and treated as a public utility in the sense in which that term was used in the work entitled *The Public and the Motion Picture Industry*.

This French decree marks an epoch in international cinema history the importance of which, while at present little understood, cannot be over-estimated, particularly in its future effect upon the industry in America.

The course thus adopted by France will be followed inevitably by other nations to the extent to which it is applicable to each, at least until an adequate and just reapportionment of the world's trade in this industry has been effected thereby, or by the intelligent voluntary act of the industry in America.

There is an increasing need both from the American and the European standpoint for the cinema alliance of nations and for the creation of the cinema committee of the League of Nations proposed in this work.

—W. M. S.

TABLE OF CONTENTS

Preface

Motion picture problems are broadly of two kinds—those which primarily affect the public welfare from an educational, moral, artistic and cultural point of view, and those which primarily affect the trade, which involve economic, industrial and commercial considerations.

The problems are international, national and local.

This work deals chiefly with the international phases of the subject and is written to apprise the nations of the world of the necessities of the present situation and to induce the League of Nations to create a cinema committee or organization of the League to deal with all phases of the subject now within its jurisdiction and to treat such matters as may be specifically committed to it by the proposed International Cinema Alliance and Accord hereinafter discussed   Page 7

I
THE FACTS THAT COUNT

The facts that count are those which show that pictures produced in America, many of which are undesirable, unwholesome and unworthy of America, monopolize as much as 90 per cent of the screen time of the cinema theatres in many countries throughout the world, with consequences which are extremely serious to public welfare in America as well as elsewhere, and to the trade in all countries.   Page 19

II
THE PROBLEMS

The major problem is to induce the production and exhibition of wholesome and desirable pictures rather than those of an unwholesome and undesirable nature.

The means by which this objective may be attained present problems of great variety and of infinite difficulty. Page 25

III
PICTURES, PROPAGANDA AND PEACE

Propaganda pictures, with a predominating theme glorifying war and which incidentally hold up to ridicule and disparagement race, religion and nationalistic attributes, are produced and exhibited in increasing numbers.

Their inevitable effect is to stimulate racial and national dislikes which readily ripen into hatreds and ultimately lead to and encourage war, and since most of these and other undesirable pictures emanate from America they seriously impair American prestige abroad and stimulate world animosity and unfriendliness against America and everything American.

The first step in the organization of an effective world peace in support of the anti-war Treaties of August 27, 1928, will necessarily be the formulation of appropriate ways and means to induce all of the instrumentalities of public communication and influence to "scrap" the war mind and to think in terms of world peace, and the first of the instrumentalities of public communication and influence to be appropriately controlled and made amenable to a reasonable and universally beneficial use of its immense power to influence the masses of the world, is the motion picture. Page 43

IV
THE LEAGUE OF NATIONS AND THE INTERNATIONAL PROBLEMS

Several committees of the League of Nations have already considered certain phases of the motion picture problems.

The supposed violation of the Economic Convention of November 8, 1927, by France's cinema decree of February 18, 1928. The American protest at Geneva July 7, 1928.

Dr. Humbert's report to the Child Welfare Committee at Geneva in May, 1926.

M. Julien Luchaire's report of July 28, 1924, to the Committee on Intellectual Cooperation and the International Cinema Congress at Paris in 1926 under the auspices of the International Institute of Intellectual Cooperation. Page 131

V

HOW THE PROBLEMS MAY BE SOLVED

By an International Cinema Alliance and an Accord of the kind presently described, and by the creation of a special committee or organization of the League of Nations to deal with all cinema matters now within the League's jurisdiction and to treat such other matters as are expressly committed to it by the nations participating in the proposed Alliance and Accord. Page 167

VI

THE BROKEN REEDS, CENSORSHIP AND THE INDUSTRY

Censorship regulations throughout the world disclose a practical unanimity of thought and of agreement upon the kind of pictures which ought not to be shown publicly anywhere.

The nations should agree upon a few fundamental specifications of pictures the showing of which should be prohibited internationally by such agreement and nationally by appropriate executive or legislative enactment.

The difficulty is the intelligent and the effective application of the prescription, whatever it may be.

As a means of suppressing the exhibition of undesirable pictures, censorship, as now administered, and the industry are both broken reeds upon which to lean or rely.

Inspection, instead of censorship, applied at the source of production, by inspectors designated by the League of Nations, in behalf of all of the nations requesting such action, would achieve highly desirable results.   Page 183

VII
The Proposed International Cinema Alliance and the Proposed Accord

Several nations should enter into a Cinema Alliance evidenced by a brief Accord of the kind presently described, in which each participant should agree not to permit pictures of a specified kind to be shown within its borders and not to permit any pictures to be imported into such country until such pictures have been inspected, at the place of origin, by inspectors designated by the League of Nations in behalf of the participating nations.

Each such nation should request the League of Nations to create a Cinema Committee or organization to designate and supervise the work of the inspectors, to supervise the execution of the Accord, and for the other purposes presently described.   Page 191

VIII
The Proposed Cinema Committee of the League of Nations

Since the problems presented are of a mixed nature affecting public welfare and the trade, which cannot be separately considered or treated, it is desirable that the

MOTION PICTURE PROBLEMS

*This is a volume in the
Arno Press collection*

ASPECTS OF FILM

Advisory Editor
Garth S. Jowett

*See last pages of this volume
for a complete list of titles.*

MOTION PICTURE PROBLEMS

William Marston Seabury

ARNO PRESS
A New York Times Company
New York • 1978

Editorial Supervision: MARIA CASALE

Reprint Edition 1978 by Arno Press Inc.

Reprinted from a copy in The Princeton
University Library

ASPECTS OF FILM
ISBN for complete set: 0-405-11125-8
See last pages of this volume for titles.

Manufactured in the United States of America

Library of Congress Cataloging in Publication Data

Seabury, William Marston, 1878-1949.
   Motion picture problems.

   (Aspects of film)
   Reprint of the ed. published by the Avondale
Press, New York.
   Includes index.
   1. Moving-picture industry. 2. League of
Nations. I. Title. II. Series.
PN1994.A1S4   1978   791.43'09   77-11383
ISBN 0-405-11143-6

Cinema Committee be composed in part of members of existing committees whose interests are in part involved.

These include the Committee on Intellectual Cooperation and on Child Welfare, and the so-called technical organizations sometimes described as the Committees on Economics, on Transit and Communications, the Health Organization and the International Labor Office.

Page 205

IX

THE PROPOSED NATIONAL COMMITTEES

The national committees which should be created by the Cinema Committee or organization, at least in every cinema producing nation, should supervise the work of inspectors, at the source of production, of all pictures intended for importation into any of the countries which participate in the proposed Cinema Alliance and Accord, and should undertake such other work as may be committed to them by the proposed Cinema Committee or organization of the League.

The influence which the work and rulings of these inspectors and of the national committees would soon exert upon the quality of pictures from an educational, moral, artistic and cultural standpoint, even though the decisions of the inspectors would be advisory only, would soon prove to be incalculably great and a permanent benefit to mankind.

The pursuit of the program outlined in this work would also facilitate and induce a reapportionment of the world's trade in this industry which would result in a harmonious disposition of the international controversies which are inevitable until that reapportionment is made upon a basis which is just to all concerned. Page 223

APPENDIX

(1) M. Luchaire's report of July 28, 1924, to Committee on Intellectual Cooperation.   Page 235
(2) Dr. Humbert's Report to Child Welfare Committee, Geneva, May, 1926.   Page 265
(3) Resolutions of International Motion Picture Congress held under the auspices of the International Institute of Intellectual Cooperation, Paris, 1926.
   Page 357
(4) Censorship Regulations.   Page 383
(5) French Cinema Decree, February 18, 1928.
   Page 407
(6) Brief American Statistical Data.   Page 413

MOTION PICTURE PROBLEMS
The Cinema and the League of Nations

CHAPTER I

THE FACTS THAT COUNT

The facts that count in the following discussion are those which enable us to comprehend the cinema problems of each nation.

They are mainly ultimate facts which in many instances necessarily involve conclusions.

These conclusions, however, are supported by inferences many of which are irresistible and indisputable and consequently they present a sufficient basis to support the convictions to which they inevitably lead.

Motion pictures which are made in America monopolize the screens of the theatres of the world in many countries to the extent of 90 percent of their capacity,[1] Probably the most important single element which has induced this result is the ownership and control of the best theatres, known as first run theatres, in the chief countries of the world by those who also produce and distribute large quantities of pictures.[2]

This policy has been induced and made possible only by the exclusive character of the exhibition contracts entered into between the renters or distributors of motion pictures and the exhibitors or theatre owners.[3]

The ownership or control of motion picture theatres in

---
[1] *1927 Film Year Book*, 931-945.
[2] *The Public and the Motion Picture Industry*, 31-48.
[3] See pamphlet, *Cinema Legislation Proposed in England and America*, by William Marston Seabury.

large numbers in the most important cities of the world by a few producers and distributors of pictures resident in America, has placed in the hands of these producers a substantial part of the world market for motion pictures.

Motion picture theatres everywhere constitute and are the market of all producers and distributors of pictures.

Theoretically the screens of the theatres of the world should be open to free and fair competition among the producers of all nations, and competition should be based exclusively upon the merits of the pictures produced for exhibition in such theatres.

The effect of the purchase of the best theatres everywhere by these large producers and distributors is to monopolize the screen time of such theatres, to restrain trade in the industry and to lessen and restrict free and fair competition for the screen time of such theatres and such other theatres as are influenced by the exhibition of motion pictures in the best theatres throughout the world.

The vigorous pursuit of these policies and of others which harmonize with them, internationally, by a few of the largest producers and distributors of motion pictures in America has had the effect of unduly restricting cinema production everywhere except in America, and as a consequence, has enabled these producers to monopolize the screens of the world with pictures controlled by them. In America it has had the effect of placing the control of the industry in the hands of a very few men who dominate and control the three or four largest companies in America.[4]

[4] Mr. Terry Ramsaye, the well informed historian of the industry says: "The motion picture industry of the world in all practical con-

THE FACTS THAT COUNT

These companies headed by these few men constitute the major part of the so-called American industry.

The cinema has become the most influential medium of expression in the world and is in daily communication with countless millions of people of all degrees of intelligence. It is "a powerful medium for the diffusion of moral, social and even political ideas and modes of thought."[5] Its appeal is now primarily and deliberately emotional. It is addressed to the unintelligent masses,[6] the mentality of which is estimated by producers in America as that of a 14-year-old child.[7] The baser and not the higher emotions are played upon for profit. Its intellectual quality is negligible.[8] There are many who believe that the standards

---

siderations is to be found in the control of about four men: Adolph Zukor of Famous Players-Lasky; Marcus Loew of Metro-Goldwyn-Mayer; William Fox of Fox Pictures Corporation and allied companies, and Carl Laemmle of Universal Pictures Corporation." *The Annals of the American Academy of Political and Social Science*, November, 1926, p. 19.

[5] M. Julien Luchaire, honorary professor of the University of Grenoble, France, Inspector General of Public Education of France, and Director of the International Institute of Intellectual Cooperation of the League of Nations, in his *Report to Committee of the League of Nations on Intellectual Cooperation*, July 28, 1924. See Appendix.

[6] Mr. Terry Ramsaye, November, 1926, *The Annals of the American Academy of Political and Social Science*, p. 19.

[7] Arthur Edwin Krows, *ibid.* 72.

[8] Thus Mr. H. L. Mencken, the talented editor of the *American Mercury*, in the *New York World* of July 3, 1927, describes the substance of the motion picture scenarios of current American successes to be "precisely what the servant girls of my youth used to find in the *Fireside Companion*. In other words, what I found there was simply mawkish and maudlin bilge." The same writer describes the substance of such pictures as mere "garbage."

Mr. H. G. Wells recently expressed some appropriate generalities on the lack of intellectual qualities in motion pictures in his interesting condemnatory review of the Ufa picture "Metropolis" in the *New York Times Magazine* of April 17, 1927, in which he said in part: "After the worst traditions of the cinema world, man strongly self-satisfied and self-sufficient, convinced of the power of loud advertisement to put things over with his public, and with no fear of searching criticism in

exploited in the pictures of the day encourage the violation of every moral precept, induce a disregard of law and order and stimulate the commission of crime.[9] False and erroneous views of life are impressed upon the ignorant and youthful audiences of the world.[10] A tendency to exaggerate class distinctions, wealth and poverty, is undesirable and the influence of the pictures upon the races of the Far East and upon the illiterate people of the world is by many regarded as harmful and as a menace to the prestige of white civilization,[11] while pictures made in America con-

---

their minds, no consciousness of the thought of knowledge beyond their ken, set to work in their huge studios to produce furlong after furlong of this ignorant, old-fashioned balderdash and ruin the market for any better film along these lines."

[9] The Rev. Canon William Sheafe Chase, D.D., has frequently referred to the unregulated motion picture screen as the school of crime in every country of the world. (*New York Evening Sun*, April 21, 1926. See also *The Public and the Motion Picture Industry*, 157.)

[10] As Dr. Nicholas Murray Butler said: "Just to what degree educational and fictional pictures are affecting the manners and morals of the present generation of the world, it is not difficult to estimate. * * * The daily broadcasting of the passions and caprices and adventures of men and women in plays of the screen, interpreted by ill-equipped authors and directors cannot but be destructive of ideals that for centuries have proved to be wholesome and worthy of preservation." (*Motion Pictures Today*, October 16, 1926.)

[11] "There is one serious reason why everyone of us is interested in British films being shown abroad, and that is that British films should uphold to foreign nations a better conception of the moral conduct and social habits of people who profess to belong to the leading nations of the world than, unfortunately, is the case with so many films that are being exported, for instance, to China. Only a few months ago I happened to be wandering up and down a little village in one of the outposts of civilization and not only an outpost of civilization but an outpost of life. There I came across a cinema. I was in the company of a very noble and dignified member of the foreign race in whose land I was at the time and, when we passed that cinema, it was emblazoned with advertisements which ought to have brought the blush of shame to the cheek of the thickest-skinned and most corrupt and abandoned of men; and the actors in that film were white people. And yet certain markets seem almost to be abandoned to that kind of sinful and abominable rubbish, which is held up to these people who, a few years ago,

The Facts That Count

stantly misrepresent American and English ideals and culture.[12]

Indeed, the recent statement of a writer in the *Osservatore Romano*,[13] the official organ of the Vatican, even though subsequently repudiated as unofficial, is the view entertained by an ever increasing number of well-informed persons, in so far as the character of many pictures now made in America is concerned.

Even the incidental comments are all symptomatic of the general dislike encouraged by the distasteful pictures which emanate from America.

No other instrumentality and no other industry presents the problems which are thus forced upon the attention of every nation for consideration.

These facts, and those subsequently stated, are the ones that count.

---

regarded us as being a dominant and ruling people. That sort of rubbish is given to them every day of the week and every week of the year." (Mr. Ramsaye MacDonald speaking before the House of Commons in opposition to the proposed form of the British Cinematograph Film Bill, March 16, 1927. *Parliamentary Debates*, Vol. 203, No. 27—2049.)

[12] As the former Secretary of State of the United States of America, Charles Evans Hughes is reported to have said, "I wish indeed that the important educational instrument, the moving picture, was not so frequently used in foreign countries to give false impressions of American life. It is most discouraging to reflect upon the extent to which the best efforts of educators and the men of public affairs are thwarted by the subtle influences of a pernicious distortion among other people with respect to the way in which our people live and the prevalence here of vice and crime." *Film Daily*, October 15, 1923, and January 13, 1927. See also *The Public and the Motion Picture Industry*, 156-157.

[13] *New York Times*, July 22, 1927, quoted a writer in the *Osservatore Romano* as follows:

"America, which has brought the film industry to an extraordinary degree of perfection, now promises not only to amuse but also to instruct us with educational films. Let us be on our guard.

"America is a very great country which has been led to believe by the undoubted superiority of the dollar that it also possesses spiritual superiority.

"A certain American spirit, possessed of extraordinary practical qualities, considers force as a philosophy and the aphorism of Ford as criticisms of pure reasoning, and can perhaps adapt itself to the ultra-modern mentality, but we find it very defective.

"The Americans have constructed monstrous palaces of forty or fifty stories to scrape the skies. But when America was still unknown to us we constructed our cathedrals to raise ourselves to heaven.

"And this old Europe, whose soil is formed of the glorious dust of ten civilizations, cannot easily forsake its past to accept with eyes closed the improvised civilization from beyond the Atlantic.

"It is for this reason that we consider dangerous for our civilization the supremacy which the film producers of Hollywood are gaining over us. Consciously or unconsciously they are dosing us with a most lethal poison, which may lead to serious consequences. Let us be on our guard and free ourselves of the yoke which is most ably being placed on our necks.

"The movies can become a magnificent medium of education provided we can draw from our thousand-year-old civilization the elements necessary to keep the spiritual leadership which no dollar king will ever be able to learn.

"Let certain Americans keep their material leadership. We wish only to keep our spiritual leadership."

The *New York Times* of July 29, 1927, printed the repudiation reported to have been made by the Vatican which, however, said, "while it deplores all distribution and showing of immoral and frivolous motion pictures, it does not approve the writer's general criticism of the United States."

CHAPTER II

THE PROBLEMS

In stating the cinema problems of the nations, a difference must be recognized between those nations which have heretofore produced motion pictures upon a substantial scale and those which have not.

Moreover it must not be assumed that because the industry in America dominates the world in this field that America and its people, or even its industry, have no cinema problems which require solution.

As a nation, America suffers from serious misrepresentation in pictures at home and abroad. Many feel that pictures made in America promote hostility to America and her people. The stimulation of increasing dislike for Americans as a people cannot but prove harmful to America as a nation. The American public suffers from the same undesirable stream of motion pictures from which the people of the world are suffering, and these pictures produce the same unfortunate effects and consequences upon the public in America as they do upon the public elsewhere.

America's cinema trade problems are many. They are intricate and most serious.[1]

Fundamentally, however, the problem of each nation is threefold.

Its governmental aspect is quite distinct and separate from the problems of its public and of its trade.

---

[1] See *The Public and the Motion Picture Industry* (Macmillan).

Considerations of public welfare, which sometimes overlap or are overlapped by the governmental phases, are entirely distinct from the problems of the trade. The trade itself in turn is divided into three different branches which, unless unified in the same financial control, have quite divergent and often conflicting interests. These branches consist of producers who make the domestic pictures, of renters or distributors who may market pictures of domestic or of foreign origin, and the exhibitors who may exhibit either or both classes of such pictures.

In non-producing nations only two branches of the trade are present—the importers and renters, who are often treated as one, and the exhibitors.

Governments are awakening to a realization of the rapidly increasing importance of the cinema from a governmental standpoint.[2]

---

[2] On June 29, 1925, Mr. Stanley Baldwin, in a speech before the House of Commons, said:

"I think the time has come when the position of the film industry in this country should be examined, to see if it is not possible, as it is desirable on national grounds, that a large proportion of films exhibited in this country are British, having regard to the enormous power which the film has developed for propaganda purposes, and the danger to which we in this country and our Empire subject ourselves if we allow that method of propaganda to be in the hands of foreign countries."

The *New York Times*, July 30, 1925.

The Public and the Motion Picture Industry, 202.

See also *Parliamentary Debates*, March 16 and 22, 1927, on Cinematograph Films Bill:

"England and no less than ten countries of Europe within the last year have had under consideration and study various phases of the subject. These inquiries were prompted and induced by the ever-growing influence of the motion picture upon all people and by the fact that American pictures are absorbing all of the screen time of American theatres and as high as 90% of the screen time of the theatres of England, and of many other countries."

The Public and the Motion Picture Industry, xiii, ix.

The Problems

The effect of the cinema upon its nationals has come to be a matter of grave governmental concern.[3]

The power of the screen to influence the public is quite definitely recognized.[4]

The problem is to induce or, if necessary, to compel the production and exhibition of wholesome rather than unwholesome pictures.[5]

---

[3] *Ibid.*

[4] Secretary of Commerce Herbert Hoover at a recent Latin-American banquet said in part:
"The motion picture industry has a distinctive place in the upbuilding of this acquaintanceship. The motion picture is not solely a commercial venture; it is not solely an agency of amusement and recreation; it is not solely a means through which the world has gained a new and striking dramatic art; nor is it solely a real and effective means of popular education. Beyond all this it is a skilled and potent purveyor between nations of intellectual ideas and national ideals. But it can also transfer the worst within us as well as the best * * * herein there lies a heavy obligation upon this industry. * * * I trust in the good faith of this great body of men who dominate the industry in the United States to carry out this profound obligation; that is, that every picture of South American life shown to our people and every picture of North American life shown to the South American peoples should carry also those ideals which build for that respect and confidence which is the real guarantee of peace and progress.
Motion Pictures Today, April 9, 1927.

[5] The development of the cinematograph is one of the most important movements in the history of intellectual life during the last twenty years. In that short space of time the conditions which stimulated and nourished the imagination, feeling and thought of the masses in every country has been transformed by the new invention. * * * We cannot question, therefore, that the cinema is a powerful medium for the diffusion of moral, social and even political ideas or modes of thought. * * * The motives (of the films) may be the basest or the loftiest, and therein lies the most important problem of the cinema. Is it to have the high educational value and the elevating and ennobling influence which the theatre seems to have had on the masses in Ancient Greece? Or is it to have the debasing influence of vulgar music hall shows or cheap novels? Doubtless its influence will be in both directions for so vast and varied a class of production must inevitably contain some admixture with the good. No man can attempt to control the colossal cinematographic industry of our times any more than he could endeavor to control the vast activities of the printing press. Nevertheless, in the former as in the latter case, good influences acting

MOTION PICTURE PROBLEMS

The dissemination of alien ideas and conceptions of thought through motion pictures in every country, the tendency to create domestic discontent abroad by the constant depiction of American riches and extravagances of all kinds and the tendency to spread unrest by such pictures is necessarily a matter for governmental consideration.

The opportunity to express and to communicate national ideals is important internationally as well as nationally.

The propaganda aspects of the subject are of such importance, especially in relation to the cultivation and preservation of the world's peace, that they are discussed at length in the succeeding chapter.

So also the stimulating effect upon a nation's trade and commerce in general, induced through the dissemination of its motion pictures abroad is of substantial consequence and importance.[6]

The industry declares trade now "follows the film"[7] rather than the flag, as formerly.

---

in harmony, and the intervention of high authorities may be of some avail in increasing the proportion of good and diminishing that of evil."
M. Julien Luchaire's report of July 28, 1924, to Committee on Intellectual Cooperation of the League of Nations. See Appendix.

[6] " * * * there has been a complete change in the demand for commodities in dozens of countries. I can cite four instances of the expansion of trade in the Far East, traceable directly to the effects of the Motion Pictures." Dr. Julius Klein of the Department of Commerce of the United States. Quoted by Sir Phillip Cunliffe-Lister, *Parliamentary Debates*, March 16, 1927.

"From the trade point of view the influence of the cinema is no less important. It is the greatest advertising power in the world." Sir Phillip Cunliffe-Lister, *ibid.* See also *New York Times*, August 18, 1926.

[7] *The Story of the Film*, 38.

THE PROBLEMS

Governments are concerned in the maintenance and promotion of their international and national position and prestige which ought not to be endangered or impaired by the exhibition anywhere of undesirable pictures from any country.

The gravity of the prejudice to Great Britain's position and prestige, and indeed the harm done to the position of the whole white race through the widespread dissemination of thoroughly unwholesome pictures throughout the Far East, cannot be overestimated.

The Parliamentary Debates [8] on the British Films Bill are full of references to this subject and the press of England has long contained many protests against it.

The matter was brought to the attention of the International Cinema Congress at Paris and resulted in a resolution designed to encourage a correction of the harm which has unquestionably been done in the Far East by pictures of the kind described.

The able report of Dr. F. Humbert, submitted in May, 1926, at Geneva to the Child Welfare Committee of the League of Nations, is a sufficient demonstration of the duties and responsibilities of governments with respect to this phase of the subject.[9]

In part Dr. Humbert said:

"The most illuminating reply on the part played by the cinema in the life of children of today has been given us by the Polish Red Cross

---

[8] *Parliamentary Debates On Cinematograph Films Bill*, March 16, 1927, vol. 203, No. 27, 2038-2040.

[9] C. 264 M. 103, 1926, iv, page 122. See also World Drift by Edward Alsworth Ross, Chapter 10, "What the Films are Doing to Young America." See Appendix.

in an extremely full article by Dr. Bogdanowicz, which supplies the following statistics compiled from the replies of 1,056 boys and 418 girls at secondary schools and 824 children in the lower forms, to a questionnaire on the frequentation of the cinema and its effects. Of the secondary school children 96% of the boys and 89% of the girls go to the cinema. Of the pupils attending the supplementary courses—children of the working classes aged between 13 and 20 years,—80% of the boys and 56% of the girls go to the cinema. In the lower forms 51% of the boys and 39% of the girls go at least once a week to the cinema. An interesting question put to the boys and girls of the secondary schools was the order of their preference for the theatre, the circus, sports and the cinema. In all the forms the preference was in the order given.

"This confirms the fact that children are attracted more by the process of the cinema than by what it displays. Nevertheless, to many children who are very fond of the cinema the danger consists of its *power of persuasion* taken in conjunction with the weakening of the critical sense by the emotion of the moment.

"Dr. Boganowicz divides films into three categories: adventure films, modern dramas and comic films. The first category seems to be particularly appreciated by very young boys or by older or rather undeveloped children, who have a passion for criminal and detective stories, full of fighting, murders, etc., in which the imagination is stirred by scenes of torture, pursuit or struggles against armed force. Girls show a preference to more sentimental themes; for example: 'the lives of princes,' 'the lives of counts,' 'the furniture of drawing rooms,' 'the tragedy of the soul,' etc. All these films naturally exercise a bad influence.

"The inquiry undertaken by forty Australian teachers which is interesting in more than one respect, gives very valuable figures concerning regular visits to the cinema. One of the most careful inquiries shows that 54% of the children visit the cinema once a week and 46% less regularly. The preference of children for good instructive films is very marked.

"In all these replies no voice is raised against the cinema as a technical invention and as an educational medium. It cannot be abolished today, as it seems to give scope for the natural instinct of children towards visual observation of movement and as it can thus certainly help them to assimilate fresh knowledge. On the other hand,

The Problems

all are unanimous in condemning the ordinary sensational film which is infinitely below the level of popular taste. The latter, indeed, often condemns it, but, being forced to take what it finds, it is attracted by the cheapness of the amusement offered.

Summing up these judgments, we can say that the life of the child today is being invaded by the cinema and unfortunately by a cinema almost entirely unadapted to its needs. Numerous replies given by children show that their preference is not for the sensational films considered by certain producers to be the most remunerative. The films, which might interest and captivate children and the general public in so many different ways, has violently abused its power of pushing sensation to the extreme by visual representation, of pushing it to the point of exasperation through the medium of the picture and of thus giving rise to criminal suggestions even under the cloak of morality. It is for this reason that the censorship of pictures must be established on quite a different basis from the censorship of the Press.

"Dr. Gaupp of Tubingen, sufficiently stigmatizes the character of the majority of popular adventure films. He quotes the statistics of Konradt, who in 250 films successively viewed, found no less than 97 murders, 51 cases of adultery, 19 seductions, 22 abductions and 45 suicides. The principal protagonists of these films were classified as follows: 176 thieves, 25 prostitutes, 35 drunkards, etc.

"The part played by the cinema in the life of a child today should clearly not be to make him live for several hours a week in such surroundings. Its sole function should be, on the contrary, to assist him by visual methods to assimilate certain parts of his educational program. * * *

"More categorical still and at the same time more general is the report submitted to the Belgium Red Cross by M. Paul Wets, Judge of the Children's Court at Brussels. 'The children's judges of the country,' he says, 'are unanimously of the opinion that the harmful influence of the cinema on the Belgian youth is one of the principal causes of crime among children.' He asserts that the bad influence of the cinema on minors is proven by the character of the statements they make when questioned in court, which reflect details taken straight from the cinematographic films they have witnessed. M. Wets remarks that the criminal psychology of children is very different from that of adults. Children generally bring no element of passion into the offenses they commit, but act under the direct influence of the films they have seen and followed, as it were, mechanically the examples they have been set.

"The cinema is a wonderful instrument of education, but if the teaching is bad the result is easy to anticipate. * * *

"As regards the moral influence, numerous replies from the Australian Red Cross emphasise the demoralizing effects of the sensational film, the falseness of the impression given, the debasement of taste, the deterioration of style and of a taste for reading, the introduction into the child's mind of unhealthy associations and of emotions and situations which otherwise would never spontaneously enter his imagination."

It should also be the concern of each government to keep the channels of trade within its borders open and free to all, and sound methods and means of obtaining this desirable result should be the subject of careful consideration and study in order that harmful and ineffective methods intended to achieve this desirable purpose may be avoided.

The nationals of each country have a right to the preservation of their nation's market for pictures free from artificial and monopolistic restraints of any kind, to the end that as and when such nationals produce meritorious pictures their access to the screens of their own country may not be unfairly blocked or impeded.

Each nation is entitled to assurances from the other of an equality of opportunity in this field and a freedom from national conditions which makes fair competition, based upon merit in product alone, impossible or unequal.

Many nations intended long ago to give these assurances generally to one another.[10]

---

[10] The Paris Agreement of the International Union for Protection of Industrial Property, of March 20, 1883, with supplementary provisions and modifications, was signed at Washington on June 2, 1911, by Germany, Austria, Hungary, Belgium, United States of Brazil, Cuba, Denmark, Dominican Republic, Spain, Portugal, Serbia, Sweden, Switzer-

THE PROBLEMS

This equality of opportunity to which reference is made
land and Tunis. By Articles 2 and 10 of this Agreement nationals of these countries were guaranteed equal protection with reference to patents, trade marks and trade names, and the suppression of unfair competition, and all contracting countries agreed to assure to the members of the Union an effective protection against unfair competition. (See *Trust Laws and Unfair Competition*, 699).

See also the Industrial Property Convention as revised at The Hague Conference of November, 1925, and the memorandum of the International Economic Conference, Geneva, May, 1927, on the subject of Unfair Competition.

This memorandum quotes as the most comprehensive list of unfair practices that which appears in Chapter 6, pages 303 to 331 of *Trust Laws and Unfair Competition (supra)* which was issued by the Department of Commerce of the United States of America in 1915.

Many of the unfair practices described in this list are prevalent in the motion picture industry in America under different names:

They are identified parenthetically by the writer as follows:

Local price cutting; one commodity price cutting; price reductions in general (the trade practice described as block booking and circuit booking involves price reductions in general and discriminations in many instances which are unfair); use of trading stamps, coupons and the like; excessive credits; reduction in price for quantity (this also is involved in block booking and circuit booking); special advantages in transportation, rebates, etc.; fixing resale prices; bogus independents (this practice was formerly in use by the Famous Players-Lasky Corporation and was condemned by the Federal Trade Commission in its proceedings against that company); exclusive dealing requirements (the whole contractual structure of the dealings between the distributors and the exhibitors is based upon exclusive exhibition contracts of which system the first run theatre is the outgrowth. It is largely through the ownership, control and monopolization of these first run theatres surrounded as they have been with special protection clauses and other incidents of special privileges which has made the monopolization of the industry by a few companies which combine the function of production and distribution with that of exhibition possible and effective); full line forcing (this is block booking in the motion picture industry); inducing breach of contract (the following illustrations of this practice in the motion picture industry may be cited:—Vitagraph Co. of America v. Anita Stewart and Louis B. Mayer, 170 N. Y. Supp. 527; Triangle Film Corporation v. Artcraft Pictures, 250 Fed. 981, 982; Carmen v. Fox Film Corporation, 258 Fed. 708; same v. same, 269 Fed. 928, 255 Fed. 569; same v. same, 204 App. Div. 776); enticement of competitor's employes (see also the cases last cited); espionage by corruption and bribery; secret commissions; misrepresenting competitors; abuses in advertising (under this heading may be included the unfair trade practice of changing the titles of motion picture subjects, thus enabling producers and distributors to reissue old pictures under new names.

from time to time, is not dissimilar to the phrase "equality

The Federal Trade Commission condemned this practice in the following cases:—Fox Film Corporation v. Federal Trade Commission, 296 Fed. 353; Federal Trade Commission v. Eskay Harris Feature Film Co., 5 F. T. D. 219; for other cases see *The Public and the Motion Picture Industry*, page 308. The unfair trade practice known as picture substitutions, whereby a distributor advertises or otherwise identifies a picture by describing its title, subject matter, the author and the star, accept contracts for the rental of such pictures from the exhibitors and then substitutes an entirely different picture without the consent of the exhibitors, may also be considered under this heading); passing off goods for those of another; shutting off materials, supplies or machines from competitors (this includes combined refusals to deal with retailers and this result is involved in the activities of the trade association known as the Motion Picture Producers and Distributors of America, popularly known as the Hays Association, and its members. The members of this association include every national distributor in America and consequently comprise the sole regular supply or source of motion pictures available to the exhibitors throughout the country. With the aid of the Association each of these distributors has adopted a so-called uniform contract for use between the distributors and the exhibitors. All of the national distributors agreed among themselves that they will use no other contract. Consequently, unless the exhibitors accept this contract when it is offered to them they cannot obtain any pictures for regular and continuous exhibition in their theatres. The distributors have inserted in this contract a so-called additional security clause which enables them to demand "additional security" from any exhibitor at any time for the faithful performance of his contract, and a so-called arbitration clause of the particular kind therein described. Thus arbitration of the kind described by the distributors is made compulsory upon every exhibitor in the United States of America. The arbitration machinery erected under this contract consists of 32 so-called Arbitration Boards which function in conjunction with 32 so-called Film Boards of Trade in as many different localities throughout the United States, all of which are supervised and directed by the Producers and Distributors Association. In the last analysis the demands of the producers and the distributors and the decrees of the so-called arbitrators are enforced by the refusal of each and all of the members of the Producers and Distributors Association to deal with or to supply pictures to any exhibitor found by any Arbitration Board to be delinquent with respect to such controversies as come before them for decision. Thus these decrees are enforced by what in effect is a boycott or a combined refusal to deal with an exhibitor alleged to be delinquent, and the list of such exhibitors necessarily becomes and is a blacklist. The ineffectiveness of the Federal Trade Commission and of the Department of Justice in dealing with this system is the subject of a resolution introduced by Senator Walsh of Montana in the Senate of the United States on May 3d, 1928, which is as follows:

The Problems

of trade conditions" used by President Wilson in the third

"RESOLVED, That the Senate direct the Committee on the Judiciary to inquire what proceedings are now pending before the courts upon the initiation of the Department of Justice or otherwise, or before the Federal Trade Commission, involving the acts or practices of the Film Boards of Trade; what investigations have been prosecuted leading to such proceedings and the amount expended in the same; what complaints have been made, concerning such acts or practices, with what diligence and fidelity such complaints have been investigated, and proceedings to restrain or punish any unlawful or apparently unlawful acts or practices of the said Film Boards of Trade and the Famous Players Lasky Corporation, or the officers, agents or servants thereof, have been instituted or prosecuted."

The illegal character of the present structure of the industry and of the unfair practices and policies pursued by it, are set forth at length in the petition of W. W. Hodkinson filed with the Federal Trade Commission on or about October 8th, 1927.

They also apear, in part, in the present conspiracy cases recently instituted by the Department of Justice, all of which charge conspiracies to violate the anti-trust laws of the United States of America.

[1] United States vs. Metro-Goldwyn-Mayer Distributing Corporation, et al., filed in the District Court of the United States for the Northern District of Illinois, Eastern Division, at the March, 1928, Term.

[2] United States vs. Paramount Famous Lasky Corporation, et al., filed in the District Court of the United States for the Southern District of New York, in Equity, on or about May 4, 1928.

[3] United States vs. First National Pictures, Inc., et al., filed at the same time and place.

[4] United States vs. West Coast Theatres, Inc., et al., filed in the District Court of the United States for the Southern District of California on or about September 8, 1928); acquiring stock in competing companies for purposes of reducing or destroying competition (this practice, although plainly violative of Section 7 of the Clayton Act, has been vigorously pursued by many of the major motion picture companies, particularly in the acquisition of their circuits of theatres by which they successfully monopolize and restrain interstate and foreign trade, all without let or hindrance from the Federal governmental agencies which are supposed to prevent such abuses and violations of the law); wrongful and malicious suits; intimidation (the record of the proceedings of the Federal Trade Commission v. Famous Players Lasky Corporation and others, consisting of upwards of 17,000 pages of testimony, is replete with instances of intimidation directed against small theatre owners whose theatres the respondents sought to acquire. See also Peekskill Theatre, Inc., v. Advance Theatrical Company, 206 App. Div. 148); fixing channels of trade (the elaborate system of marketing motion pictures now in vogue in America has

of his celebrated Fourteen Points,[11] although it is more comprehensive.

This, it is said, meant "not that an era of international free trade should be inaugurated, but," as President Wilson explained later, "that whatever tariff any nation might deem necessary for its own economic service, be that tariff high or low, it should apply equally to all foreign nations; in other words, that there should be no discriminations against some nations that did not apply to others." [12]

---

successfully fixed the channels of trade against all competitors to such an efficient extent that today not a single motion picture can profitably be marketed on a national scale without the consent of one of the very few national distributors of consequence which now control this industry, not only in America but elsewhere throughout the world. The major means by which this result is accomplished include the use of the uniform exclusive exhibition contracts of the kind and in the manner already described, the first run theatre and its incidents, particularly their ownership and control by the few national distributors and their friendly theatre-owning associates and the producers' and distributors' trade association and its incidental machinery, particularly the so-called Film Boards of Trade and the so-called Arbitration Boards. This system enables the important members of the Producers and Distributors Association to control completely the market for motion pictures in America, and this control results in the inevitable exclusion of all foreign competitors who are unable to contract with one of the members of this association for the distribution of foreign pictures throughout America. This makes the approach to the market in America dependent wholly upon the consent of one of the companies now in control of that market and this situation presents the most vicious type of private monopolization and restraint upon domestic and international trade which has ever been known, in any industry, anywhere.

[11] "The removal, so far as possible, of all economic barriers and the establishment of an equality of trade conditions among all the nations consenting to the peace and associating themselves for its maintenance."

[12] *The International Economic Conference*, by Allyn A. Young and H. Van V. Fay 1, citing President Wilson's letter to Senator Simmons. *Commercial and Financial Chronicle*, vol. cvii, page 1703 (November 2, 1918).

M. D. Serruys, the able French member of the Economic Committee of the League of Nations and of the Preparatory Committee for the International Economic Conference, in a memorandum submitted at Geneva in May, 1927, entitled "Treaties—Tariff Systems and Contractual

The Problems

Obviously, any discrimination which results from the existence of a private monopoly of an industry within any country is equally offensive and intolerable and contrary to the plain spirit of the Paris agreement and to that part of the third of President Wilson's Fourteen Points in which he uses the phrase "equality of trade conditions."

Methods" (C. E. 1.131), declared that the means of bargaining which governments seek to obtain by their tariff systems are selected with regard to the objects which they have in view when concluding commercial conventions, and that the oldest and most general of these motives is the desire to obtain equal trade conditions described in the third of President Wilson's Fourteen Points as one of the necessary guaranties of economic peace.

The phrase "equality of opportunity" is retained, notwithstanding its amusing condemnation, by Mr. George Bernard Shaw in the *Intelligent Woman's Guide to Socialism and Capitalism* (Brentano), pages 93 and 94.

"But, after all, said Mr. Shaw, "you are an Intelligent Woman, and know this as well as I do (i. e., that on the whole Conservatives, Liberals, Socialists, Protestants, Catholics, Dissenters and other groups lumped by Carlisle, as mostly fools, deserve this classification). What you may be a little less prepared for is that there are a great many people who call themselves Socialists who do not clearly and thoroughly know what Socialism is, and would be shocked and terrified if you told them that you were in favor of dividing up the income of the country equally between everybody, making no distinction between lords and laborers, babies in arms and abled body adults. They would assure you that all this is a mere ignorant delusion of the man in the street and that no educated Socialist believes such crazy nonsense. What they want, they will tell you, is equality of opportunity, by which I suppose they mean that Capitalism will not matter if everyone has an equal opportunity of becoming a Capitalist, though how that equality of opportunity can be established without equality of income they cannot explain. Equality of opportunity is impossible. Give your son a fountain pen and a ream of paper, and tell him that he now has an equal opportunity with me of writing plays, and see what he will say to you. Do not let yourself be deceived by such phrases, or protestations that you need not fear Socialism because it does not really mean Socialism. It does; and Socialism means equality of income and nothing else. The other things are only its conditions or its consequences."

Thus, according to Mr. Shaw, incomes but not opportunity may be equalized.

Of course ability and other purely personal or individual attributes cannot be equalized and no one supposes that they can be. But business

Motion Picture Problems

Finally, revenue also becomes an important elemental phase of this subject under which naturally falls tariffs, taxes based on admission prices at the theatres, taxes upon the gross receipts of distributors or renters, reel taxes and other sources of income.

Those interested in public welfare are particularly concerned in obtaining pictures which are better in a moral, educational, cultural and ethical sense.

Any means which will achieve this desirable result will find unanimous support from those interested in this phase of the subject.

The chief reliance to attain this object has thus far been placed in censorship, but the conviction is dawning upon enlightened publicists in America that legal censorship is futile and ineffective.

---

opportunity and trade conditions can be equalized by legislative or executive prescription and by the prohibition and suppression of the unfair practices by which the unethical and unscrupulous take advantage of their more conscientious or less intelligent competitors.

Our constitutional phrase that all men are born free and equal has been the frequent butt of cynics and self-conscious sophisticates who delight to point to its absurdities. Yet our courts have had no difficulty in placing an intelligent and effective interpretation upon it which indicates that it still serves a useful function in the preservation and protection of the rights of all.

The irony of attempting to equalize the opportunity of a boy to write plays in competition with Mr. Shaw by presenting the boy with a fountain pen and a ream of paper is amusing but not convincing, since Mr. Shaw's success is dependent upon something more than possession of pen and paper; but if Mr. Shaw were a motion picture producer and the boy in question also produced pictures and, incidentally, owned in conjunction with other playmates, exclusive of Mr. Shaw, the best theatres of the world in which the amateurish pictures of this boy and his playmates were daily exhibited while none of Mr. Shaw's brilliant pictures could find a market, however scintillating and meritorious they might be, then the effort to apply the phrase equality of opportunity to the unfair and uneconomic practice of the ownership or control of large numbers of cinema theatres by cinema producers would be more appreciated by Mr. Shaw.

The Problems

The conviction is also dawning in the minds of these publicists that the supposed effort of the industry in America to correct the conditions of which the public justly complain is equally futile and is and has been a mere pretense and a sham.

Publicists are today searching where their efforts will be rewarded, in the economic, industrial and commercial fields, from which alone can come the changes which they justly demand, in the form of pictures which are better in the respects stated.

The trade itself has no adequate conception of social or of public service or responsibility. It is still purely commercial.

It has been and is engaged primarily in the intensive pursuit of money. It is not interested in an effort to make pictures which, while affording a maximum amount of wholesome entertainment, will at the same time supply the greatest public service. The fact that wholesome pictures are profitable is disregarded as of no consequence because unwholesome pictures are believed to be more profitable.

True, the existence in the trade of the highest conceptions of public service has been asserted and preached by the representatives of the trade in America.

Incalculable quantities of publicity have been disseminated through these channels in an effort to convince the public that the picture millennium has arrived, that the few who control this tremendously important instrumentality are aware of their responsibility and are discharging it magnificently, and that the producers and their agents are obsessed with their devotion to the single purpose of making pictures which are better in the sense already described.

Unfortunately the publicity is mere industrial propaganda.

Some years ago a representative of the producers frankly stated that the producers can make better pictures.[13]

For years thereafter the producers, through their agents in America, informed the public that better pictures were then being produced and would thereafter continue to be made.[14]

The trade and a few intelligent publicists have for some years known better and writers for the trade have recently admitted, with unusual candor and frankness, that the producers have no idea of making pictures which are better in the sense described for a generation or more for no sounder reason than the belief that better pictures under present ineffective distribution methods do not pay.[15]

Each country's national and international prestige, its

---

[13] Thus Mr. H. D. H. Connick, then an officer of the Famous Players Lasky Corporation in a speech before the Governor of the State of New York in April, 1921, referring to the four or five men who still control the industry, said in part: "These four or five men together can absolutely insure the quality of their pictures to any standard that might be agreed upon." *The Public and the Motion Picture Industry*, 149.

[14] *Ibid*, 152-158.

[15] November, 1926 *Annals of the American Academy of Political and Social Sciences*, 19; Mr. Terry Ramsaye and 72-73 Mr. Arthur Edwin Krows. Mr. Benjamin De Casseres (*Motion Pictures Today*, September 3, 1927) declares in substance that he worked with the motion picture scenarioists in America for some years "dumbing up big ideas for the papoose brain. We giggled and gurgled over our creative idiocies. We were in the great conspiracy to keep the squareheads square."

See also the *Educational Screen Magazine*, May, 1927, 215, *et. seq.*

THE PROBLEMS

national, economic and commercial advancement, its right to utilize its screens for the dissemination of worthy ideals, its moral obligation not to use, or to permit them to be used, to incite national hatreds which foment war and conflicts, not to use them in the ridicule or disparagement of any religion or to incite racial or national prejudices; in other words, not to make or permit any use of this immensely powerful instrument, contrary to good morals, or against the peace of the world, are all part of the cinema problem of each nation, and of all nations.

These matters necessarily involve a critical study of the commercial and economic structure upon which the industry, in each of the chief picture-making countries of the world, rests. They require a similar examination in countries which are still merely markets for motion pictures.

The problem of each nation presents substantial differences from that of any other, but the nations have large international as well as national interests in common and it is therefore necessary to set up the international facilities, supplemented by appropriate national means, competent to make an authoritative survey of the trade and other conditions attributed to motion pictures throughout the world and thereafter appropriately to deal with the subject.

While it is desirable to preserve the initiative of private enterprise, nevertheless the national and international interests at stake are such that the industry can no longer with safety to any country be permitted to continue to pursue its present ill-considered course and to disseminate, uncontrolled, as it has in the past, its undesirable pictures throughout the world.

The necessity for a sufficient governmental and international check and for an agreement among the nations concerning a common international purpose and determination to attain the results described, has now become clear and apparent.

CHAPTER III

PICTURE PROPAGANDA AND PEACE

Propaganda pictures are being produced in increasing numbers, and effective ways and means must be found to deal with them not only on a national scale but to prevent their harmful exhibition internationally.

This latter problem is one of great difficulty.

Consideration of motion pictures as an instrument of propaganda requires the examination of an extensive field of which the motion picture itself is only a fractional part.

The remainder of the field includes every channel or medium of communication with and influence upon the public mind.

Specifically these instrumentalities include the press, the periodical and the book, the church pulpit and lecture platform, the school, college and university, the stage, the radio, the use and application of sound in motion pictures, and the most modern of all, television motion picture and radio combined for presentation in the home.

Yet, notwithstanding the treatment of motion pictures as one of the group of propaganda instrumentalities, the motion picture has attributes not possessed by the others which requires that it be specially considered and treated in a class by itself, although to ascertain the appropriate prescription for the use of propaganda pictures the whole field must be kept in mind.

Motion pictures, unlike the stage, the church, the platform, the school and university, are based upon an industry which involves economic and commercial problems and principles of national and international trade.

Its commercial problems are far more intricate than those which the distribution and circulation of the press, the periodical and books involves. And the approach to the mind and the effect made upon it by pictorial presentation surrounded by the usual incidents of theatrical display and exhibition, creates a far more vivid and lasting impression than that made by any of the other media in question.

This extraordinary instrumentality is aimed directly at the public mind and at its emotional senses.

Its primary objective at present is to amuse and to entertain, but this result is achieved through appeals chiefly to the emotional senses.

The problem of inducing the production and exhibition of pictures which possess a larger informative content than those which are now prevalent, is one of immense difficulty largely because the subject matter is one of constant variation addressed to an ever changing audience and designed to reach the largest numbers, which encourages the production of pictures which appeal primarily to elemental emotions common to all, rather than to the production and exhibition of the pictures of greater informative substance or even of an intellectual quality.

(1) *Discussion of What Propaganda Is*

Before approaching a discussion of the propaganda pictures themselves, it is desirable to have a clear comprehension of just what propaganda is. Mr. Peter Chalmers Mitchell, C.B.E., F.R.S., D.S.C., LL.D., a member of the editorial staff of the London *Times*, who was attached to the Directorate of Military Intelligence in the British War Office during the war, wrote a brilliant discussion of the subject for the Encyclopedia Britannica.[1]

He tells us that propaganda is a term applied to a concerted scheme for the promotion of a doctrine or practice; more generally the effort to influence opinion by a false analogy from such plural words as "memoranda" frequently applied to the means by which a propaganda is conducted.

The objective of a propaganda, we learn, is to promote the interests of those who contrive it rather than to benefit those to whom it is addressed; in advertisement, to sell an article; in publicity, to state a case; in politics, to forward a policy; in war, to bring victory.

This differentiates propaganda, it is said, from the diffusion of useful knowledge; the evangel of a mission; the publication of the cure of a disease.

In such objectives, says Mr. Mitchell, there may be a secondary advantage to the contriver, but to convince the subjects of the effort is the leading motive. Similarly, those engaged in propaganda may genuinely believe that success will be an advantage to those whom they address, but the stimulus to their action is their own cause.

The differentia of propaganda, it is said, is that it is self-seeking, whether the object be worthy or unworthy intrinsically in the minds of its promoters.

---
[1] Vol. XXXII, 176, *et seq.* See also The Meaning of a Liberal Education by Everett Dean Martin, 45 to 67.

Indifference to truth is declared to be a characteristic of propaganda and truth is said to be valuable only so far as it is effective.

In every effort to control opinion there are said to be persons, either indifferent to justification or who justify the means to the end.

"But," continues Mr. Mitchell, "the more the emotions are excited, whether by patriotism or by cupidity, by pride or by pity, the more the critical faculties are inhibited. It is a quality of propaganda, as of counter-propaganda, that high-minded persons on both sides commend their cause by identical arguments, and that they soon come to believe what they wish to be true. * * * The suspicions aroused by an admitted propaganda lessen its effectiveness, from which it follows that much of the work has to be furtive."

It is said that in the atmosphere of war, truth, like many other fine qualities of humanity, is judged by expediency with varying success.

(2) *Supposed Necessity or Justification for False Wartime Propaganda.*

Bismarck's cunning "doctoring" of the famous Ems dispatch is a powerful illustration of the effectiveness of well directed false propaganda, as a means of precipitating war.

It has been well said,[2] referring to the Franco-Prussian War:

---
[2] *Europe in the 19th Century* by A. J. Grant, M. A., Professor of History in the University of Leeds, and Harold Temperley, Litt D., Reader in Modern History at the University of Cambridge (Longmans, Green & Co.), page 341, see also Memoirs by Lord Redesdale Vol. II 529, 532.

"The war was brought about not by what happened at Ems but by the false report of what had happened. There was no effort to discover whether the report was false or true. The statesmen of France—even the pacific Ollivier—treated a question which involved the lives of millions in the temper of duellists. France had been insulted; she had received a box on the ear (un soufflet sur la joue) and honor demanded immediate war. On the 15th the assembly supported this decision. Hardly a voice was raised on the other side, though Thiers demanded further information as to the exact proceedings at Ems. Ollivier saw his deeply cherished hopes of peace disappear; but he accepted war, he said, 'with a light heart' because his conscience was clear.

"There were, of course, greater and deeper causes of war than Bismarck's 'doctoring' of the Ems telegram; but it was the communication prepared by Bismarck for the press at the Berlin dinner table which actually set alight the flames of the great war which led up to the vastly greater war of 1914. A little delay to allow nerves to grow steady and passions to cool, the possibility of reference to an external judgment which might have appeased the sense of honor, the application of some part of the ideas which have led to the formation of the League of Nations, might have prevented the war, at any rate in the shape in which it came."

The slogan "win the war at any price" has swept many from their moral moorings.

Those who have written on the subject of propaganda seem to concede the necessity for the use of false propaganda in time of war.

Lecky declares[3] that—

"A large and difficult field of moral compromise is opened out in the case of war, which necessarily involves a complete suspension of great portions of the moral law. * * * Destruction is one of the chief ends. Deception is one of its chief means, and one of the great arts of skilful generalship is to deceive in order to destroy.

"Whatever other elements may mingle with and dignify war, this at least is never absent; and however reluctantly men may enter into war, however conscientiously they may endeavor to avoid it, they

---

[3] *The Map of Life*, by William Edward Hartpole Lecky, 92.

must know that when the scene of carnage has once opened these things must be not only accepted and condoned but stimulated, encouraged and applauded."

Mr. Norman Angell[4] asks the pertinent question whether it was and is necessary to promote and engender hate quite so successfully as it was promoted during the World War, and he points out significantly the impossibility of the achievement of practical peace terms with any enemy against whom the hatred of the world had been directed for many years.

It is believed that not only do the ends to be attained by false wartime propaganda fail to justify the means to which a nation is obliged to descend in its use, but that the after and lasting effect of such a policy and practice seriously jeopardizes public confidence in information from government sources, retards the resumption of normal relationships essential to continued peace of the world and hence that its use is unjustifiable.

Some 400 years before the Christian era began we were told that "It is better not to live at all than to live disgraced," that "A lie never lives to be old," and again, "Do nothing secretly, for time sees and hears all things and discloses all."[5]

This philosophy of the tragic poet seems preferable to that which countenances the use of false propaganda and demonstrates besides the ultimate futility of its use.

---

[4] *The Public Mind, Its Disorders; Its Exploitation.*
[5] Sophocles.

(3) *Concealed or False Propaganda In Peace Time for Mercenary Purposes Is Inexcusable.*

But, however doubtful the wisdom of refraining from the use of false wartime propaganda may be regarded by some, all should unhesitatingly agree that the wilful falsification of facts in times of peace, for the mere mercenary advancement of those who circulate them, ought to be suppressed if appropriate means can be found by which to suppress them, which will not prove to be worse and more harmful than the disease of false propaganda itself.

(4) *The Informed Have No Illusions Concerning the Inferior Mentality and Morality of the Public.*

The informed students of mass psychology have no illusions concerning the mental and moral inferiority of the public or of its susceptibility to influence by all propaganda however partisan it may be.

A discouraging and depressing picture is painted by all who have described it.

M. Gustav Le Bon, who made a scientific and critical analysis of the subject, declares that crowds display a singularly inferior mentality.[6]

Mr. Benjamin de Casseres, a brilliant writer, who for some time past, according to his own statement, has been engaged in debasing literary material to the supposed level of the public's capacity to enjoy it, declares,

"The American picture mind is a tabloid mind. * * * It is only

---

[6] *The Crowd, A Study of the Public Mind* (London, T. Fisher Unwin) first translated, 1896.

concerned with crime, sex and money played down to its crudest and most elemental form." [7]

Mr. George Bernard Shaw applies the phrase "artificial happiness"[8] to the effect which the use of alcohol and drugs exerts upon the public. He shows the unreasoning attitude of the public towards its own debasement and makes some interesting comments on the subject.

Motion pictures have long been a form of artificial happiness. Mr. de Casseres uses them "as sleeping powders" to "reduce mentality."

Mr. Norman Angell, in a very searching discussion of the public mentality[9] declares that the errors of public opinion are far more damaging than they used to be, both because they affect governments more decisively and because society has become more vulnerable as it has become more complex.

It is increasingly important, he declares, to understand the nature of the public mind; the disorders to which it is subject, the way in which political and journalistic demagogy affect it, and the educational or moral deficiencies which need to be corrected.

He shows the amazing susceptibility of the masses to emotional appeal, their preference for triviality when confronted with serious problems the decisions of which, by them, mean peace or war or life or death.

He shows the tremendous influence of propaganda upon

---

[7] *Motion Pictures Today*, September 3, 1927.
[8] *The Intelligent Woman's Guide to Socialism and Capitalism*, 395.
[9] *The Public Mind—Its Disorders, Its Exploitation* (E. P. Dutton & Co., New York).

the public and confirms in substance the well expressed statement of M. Le Bon in which the latter declares:

"How slight is the action upon them (the masses) of laws and institutions, how powerless they are to hold any opinions other *than those which are imposed upon them*, and that it is not with rules based on theories of pure equity that they are to be led, but by seeking what produces an impression on them, and what seduces them."

According to Mr. Angell, all classes of the community are equally susceptible to propaganda and emotional appeal.

Educators and the clergy are declared to be no wiser and no more immune from these subconscious influences than the politician or the merest moron.

He deals interestingly with the so-called demagogy of the press and says:

"It is nothing new in our society for a large economic interest to become linked to the maintenance and encouragement of some common human weakness. The position of the liquor traffic at certain times would occur to one as a typical case. There has grown up in recent years another great economic interest (by its very nature in a position to exercise enormous influence in a much more direct fashion than the liquor trade could) which is pushed, as an indispensable condition of sure and rapid profit-making, *to maintain and develop certain passions and weaknesses socially very much more destructive than the taste for strong drink.* At no time did we ever see alcohol take such possession of whole nations and groups of nations for years together, that governments and people alike indulged in orgies of self-destruction and drank themselves back to barbarism."

"I suggest," continues Mr. Angell, "not that the press is the cause of that lack of balance in public judgment which has so often in the recent past made democracy unworkable (for the cause must include deeply rooted anti-social instincts of human nature), *but that a certain section of the press is pushed, as a first condition of its existence, to intensify the human weaknesses which lie at the root of most public folly;* to render them more unmanageable, to become the exploiter and developer of immensely dangerous, disruptive forces. This does not, of course, apply to the press as a whole—'the Press' must include an infinite variety of publications. But it does apply generally to that section which is organized into great industrial combinations involving capital running into millions, and which must, consequently, in order to pay dividends, maintain enormous circulations at all costs and so take the shortest of all possible cuts to exciting the interest of all and sundry—factory girls, school boys, teashop waitresses—in such public questions as may happen to come up. * * * Minds are unbalanced because one part of the facts has been obscured by another part. Yet the popular paper must, at the cost of sacrificing its circulation, still further upset the balance. * * * A paper which during the war refrained from printing dubious German atrocity stories could not hope to do as well as one which appeared with alluring tales of German corpse factories. Thus in the competitive process, a vicious circle is established.

"Public taste calls for corpse factory stories from this ingenious editor! These, inflaming the temper of the public, render that public less able to hear patiently or to give any consideration to facts which might offset in their minds the effects of the atrocities. The editor finds himself obliged to be aggressively one-sided. It is not, be it noted, a matter of expressing editorial opinions, but of selecting the news which the readers shall know."

(5) *The Excuse of "Giving the Public What It Wants."*

Mr. Angell attempts to palliate the offense of the sensational press in "giving the public what it wants" by attributing its failure to pursue a better course to the competitive struggle for existence, and points out that if the whole press does not pander to the lowest elements of human character, that portion of the press that does pursue that course transacts all the business.[10]

But that is, of course, no adequate excuse or justification, and happily we have some notable exceptions.

---

[10] *The Public Mind*, pages 123-127.

What a monstrous absurdity that permits the sensational press, particularly in its tabloid manifestations, or the motion picture industry, deliberately to cultivate the deterioration of the public taste and morals solely because it is profitable to these agencies to do so.

The real answer is that governments should be sufficiently concerned in their public's welfare, at least to declare that whatever contributes to the injury of the public shall be illegal, and leave the question of guilt or innocence in specific instances to the established channels for determination.

Thus the competitive situation would be equalized and the pressure to outstrip others in any of these trades by this type of sensationalism would, at least to some extent, be modified and perhaps removed.

(6) *Since Every Picture Contains Intentional or Unintentional Propaganda, Pictures Must Be Treated as Far More Than a Mere Amusement or Industry.*

In discussing the subject of propaganda in its relation to motion pictures this instrumentality must be recognized and treated as far more than a mere amusement.

Even in the process of supplying popular amusement and entertainment, motion pictures inform or misinform the public mind and so, inevitably, contribute something either toward the public improvement or toward the deterioration of its taste, culture, education and morality.

Hence, pictures which contain unintentional propaganda must not be overlooked in the discussion which follows.

MOTION PICTURE PROBLEMS

One does not expect to find what many regard as anti-American propaganda in pictures which emanate from America.

Yet that is exactly the poison, to us in America, which many of our films quite unintentionally contain.

The pictures which portray and display Americans at their worst, as a rich, extravagant, vulgar, lawless and even as a criminal people, boastful of our economic, financial and industrial achievement, "telling the world" about them and ourselves and "selling America to the world," indisputably do us incalculable harm and injury both here and abroad.

Mr. Sidney R. Kent, the able general manager of Paramount Famous Lasky Corporation, supplied convincing testimony on the subject in his interesting address before the Harvard Graduate School of Business Administration.

Mr. Kent declared:[11]

"American motion pictures at the present time (1927) are meeting with a great deal of opposition in foreign countries because they carry something that no other merchandise in the world carries. Motion pictures are silent propaganda, even though not made with that thought in mind at all. You cannot prevent it. Imagine the effect on people in the Balkan States who constantly see flashed on the screen, American modes of living, American modes of dressing and American modes of travel, all the comforts and luxuries to which we are accustomed.

"I remember shortly after the war being in a little town in Roumania that had been destroyed and was being rebuilt. I stayed throughout the day and went to the little theatre, which was in an old livery stable. An old projection machine was run there at night with an American motion picture. Women were working in the brickyards, a great deal of brick being used to rebuild the town, and these women

---

[11] *The story of the Films*, p. 208.

PICTURE PROPAGANDA AND PEACE

were hitched to two-wheel carts alongside of big dogs. At night their only form of recreation was to come in and see an American motion picture. As I sat there I wondered what was going through the minds of these people who were looking at those palatial homes and the marvelous skyline of New York, what restless thoughts and ambitions must be awakened when they compared them with the circumstances under which they themselves were living.

That is one of the things that foreign governments and foreign peoples are fighting against and not without just cause. It is a situation that has to be handled with a great deal of sympathy and understanding, because the American motion picture bears a great and direct relation to the American trade balance abroad. Do not forget that. If you investigate the automobile situation you will find that the American automobiles are making terrific inroads on foreign makes of cars and that the greatest agency for selling American automobiles abroad is the American motion picture. Its influence is working insidiously all the time, and even though all this is done without any conscious intent, the effect is that of a direct sales agency.

Every one of these foreign countries in which we distribute has its own background and its own history. Each wants to produce the stories that are native to its own country; each wants to have its own industry. Take the case of a nation like the English nation, with colonial possessions all over the world, a nation which lives on trade and barter. The motion picture is the most vital thing in the life of that people. England is making a terrific effort to build up a motion picture industry by forcing on its exhibitors a quota that obliges them to show a certain percentage of home-made pictures. They are trying to meet American competition by making a market for their own product by law."

These admissions from an able and high authority in the American industry remove the subject from the field of controversial debate.

Sir Albion Banerji, Prime Minister of an Indian State, was reported to have said:[12]

"Sensationalism and commercialism in pictures are proving a hindrance to amicable relations, because foreign audiences gain false and unfavorable impressions of the United States.

---
[12] *Film Daily*, November 5, 1926.

"America is not the only country guilty of this mistake," he declared, pointing out that "other nations should seek to depict national life in a true light.

"Because of the preponderance of American films," he continued, "greater effort should be made by this country to prevent foreigners from gaining the impression that the United States is 'a land of bandits, bootleggers and social high flyers'."

(7) *Persistent World Americanization and Continuous Misrepresentation of America, a Potent Species of Anti-American Propaganda.*

Among the many protests against the process of world Americanization in various forms, of which the motion picture is probably the most effective, Mr. G. K. Chesterton's comments at the Delphion Coterie Dinner in London in 1927, are interesting and amusing.[13]

"The English habit of life," said Mr. Chesterton, "the look of an English town, the whole tone of existence in this country, is being altered entirely by the economic and commercial presence of America."

While Mr. Chesterton said he objected, and objected most violently to the Americanization of England, he generously declared that he had no objection to the Americanization of America.

"We Englishmen," said he, "have no right to be pharisaical about the present commercial insolence of America.

"I am afraid most of the things that all civilized people in Europe are now complaining of about American manners, their habit of showing off their wealth and insulting poorer but much more civilized countries, bears an uncomfortable resemblance to the reputation the Englishman had in the early part of the nineteenth century when he traveled abroad.

"I am afraid that at the height of our commercial triumph we also were a little bit inclined to interpret commercialism in terms of caddishness.

---

[13] *Manchester Guardian Weekly*, December 23, 1927.

PICTURE PROPAGANDA AND PEACE

"Granted then that the American has many noble and charming qualities, that he has retained a great fountain of simple enthusiasm, almost always turned to absurd objects, but still genuine,—affairs here come, I think, to the point of defending our native land and damning all Americans to Hell.

"If you go to New York as a visitor," he continued, "it is rather amusing to walk down Broadway and see the idiotic electric signs wriggling about like dancing devils. You say to yourself, 'after all, I haven't got to live here, and it is always interesting to watch strange tribes, but please God I shall soon be at home again.' If I had thought that when I got home I should find exactly the same red-hat devils standing on their heads as advertisements of chewing gum I think that, as an aged and almost decrepit optimist, I should have contemplated suicide. Yet that sort of thing has happened."

It is probable that Mr. Chesterton rarely if ever attends the cinema, yet it is clear that American pictures abundantly convey the impression of America which he so amusingly describes.

It is a distinct pleasure to direct attention to the extremely sensible editorial comment of the *New York Times*[14] entitled "Our Films Against the World," which deals in part with some of the international aspects of the subject.

"If the indicated compromise is reached between French and American motion picture producers, to forestall the quota arrangement proposed by the Herriot Commission," said the *Times*, "it is possible that the citizens of this country may begin to appreciate what is animating Europe in its determination that American films shall not dominate its theatres. For on the basis of that compromise Hollywood, in order to obtain more representation in European theatres, will be obliged to distribute more German, French and British pictures. And then shall we hear the cry from patriotic societies—and Mayor Thompson—that European propaganda is seeping into the pure spring of our national life? If we do, and it is probable, we may have more sympathy for the

---
[14] December 28, 1927.

Motion Picture Problems

same cry that is now filling Europe, where films portraying American life have been the chief entertainment of the foreign audiences. Writing in the *Atlantic Monthly*, an Irishman notes that what his country fears is not Anglicanization but Los Angelesization.

"Of course, so far as the foreign producers and our own are concerned, the chief matter is financial. All parties in interest want to make all the money possible, and since the United States has 25,000 cinemas in comparison with about 4,000 each in Germany, Great Britain and France, this is the market which foreign picture producers want to reach. They have been held out so far on the ground, and a generally true one, that American audiences do not especially favor foreign films.[15] They feel they have not been given a fair trial, and they now propose by the use of certain clubs familiar to all nations engaged in international tariff matters, to force that trial. If the American producers want to avoid a harsh quota law abroad and continue to have the lion's share of the foreign market, they will probably have to come to some such agreement, particularly since it is indicated that France, Great Britain and Germany are disposed to make a tripartite combination against Hollywood.

"One word may be said in the hope of assuaging the fears of those who have been brought up to feel that foreign films, particularly French, are likely to be wicked. It is principally in Hollywood that France appears as a land devoted exclusively to the more glamourous sins, England to 'silly awsses' and Germany to fat people and the guzzling of beer. Their own producers search more deeply beneath the surface for national traits and experiences. Perhaps the outcome of this discussion, as is often the case, will be to translate the peoples of the world more truthfully to one another."

It is unfortunate, but it is nevertheless the fact, that the pictures made in America fail in realism and depict the

---

[15] Of course, American audiences do not especially favor foreign films. How could they? They have not been permitted to see them nor has there been any exploitation of them in America since about 1915, when the old General Film Company, the motion picture trust of its day, was rapidly approaching its demise. Had the American market in the past decade been open to free competition, and if it were not now controlled by an extremely small number of the members of the Producers' and Distributors' Association, meritorious films of European and British origin would easily have found their way to the favor of the American public.

several nations including America, their manners, customs, life and culture, not as any of them are, but as ill-equipped and ill-informed producers conceive them to be, or as they elect for purely commercial reasons to have the world see them and in consequence there is a wide and natural prevalence of utterly misleading and erroneous conceptions of these subjects, all lowered to make the broadest popular appeal for the sake of larger profits at the box office.

(8) *The Subjects of Propaganda Pictures and the Countries From Which They Come.*

The subjects of propaganda are numerous and almost limitless, but for purposes of this discussion an effort will be made to consider the following types of pictures.

Among the most important are nationalistic pictures with which racial and religious or anti-racial or anti-religious pictures may be included.

These pictures so often include those which glorify and encourage war, even in times of peace, that it is perhaps simpler to review some of the nationalistic themes, the anti-racial attacks, the religious and anti-religious pictures, and those which contain war propaganda, simultaneously.

In the mass of nationalistic subject matter which will presently be discussed, it is gratifying to note propaganda, or more correctly speaking, pictures of a general publicity nature which are thoroughly wholesome and which ought to be encouraged since they tend to display to the world the advantages and charms of the several nations in a thoroughly friendly and desirable way.

MOTION PICTURE PROBLEMS

Thus, a Norwegian company, subsidized by the Nautical Society *Amerikaninge Deu Norse*[16] was said to be engaged in the production of a propaganda picture about 8,000 metres in length, depicting winter sports in Norway, salmon fishing, regatta racing and all of the tourist attractions of the country.

Canada, through the Dominion's Picture Bureau and Natural Resources Intelligence Service is said to have deposited ten reels of motion pictures and four sets of lantern slides, presenting the agricultural and scenic attractions of Canada, with the American Museum of Natural History in New York.[17]

These films and slides are intended for circulation without charge among the schools of New York City.

In November, 1927, it was reported that one of the large American film companies planned to produce two motion pictures abroad, one sponsored by the Hungarian and the other by the Spanish government.

The reasons given by one of the motion picture trade papers for this undertaking are interesting.

"This," it is said, [18] "is in line with a policy to further good will for American production on the continent by working with government officials. The extent of the foreign picture market now commands increasing attention to details of policy as well as saleability.

"Film producers, leading the foreign market sales, are making greater efforts in press agenting the acquisition of European players and directors in the countries where these people are engaged.

---

[16] *Variety*, June 1, 1927.
[17] *New York Times*, May 15, 1927. Teachers desiring to use these films were requested to communicate with Mr. George H. Sherwood, Department of Public Education, American Museum of Natural History, New York.
[18] *Variety*, November 10, 1927.

Picture Propaganda and Peace

"Some of the producers are trying for casts of players, directors and writers mainly of foreign birth as a sales angle when the productions are shown abroad. This plan is an elaboration of the idea of the whole community turning out to see a picture in which a home-town boy is featured. In Europe, more than here, national players are figures to draw, irrespective of their merit, in films."

Another illustration is the announcement that the present and future development of Havre as a world port will be shown internationally through a film just completed by the Pathe Consortium.[19]

Of a very different character are the following pictures.

France has complained bitterly of the manner in which her nationals have been depicted in films, largely of American origin, and circulated everywhere.

The distinguished French Ambassador to the United States, M. Paul Claudel, referred to the subject in an address at a dinner tendered to him by the Association of Foreign Press Correspondents in New York on November 15, 1927. Describing a recent visit to Hollywood and some of the motion pictures he had seen or heard about, he continued:[20]

"I saw, or I was told, that in those pictures colonial wars of France, African wars of France, are quite the fashion and generally French soldiers and French officers are represented in a way which is not at all flattering. I know that it takes much time to change a type which has once caught the eye and fancy of the public.

"I know also that the movie drama cannot do without villains and as it is difficult to find villains among one's own countrymen it seems better to choose them among people of other nations. But I have a right to say, and I have here as witnesses people who have seen French soldiers and officers under every latitude, that they are not what the

[19] *New York Times*, April 28, 1927.
[20] *New York Times*, November 16, 1927.

film producers judge proper to show to the American public and to the public of all nations of the world, since there is no nation where American films are not seen and enjoyed. The French soldiers and officers are exactly the same in Indo-China and Africa as they were at the Marne and in Verdun. * * *

"Some people seem in America to entertain the foolish idea that Frenchmen have a natural taste for war, that they positively cherish war-making, that they are always ready to make war just for the fun of the thing. It is just the same as if you said that South Americans were fond of yellow fever and Japanese of earthquakes. No people in the world suffered more from war than France in the last century, and nobody but a madman can imagine that a nation which has just emerged from the horrors of the last conflict is not decided and, I may say, frantically decided to do everything in its power to avert a new catastrophe.

"A new word has been coined in America "to outlaw war." It is a splendid word and a good idea. France is as ready to try it as any other, and the word and idea were embodied in a recent communication from M. Briand to the American people by way of the Associated Press."

After referring to America as "this splendid country" and the magnificence of being an American, M. Claudel continued,

"Or is it better to say that it is not only a nation, it is a continent, it is a climate, rain and fine weather in all the world depend on her permission.

"America is a whole league of nations by herself; if she vetoes war there can be no war, and I quite agree with Mr. Wickham Steed that all by herself she can do more, she can in fact do more for the cause of peace, only by opening or by closing her doors, than any Covenant and than any league of nations. It is a tremendous power and a tremendous responsibility, but I am confident that they cannot lie in better hands than in the hands of our dear friends and old and recent associates."

An interesting hint at the correct point of view with reference to the use of many war scenes in motion pictures is presented in the comment attributed to the French government.

Measures, it is said, have been taken by the French government to regulate the use of war scenes in pictures and instructions have been issued to censor and to refuse to approve war scenes that are dragged into a picture for no better purpose than to improve its commercial success. The government is said to have stated that the tragic events of the war "should not be travestied for commercial ends," but pictures which present war in an authentic and historical way are not interfered with.[21]

The American picture "The Big Parade" occasioned considerable disquietitude in France.

Some declared "that the version of the film which was exhibited in the United States presented French womanhood in an extremely unfavorable light and showed a French officer at the battle front trembling with fear and an object of scorn to American soldiers."

The American picture "Beau Geste" is another which was adversely criticised and occasioned national animosities in France.

It is not surprising that France has protested against such pictures.

Almost simultaneously with Ambassador Claudel's speech in New York came the announcement of a resolution of the French Association of Motion Picture Exhibi-

---

[21] *Film Daily*, January 24, 1928. It has also said that recently the French censors have barred several war films from the Rhineland upon the ground that they were offensive to French ideas.

tors representing nearly all of the cinema theatres of France.

The resolution began by expressing great alarm over the large number of American films presented throughout the world, in which France is "deliberately and wantonly" depicted in a role which is totally foreign to her actual character.

"Frenchmen are always shown as villains and French women as vamps," the resolution said. "Further, it is considered false to give the idea that the French people, the French army and the French colonial troops are made up of heartless adventurers and escaped convicts, and that in the noble Foreign Legion discipline is unknown." "We consider further," continues the resolution, "that it is wrong to allow these misconceptions to continue on the part of a nation which has always been on the friendliest terms with France, and that the time has come for an amicable understanding on the subject.

"We therefore, in a spirit of confraternity, call the attention of all those who have anything to do with making films in the United States, to this deplorable situation, and we are confident that the wisdom which has guided the friendship between the two nations for over one hundred years will remove these misconceptions."

The exhibitors concluded by emphasising that their protest is totally devoid of any commercial inspiration, but is prompted solely by the pride which all Frenchmen feel in more than one thousand years of French history, "during which France has devoted herself in civilizing the world and in furthering all those beautiful ideals which have come from the universal conscience."[22]

It is gratifying to observe an enlightened point of view displayed in an editorial comment in one of New York's leading papers."[23]

In a well considered article entitled "Its An Ill Wind" the *Herald Tribune* said in part:

"The American film industry is being subjected to a growing number of restrictions by some of its best foreign customers. Germany for some time has imposed a quota on the showing of American pictures. The English film quota law went into effect recently and now France has put the importation of foreign films under the supervision of a governmental official with almost unlimited powers of censorship while insisting upon an interchange to force more French films on the American market. Spain, too, through its domestic producers, has begun agitating for a similar club to be held over Hollywood. Indeed, some observers profess to see in all of these measures a drawing together of these countries, or some of them, into a combination to halt the all-conquering advance of the Hollywood product. * * * Since this foreign business has now grown to be about 40% of its total, according to the recent estimate of its largest producers, Hollywood is bound to take cognizance of the threat and to modify its methods to meet it.

"The rest of us can look upon the struggle with some degree of complacency. The patriotic American will feel a natural impulse to 'root' for the home industry simply because its exportations bear the stamp 'made in America.' But a little reflection should convince us that as 'movie' spectators we have everything to gain and nothing to lose by the qualified success of this foreign dictation. Already as a result of the German effort American audiences have been privileged to see, in exchange for Hollywood films, some of the most startling, artistic successes in cinematography.[24] We could endure with equanimity a

---

[22] *New York Times*, November 18, 1927.
[23] *New York Herald-Tribune*, March 5, 1928.
[24] This is not quite correct. America's privilege in this respect resulted not from Germany's quota law or system but from the fact

MOTION PICTURE PROBLEMS

lot more of the same and of British and French films. The latter do not yet compare with the Germans,[25] but in matters of taste and artistic integrity they often surpass our own. We can even rejoice that a commission of Frenchmen has been empowered to pass on American films offered for exhibition in France, since its canons of taste will undoubtedly be reflected to some extent in what Hollywood offers for domestic consumption.

"If the American 'movie' were of unmixed value in making friends for us abroad and spreading among foreigners an understanding of this country and its ideals, one might find it in his heart to regret or resent any arbitrary restraint on its dissemination. But since, on the contrary, in its ridiculous exaggerations and gross sentimentality, it is more often a vehicle of an injurious misconception of American life, it is possible on this score also to welcome the growing intervention, while one might argue that we over here need to know about other people through their pictures quite as much as they need to know about us. Hence, all things considered these crocodile tears!"

Occasionally the effort of a nation to suppress the use of opprobrious terms or undesirable pictures directed against another is noticeable,[26] but as yet there is no agreement of any kind upon the subject among the nations and no inter-

---

that the Famous Players Lasky Corporation and the Metro-Goldwyn-Mayer Company had loaned the German Ufa Company in 1926 the sum of $4,000,000 on condition that Ufa would exhibit 20 pictures of each in its German theatres in exchange for the exhibition of 4 pictures by each in the theatres controlled by these two American companies in America.

[25] This assertions presents a highly debatable issue, many informed persons being of the opinion that French pictures are as good in every respect as those of any other nation.

[26] The *New York Times* of April 2, 1927, contained the following, in part, under a Paris headline: "Applying the spirit of Locarno on their own account, the French police have forbidden the word "Boche" to be used in titles or sub-titles in films lest France's neighbors across the Rhine should be offended.

"During the war no one ever found a really satisfactory clue to the derivation of the word "Boche," which was the French equivalent of the American army's "Heinie" and "Squarehead." It denoted everything that was outrageous about the Teutonic enemy, his manners, his appearance, his speech and his behavior.

national means of correcting such evils when they arise at numberless points throughout the world.

But France, of course, like other nations has her own propaganda film of which the following illustrations may be given.

A distinguished gathering in Paris, said to have been composed of Marshals Foch, Joffre and Petain, General Gouraud and many other generals and high officials of the French army and members of the government and diplomatic corps, enthusiastically received "La grande Epreuve" (The Great Test).[27]

"Those who saw this moving film history, containing many actual scenes taken in the war," said the *New York Times*, "were struck by the fact that the French producers have achieved an epic of war with a very minimum of hatred. One came away with a deep feeling of the tragedy of war and the necessity of peace, but with no sentiment of bitterness against former enemy nations.

"To reach this desired goal the producers have taken great pains. For example, the word "German" does not appear in a single title, the term "enemy" being substituted."

Again the French war film entitled "The Legion of Honor," which was presented for the first time in America on board the Ile de France on July 19, 1928, is declared to be somewhat different from the usual run of war productions.

"But now the word has been suppressed. Movie directors who are producing war films are warned that they must respectfully use the word "Allemand" or "Germany" when referring to the co-signatories to the treaty of Locarno."

[27] *New York Times*, April 27, 1928. The *New York Times* of August 14, 1928, says that this same picture is to be exhibited here under the title "The Soul of France," and in Belgium, Switzerland, Egypt, Holland, Australia, New Zealand, the Dutch East Indies and Brazil.

MOTION PICTURE PROBLEMS

"Where most of the rest have been bold and slashing—as witness 'What Price Glory'—the 'Legion of Honor' gives a softer, a certain dispassionate treatment. It is patriotic, of course, but it is not made in such a way as to offend any nation or people."[28]

The attempt to soften the natural animosities which the presentation of any war picture must necessarily stimulate is laudable but it is probably largely an attempt to camouflage the fact that the picture is in reality a war propaganda film.

The same thing was claimed for the British picture "Dawn" which pictured the story and execution of Edith Cavell.

Indeed, some of the press notices stimulated by those who controlled the picture and its exhibition even declared that the picture displayed some of the fine traits and characteristics of the German people.

The Germans themselves, however, protested against the picture vigorously as will subsequently be shown.

German war films with their accompanying publicity have been considerable in number.

Thus it was said that the German cinema industry, which, while waging underground warfare on American pictures, is trying desperately to break into American markets, released in the last year or is now producing no fewer than 34 feature films glorifying the Reich's monarchistic and militaristic past, according to data published in *The Berliner Tageblatt*.[29]

The *Tageblatt* is said to have taken President von Hindenburg to task for permitting the use of his name as

---
[28] *New York Times*, July 20, 1928.
[29] *New York Times*, September 13, 1926.

patron of a picture called "Bismarck" which is frankly anti-republican in tendency, the producer of which, when he recently ran short of funds, appealed for financial backing on the ground that his film was "nationalistic propaganda."

Another "worthy example of loyalty to the Prussian kings" cited by the *Tageblatt* is "German Woman—German Fidelity," in which the late Empress Augusta Victoria is the leading character by special permission of the ex-Kaiser.

The *Tageblatt* is said to have remarked that while the German movie censor ruthlessly suppresses radical screen productions like the much-discussed Russian film "The Cruiser Potemkin," he freely approves cinematographic attacks on the Republic by the Royalist Reich.

It was said that German producers nowadays deliberately drum up opposition to American pictures here—a leading trade paper recently inquiring editorially, "America, do you hear our hissing?", and at the same time try to break into the American market with idealized and dull tributes to the Fatherland's imperial army. In Germany today it is said there are fifty such films produced to one of any other kind. In fact, it was remarked, the production of big artistically sincere photoplays has ceased altogether.

An optimistic account of a monumental picture to be produced by the German company known as Ufa appeared somewhat later.[30]

---

[30] *New York Times*, February 28, 1927.

Motion Picture Problems

It was declared that the picture would be based upon material provided from the German official war archives, but the representative of one of the largest American picture companies declared that the picture constituted an historic document of the greatest importance and that America's role in the war would be shown in an objective manner and that the picture "would be wholly free from propaganda," statements which illustrate the type of obviously untruthful publicity for which the industry in America has so long been notorious.

The following comment shows how extensively and effectively the American film companies have been able to make the distribution and circulation of their war films as well as others, throughout the world, and it shows moreover that pictures which are indisputably war pictures, and known to be such by those informed on the subject, are nevertheless exploited by the producers and disguised under changed titles and under the thoroughly untruthful and misleading statement that they are in reality anti-war pictures.

The *New York Times* printed as news the following obvious piece of producers' publicity.[31]

"As an anti-war film 'Rivals,' the German adaptation of 'What Price Glory,' opened the Berlin film season and found popular favor. The newspaper criticisms yesterday were laudatory. The passage in which the war is announced as senseless butchery culminating in 'nevermore war' drew cheers from the house. The German war prisoner scene was eliminated.

"The same film is shown in France under the title 'The Servitude

---

[31] **August 8, 1927.**

of Glory,' in which the panoply of war is glorified, while in Italy certain scenes have been altered to give them a tendency more anti-war.

"Public censors in Belgium, Holland, Denmark, Norway, Sweden and Spain have passed the film for release in September and October. It has been running in England. Winfield Sheehan, vice-president of the Fox Film Corporation, who now is in Berlin, superintended the European productions."

Thus it appears that truth is not remotely connected with the exploitation of pictures anywhere. Titles are changed so that the subject matter may not be recognized and it is then described as an anti-war film although it is said that "the panoply of war is glorified." And censors throughout the world are led by the nose to approve subject matter based upon the representations of those who control it rather than upon a more intelligent conclusion of what the picture in reality portrays.

When the second part of the German picture entitled "The World War—A Historical Film" was shown for the first time at the Ufa Palast in Berlin, a special audience, which included a number of governmental officials, assembled.

The ex-Kaiser is said to have appeared only in one short scene and to have been greeted by "rather pronounced hisses which hesitating applause failed to drown out. Hindenburg and Mackensen drew a thunderous ovation as did Rathenau, when he was shown as attempting to persuade the government against ruthless submarine warfare and warning that the blockade would cause the fall of 'the Central European fortress'." [32]

---

[32] *New York Times*, February 11, 1928.

MOTION PICTURE PROBLEMS

The *New York Times* gave the following interesting account of the picture:

"The film shows," said the *Times*, "the years 1915-1916, emphasizing the distress suffered by the civilian population with gaunt hunger haunting the children and the aged. * * * The Crown Prince's attempt to capture Verdun early in 1916 in order to give it as a present to his father on his birthday is shown in detail, while the repulse is treated as a pure hammering campaign on the part of the French backed by the entire world. While the attempt to picture the scenes within the 'Central European Fortress' cannot be seen as purely objective, which was the hope of its directors, nothing is depicted which could be interpreted as meaning a slight or slur on opponents. Gas warfare is mentioned only once in this period and then as a weapon of the French in regaining lost ground near Verdun. There are scenes of soldiers helping wounded enemy troops, but always of Germans helping French. Brutality and horrors are left out for the most part and the dead on the battlefield are practically omitted. There is an attempt to portray rather futuristically the general delirium of war by massing on the screen at one time whirling machines, firing guns, emaciated workers, charging soldiers, sorrowing mothers and stern generals.

"The production was directed by two former officers of the Imperial General Staff and there is a grave question in the minds of prominent persons whether these efforts have done much toward the education of the general public on German history of this period or have furthered the movement to heal the wounds of war and bend efforts toward peace."

Obviously the educational content of this and other similar pictures is incidental, if existent at all, while the real appeal to the public is addressed to their emotions and not to their intelligence, with the inevitable effect that the old wounds are opened and harrowed anew, and the result must surely contribute more to the revival and stimulation of hatred than to the promotion or cultivation of peace.

The description of the first part of this German war

film in Berlin under the title "The People's Heroism" is full of interest.

"According to the advance notices," said the *New York Times*, "it was screened in a purely objective spirit, without national bias or rancor.

"Its 'objectivity,' however, is not too pronounced to displease Alfred Hugenberg, the German Nationalistic Northcliffe, who yesterday became Ufa's new head.

"The picture is in three parts, each timed to fill an evening's program.

"The first part, shown tonight, is called 'The People's Heroism.' It portrays the events of the war up to the stabilization of the Eastern and Western fronts.

"There was applause for the Kaiser when he was portrayed riding down the Unter den Linden in a full dress uniform just after the outbreak of hostilities. Tonight's distinguished audience was too well bred to express its views more forcibly than by clapping or hissing. The prospects of this scene starting a free-for-all fight at future performances seems excellent, however.

"Generals Hindenburg and Ludendorff, always together and depicted among the troops, also won loud applause, but that given to their 'Imperial Master' rang still louder.

"On the eve of the war the heads of the Allied Nations are shown amid surroundings of martial pomp while the Princes of the Central Empires are kneeling in humble prayer. The German victories in Belgium, France, Lorraine, East Prussia, Galicia and elsewhere are fully recorded. The German defeat at the Marne is dismissed with a curt subtitle, 'Then the German High Command Broke Off the Battle.'

"Ypres is listed among the German victories and no reference is made to the fact that poison gas was used there for the first time by the Germans.

"Columns of German refugees are shown fleeing before the Russians in East Prussia, but none appear in the French and Belgian war scenes.

"Of course the dead are visible on the battle field. In the hospitals, which the picture portrays, no severely wounded are in evidence, however. The suffering civilian population is omitted altogether."

Thus, as the *Times* correspondent so well says,

"In this production, which is based on the German official archives and is composed largely of camera shots behind the front made in the course of the struggle for the purpose of maintaining the civilian morale war, becomes glorious rather than dirty and brutal." [33]

From Berlin came also the report of a Silician film entitled "The Land Under the Cross" the description of which indicates the political rather than the war quality of its propaganda.

It was said to have been forbidden by the censorship commission before the Geneva League Council meeting for fear that its exhibition might injure Germany's foreign policy.

The film was shown for the first time in the presence of Chancellor Marx, Foreign Minister Stresemann and many other dignitaries. It is said to be a protest against the division of Upper Silesia and to be an appeal to the German nation to aid their suffering compatriots on both sides of the new frontier.

The performance is said to have been opened by a speech from one of the deputies who announced that the film would be shown in every German city and town in the next few months.[34]

But Poland, not unnaturally, felt aggrieved by the picture and is said to have sent an official protest to the German authorities, and at the same time to have

---

[33] *New York Times*, April 23, 1927.
[34] *New York Times*, March 24, 1927.

PICTURE PROPAGANDA AND PEACE

launched a boycott against the films released by the German firms Deulig, Echo and Emelka.[35]

The German expenditure of a large sum of money said to aggregate more than 6,000,000 marks through its representative, Capt. Lohmann, in connection with the Phoebus Films and other motion picture concerns, is of importance as indicating the efforts of the German government to utilize films for propaganda purposes.[36]

Germany, like other nations, has had occasion to protest a number of pictures deemed by her to be offensive to her national ideals and character.

The American pictures entitled "Mare Nostrum" and the "Four Horsemen of the Apocalypse" are illustrations.

"The national executive of the German film industry has obtained from the Metro-Goldwyn Corporation a formal promise to refrain hereafter from the production or distribution of pictures having a tendency to provoke international animosity. This was announced here (Berlin) today," continued the *New York Times*, "in connection with the German protests against the release of 'Mare Nostrum' the Metro-Goldwyn war film, in Paris. German indignation was aroused against the same concern first when, after Rudolf Valentino's death, his old picture 'The Four Horsemen of the Apocalypse' was revived on the New York screen.

---

[35] *Film Daily*, June 12, 1927. In an earlier issue of the *Film Daily*, (April 15, 1927) in commenting on the acquisition of control of the German company Ufa by Alfred Hugenberg, and his supposed purpose to utilize some of that company's productions as propaganda, the *Film Daily* said, in part: "News dispatches state that the Polish Minister here has protested to the German government against the exhibition of the German film 'The Land Under the Cross' which reveals the suffering of the populace of Upper Silesia under Polish rule. When this film was shown in the capital it was criticised in the liberal press here (Berlin) as propaganda which could only injure the Polish-German prospects of an understanding. As the film was produced by the Deulig Film Company which is controlled by Hugenberg through the Scherl, the inference is that the reorganized Ufa is going ahead with its reported policy of propaganda."

[36] *New York Times*, August 10, 1927.

Motion Picture Problems

Stigmatizing 'Mare Nostrum' as a provocative film, the national cinema executive demanded its permanent withdrawal from exhibition everywhere. Metro-Goldwyn replied that its contractual obligations would prevent complete withdrawal, but it voiced entire agreement with the German objection to 'pictures which may create bad blood or hate between peoples or place a certain nation in an unfair light.'

"While the Berlin press generally applauds the movie organization's action the Socialist *Vorwaerts* remarks that German productions of a provocative nationalistic character ought also to be banned.

"Apparently unaware that Ufa is now preparing a war film 'based on Germany's archives,' which can only mean the records of the Imperial General Staff, the *Taegliche Rundschau*, which is close to Wilhelm Strasse says that several entente countries are making war pictures directed against Germany.

"'This,' it adds, 'is the worst political misdemeanor that could be committed in Europe nowadays.'

"Its editorial demands that the Metro-Goldwyn Corporation's refusal to withdraw 'Mare Nostrum' immediately should be met with reprisals.

"The Monarchistic *Tage* urges that the German film market be closed to Metro-Goldwyn until its anti-German productions disappear from the screen." [37]

It is, of course, obvious to any thoughtful person that the continued and persistent circulation throughout the world of American-made pictures which arouse such natural animosities must of necessity be an extremely harmful thing so far as the American public is concerned and that the absence of any possible adequate excuse for this vicious practice becomes all the more plain when it is realized that the industry in America pursues its ill-considered course solely for the commercial benefit of those engaged in this industry.

Later it was said that a movement was under way in Germany to prevent the issuance of import licenses to any

---
[37] *New York Times*, March 11, 1927.

producing organization, no matter in what part of the world it may be located, which makes pictures, construed in Germany to be anti-German in theme.[38]

This same type of industrial boycott has been forced upon several of the nations by the ill-considered pictorial rubbish which has unfortunately emanated in such large quantities from America.

Mexico, Spain and France have each had recourse to it, but its limited effectiveness due to the restricted character of these national markets, fails to supply the efficient means necessary to prevent rather than to punish the exhibition of nationally offensive pictures in other countries throughout the world.

A trade paper in New York[39] declared Latin-America to be aroused over pictures emanating from America alleged to libel South American countries and its people.

Mexico particularly protested against the pictures, among others, entitled "Somewhere In Sonora," "Why Worry," "Mlle. Midnight," "Bad Man" and "One Week of Love."

Somewhat later the Spanish government was reported as having adopted a measure prohibiting the exhibition of all Metro-Goldwyn-Mayer productions in Spain.[40]

The particular occasion of this edict was the exhibition of the picture entitled "Valencia."

Another trade publication declared that the Spanish Premiere's action followed closely upon widespread pro-

---
[38] *Film Daily*, May 2, 1928.
[39] *Variety*, July 13, 1927.
[40] *Variety*, October 26, 1927.

tests against American films in France, Italy and other European countries. "It is felt," said this paper[41] "that the Hollywood practice of selecting Europeans of one nationality or another for the portrayal of villains, freaks, fops and scoundrels has gone far enough and the absurd generalization of Englishmen as cads and dandies, French women as immoral dolls, Spanish grandees as loathesome debauchees, and Dutch women as waddling geese, is hurting the prestige of the different countries."

If the thoroughly misguided industry in America and its equally blind trade press but knew it, it is the prestige of America which is hurt by such inconsiderate pictures.

"General Primo de Rivera," continued the article, "in denouncing 'Valencia' said that it did not constitute an isolated case of misrepresentation. The Spaniard is not a disguised bandit with fierce mustaches, tinkling away on a mandolin or guitar under the window of some innocent maiden with the object of luring her away. There may be such Spaniards, but there are also that kind of Americans, he added. Why should we be singled out to play the scoundrel in every play?

"The French object that the American people gain an absolutely erroneous idea of French men and women from Hollywood films. Everybody knows the movie Frenchman. He is generally a smart, cynical, blatant, bon viveur, or a shrewd rascal. French women have gained a reputation in the United States as being the most immoral creatures on earth."

Brazil has felt the sting of disparagement of her great national capital in a heedless picture from America, and at the recent Pan-American Conference at Havana a move was said to have been made to prevent the exhibition of motion pictures considered prejudicial or unfriendly to Latin-American countries.

---

[41] *Motion Pictures Today*, January 14, 1928.

PICTURE PROPAGANDA AND PEACE

Thus, the distinguished Brazilian Ambassador to Washington spoke a friendly warning to American motion picture companies, referring to a picture which he said showed Rio de Janeiro as "a dismal and squalid village with the inhabitants having apparently no other occupation than playing and dancing the tango at all hours of the day and night, while our Portuguese language seemed to be entirely unknown in Brazil[42]

A motion at the Pan-American Conference was said to have been made before the Committee on Intellectual Cooperation of the Pan-American Conference and was in substance to the effect that the conference should recommend to the American governments the greatest vigilance in the production of films, to avoid distribution of those representing the national character or customs of any American country, in a manner likely to offend the public sentiment of that country.[43]

The Irish race and their supposed characteristics have long been the subject of humorously intended but nevertheless offensive and objectionable characterization in pictures emanating from America.

Early in October, 1927, and later, vigorous protests were made by individuals and one or more Irish-American societies against the group of pictures deemed by them to be anti-Irish and on one or more occasions to have made disparaging or ill-considered reference to the Catholic religion.

---

[42] *New York Times*, November 16, 1927.
[43] *Motion Pictures Today*, February 4, 1928.

The pictures objected to included "The Callahans and the Murphys," "The Garden of Allah," "Bringing Up Father," "Irish Hearts," "Finnegan's Ball," "The Cohens and the Kellys in Paris" and others.

The flood of these undesirable pictures caricaturing the Irish gave further stimulus to the effort to correct these conditions through the futile means of Federal censorship. The Irish Press contained much comment on the subject.[44]

Turning to Russia, an interesting set of facts are observable.

The production, distribution and exhibition of motion pictures in Russia and the exportation of Russian pictures into other countries were originally, under the Soviet regime, matters of complete governmental control.

---

[44] Thus the *Irish World of September* 10, 1927, said in part:

"Notwithstanding all the protests made by Irish organizations and individuals the Metro-Goldwyn Corporation and the Loew theatres are still presenting the anti-Irish moving picture 'The Callahans and the Murphys' wherever it is possible to do so, and in many places under police protection. * * * It is evident that 'The Callahans and the Murphys' and 'Irish Hearts' are but the forerunner of a series of pictures holding up the Irish people to ridicule and contempt.

"Unless a definite and united stand is taken against these vile caricatures, the Irish people in America and the world over must reconcile themselves to being lampooned on the moving picture screens for years to come.

"The protest to date, while not sufficient to impress upon the producers the necessity of confining themselves to decency in their productions, has thrown a considerable scare into them. As a result it is probable that their coming films will to some extent be camouflaged. We ask our leaders to give us their cooperation in putting an end to this evil. As in the past, we will do everything that lies in our power to protest in a lawful way against these atrocities. We want our readers to do the same. We want them to keep in touch with us and inform us of what is being done in their localities."

See also the file of the publication entitled *The Spokesman* published in New York, issues of August 11, 19, September 17, 24, October 1, 1927, and the petition of the American Irish Vigilantes Committee presented to the Federal Trade Commission, October 5, 1927.

PICTURE PROPAGANDA AND PEACE

It may well be that in the process of adoption of the "new economic policy" of 1921,[45] there was at least a partial resumption of or reversion to capitalistic principles in the permission to private interests to make and retain profit on some of the transactions relating to this business.

In reference to this subject one of the trade papers in America[46] declared that the few picture-producing companies in Russia had no right to distribute their own product, this being in the control of the state until 1926.

"This system," continued *Variety*, "placed the producers in the position of being unable to realize profit out of their productions. With the abolishment of this State Monopoly the same Sovkino formed a cinematographic association assuring production, distribution and exhibition."

It is not desirable at this time to make an extensive review of the industry in Russia other than to indicate that it has become, and will in the future continue to be, of increasing importance, as is evidenced from the fact that its productions in 1926 and 1927 were said to total 272 in number.[47]

Of these subjects some 23% were estimated to be or to contain intentional Soviet propaganda.

Estimates indicate that in the next two or three years 200 pictures yearly will be produced in Russia and approximately 25% of these are intended for foreign distribution.[48] Also it is declared that Russia, realizing its necessity to

---

[45] *The Economic Organization of the Soviet Union*, by Scott Nearing and Jack Hardy (Vanguard Press, New York.) See also *The Real Situation in Russia* by Leon Trotsky, translated by Max Eastman (Harcourt Brace & Co.)
[46] *Variety*, August 17, 1927.
[47] *Id.*
[48] *Film Daily*, December 18, 1927.

reach foreign markets, is prepared to remove from its productions any subject matter which will prevent that result.[49]

Obviously, however, the statement concerning the elimination of propaganda must always be accepted with considerable skepticism, and as already pointed out these films will inevitably carry their content of propaganda, whether intended to do so or not.

It is declared that pictures are to be produced "from which all elements of revolutionary propaganda interest are absent" and among those mentioned as in this category are the "Tsar and the Poet," based on an episode in the life of Alexander Pushkin, Russia's great poet, and "The Waiter in the Restaurant," from a popular Russian novel by the same name, and a further picture from which much is said to be expected entitled "War and Peace," a film version of the Tolstoy book of the same name. Another, entitled "The Ten Days That Shattered the World," is included, but it is said that the fact that this picture deals with the events of the Russian Revolution of 1917 may be expected to limit the appeal of this picture.[50]

From Mr. Walter Duranty, who writes so interestingly of Russia in the *New York Times,* comes an interesting description of the picture entitled "Two Days." It is described as a well executed, vivid portrayal of an individual tragedy arising from the national tragedy. He says

---

[49] *Film Daily,* December 18, 1927.
[50] *Film Daily,* December 17, 1927.

PICTURE PROPAGANDA AND PEACE

it contains no love element, no comic relief, nothing but stark realism, death and destruction. But he adds:[51]

"There are extraordinarily poignant scenes and few captions *and the effect of indirect but immensely powerful propaganda aroused the enthusiasm of the picked audience.* To anyone familiar with Russia's tragedy there is nothing in the play that might not have occurred in reality and it may easily succeed abroad. But as an evening's entertainment for the worker, peasant or small employee with his wife and family after a day's work it is rather strong medicine.

"Stranger things than that are done here in the name of propaganda. Anita Loos may be surprised to learn that 'Gentlemen Prefer Blondes'[52] has just been published in Moscow with a eulogistic preface by that redoubtable feminist die-hard Communist, Madame Kollontai.

Madame Kollontai calls it a damning satire of capitalist society and after brief musings on Lorlei's wasted talents and the happier fate of the proletarian community, reaches the conclusion that such 'blondinkas' * * * serve the American gentlemen right. The book is splendidly translated, unlike most foreign novels published here, but the translator cannot reproduce Lorlei's orthographic eccentricities."

Again the effort to make propaganda more palatable

---

[51] *New York Times* December 18, 1927.
[52] Which, by the way, is a brilliant satire of life as it is in Hollywood, not in America, as seen through the eyes of a clever member of the Hollywood colony.

and less obvious is seen in the following brief reference to the subject:

"Propaganda, it is said,[53] is becoming more refined in Soviet film art. After much exaggeration and coarseness the Soviet Kino now blends propaganda with esthetic effects in an unobtrusive way. 'His Majesty's Prima Ballerina' the season's best film and the present month's sensation, is especially interesting, not only because it shows this new artistic subtlety to a remarkable degree, but also because it illuminates with brilliant fidelity a great historical background."

A writer in the *London Times* gave an excellent review of the situation in the Far East.

The article was reprinted in the *New York Sun*[54] and is reproduced here almost in full.

"Whatever may be the effect of Communist agents in the Far East there can be no doubt that the relations between Europeans and natives, especially in the large towns, are very different from what they used to be. People who revisit the Indies after a few years' absence are painfully struck by the change in the attitude of servants and laborers. Without showing overt insolence there is, in their behavior toward the whites, an undercurrent of impudence that borders on contempt. There is little now of the genuine respect toward Europeans that was formerly the rule in the East, and one cannot help feeling that the European no longer holds the same place in the minds of the native and that he has, in some way, suffered degradation.

"It is possible that this regrettable change of spirit may, in a large measure, be due to the persistent propaganda of those organizations which are bent on upsetting our present social fabric. At the same time there can be no doubt that the way for Communistic influence has been greatly facilitated by a powerful and novel element which, in recent years, has entered into the lives of semi-civilized people in all parts of the tropical world. *That element is the cinema.*

"The writer during his travels in Asia found no one who did not agree with him as to the deplorable effects of the 'pictures' on the prestige of Europeans in the Far East. Until the cinemas laid bare

---

[53] *New York Times*, June 5, 1927.
[54] October 26, 1926.

Picture Propaganda and Peace

the worst sides of the life of the white man most of the natives were ignorant of the depths of vice which afflict certain sections of white society.

"It is true that no man is a hero to his valet, and it is probable that the Sahib's 'boy' has few illusions as to the vaunted moral superiority of the European. But to the vast mass of black, brown and yellow people the inner life of the European, and especially that side of it which flourishes in centers of crime and infamy, was unknown *until the American films showed them a travesty of it.* The spread of picture houses in remote tropical countries has been remarkable in recent years, and it is now rare to find a town of a few thousand inhabitants which cannot boast of its 'picture palace.' The films shown in these places are of the most sensational description, and, although a certain amount of police censorship is exercised, the great majority of the pictures teem with episodes of crime and violence of all kinds.

"The simple native has a positive genius for picking up false impressions. By the unsophisticated Malay, Javanese, or even the Indian and the Chinese, the scenes of crime and depravity which are thrown on the screen are accepted as faithful representations of the ordinary life of the white man in his own country. The pictures of amorous passages, many of which, according to his ideas, are very indecent, give him a deplorable impression of the morality of the white man and, worse still, of the white woman. The act of kissing, save among the natives who have had the 'benefits' of education, is never practiced among the peoples of the Far East, and the prolonged and often erotic exhibitions of osculation frequently shown on the screen cannot but arouse in the minds of unsophisticated natives feelings that can better be imagined than described. To hear, indeed, the remarks and catcalls which often proceed from the cheap seats occupied by young coolies during those 'love passages' is sometimes enough to make one's blood boil.

"*The police authorities in the East are unanimous in attributing many of the more important and complicated crimes to the suggestion of the cinema.* It is, in fact, not necessary for the people to pay to see the most striking of the violent episodes of a film. Posters outside a cinema display, with every possible exaggeration, scenes of battle, murder, and sudden death. The little black or yellow child can feast its astounded eyes on the sight of a 'Sahib' strangling a semi-nude woman with blue eyes and golden hair. To his primitive mind such pictures must come as an amazing revelation. To the vast majority of those who pay to see the show the plot of the film is often quite incomprehensible. Most of the scenes depict things and situations that they have never even imagined and cannot understand. But the vivid actions of the actors are clear enough to their minds, and they are quite capable of grasping all the exciting details of a burglary or the lurid phases of a murder. One can imagine the conversations that take place in the shade of the big mango trees or in the little brown huts among those who have seen a 'picture' for the first time; the absurd impressions, the puzzling influences, the demoralizing conclusions.

"The writer was assured that in Malaya considerable care is being taken in the censorship of films and that, wherever possible, objectionable scenes are cut out. So dependent, however, are most of these films on a sequence of sensational episodes that it is quite impossible to eliminate even a tithe of the pictures which represent Europeans in criminal, or undesirable situations. If everything calculated to bring the white man into contempt were taken out very little would be left. *The native has already been taught to demand sensational scenes and is satisfied by nothing else.* The proprietors of the picture houses are already complaining of undue discrimination and protest that further interference would ruin their business."

An extremely interesting and informative article written by Mr. John MacCormack of London for the *New York Times* lists many of the war films and shows very clearly that many of the nations are engaged in the production of what in reality are war propaganda pictures.

Many of these pictures will obviously rekindle highly undesirable and dangerous international animosities which are distinctly anti-social and directly against the peace of the world.

Referring to war stories, Mr. MacCormack says:[55]

"The list of war pictures made, being made, or to be made is a long and remarkable one. Nearly every country that produces films has contributed to it. Hollywood was responsible for 'The Four Horsemen,'

---

[55] *New York Times*, July 1, 1928.

Picture Propaganda and Peace

'The Big Parade,' 'What Price Glory' and more recently, 'Wings.' That is, not to mention pictures like 'Shoulder Arms' or 'Rookies' which treated war in its humorous or what might be described as its more peaceful aspect.

"France will shortly be showing in this country 'The Soul of France,' in which over 20,000 French troops took part on the battlefields of the Marne, Champagne and Verdun. She will also present Able Gance's great spectacle 'Napoleon,' where five projection machines utilized the whole width of the stage for the more adequate screening of some of the battle scenes.

"Sweden, which was not in the great war, has fallen back for its portrayal of battle, murder and sudden death on the career of its national hero, Charles XII. Most of the scenes of the Swedish film bearing his name as title are simply reconstructions of the battles fought by a king who, if he was a heroic figure to his countrymen, has also been called 'the madman of the North' and was misled by dreams of military glory.

"Germany, besides her semi-official picture 'The War Through German Spectacles,' has lately sent us 'At the Edge of the World' and 'The Fugitive Lover.' 'At the Edge of the World' teaches the lesson, which Germany has had opportunity to learn, that the fruits of peace are more lasting than the glories of war. The story, which is picturesquely told, hangs on the fortunes of a quaint old mill near the frontier between two warring nations. 'The Fugitive Lover' is also a praiseworthy attempt to show the futility of war, but more immediately concerned with the love adventures of a German soldier during the war time in France.

"A list of English war pictures is legion. 'Ypres,' 'Mons' and 'The Somme' detailing the exploits of the army and 'Zeebrugge' and 'The Battles of Coronel and the Faulkland Islands,' setting forth some of the deeds of 'the silent service' have already been shown. 'Q Ships,' which reveal secrets of the 'mystery' craft to lure German submarines to their undoing, is being trade shown this week. In this picture Admiral Lord Jellicoe personally reacts his meeting with Vice Admiral Sims of the United States Navy. The ill-fated landing at Gallipoli is to be the subject of a later film.

"All these are nothing but fragments of war history. 'Tommy Atkins,' which has just been adapted by Major Ian Hay Beith from the play of that name was made with the cooperation of the British War Council but has a hero, a heroine and a romantic love story for all that.

Motion Picture Problems

It deals not with the great war but with highly filmable, if less sanguinary encounters with dervishes in Egypt, and optimistic persons have described it as 'The Beau Geste' of the British Army. * * * Then there is 'Dawn,' of which little need be said here, except that it is scarcely the sort of peace propaganda which carries the widest international appeal. The same will probably be said of 'The Burgomaster of Stilemonde' for whose production the whole town of Diest has been placed at the disposal of British film craft and large numbers of Belgian cavalry and infantry loaned by the Belgian government. Some of the cavalry even consented to don authentic Uhlan uniform and equipment which had been procured specially from Berlin, and to clatter through the cobbled streets of Diest as did its invaders in 1914. Two women, unaware that the town had been temporarily dedicated to film purposes, fainted when they caught sight of the Uhlans. Which is interesting if what it indicates is still at the back of Europe's mind.

"But of all British war films which paint Germany in a bad light, the very latest of them, which bears the title 'Victory' is likely to be most resented east of the Rhine. 'Victory' is a film calculated not only to keep the home fires burning but to fan the flames of hate as well. A German army headquarters occupies a French chateau, whose chatelaine is subsequently outraged by a staff officer and molested by his orderlies. Two British officers try to rescue her and one of them is shot for it. The other officer and the young mistress of the Chateau are saved by the Armistice. 'Victory' is an excellent war film in many respects, but even the London critics protested that to represent a German general as gazing with loathing on a French baby which has crawled into his room, is ridiculous. The recrudescence of public interest in the Great War has been exploited in other media besides the films. No doubt there is a generation, bulking large in cinema audiences, which had no personal experience of the late unpleasantness and is curious to realize it second-hand. Those who did participate in it, have perhaps reached the stage where it is interesting to have blurred memories revived by pictorial association. Fighting always makes a good story and screen analyses of war psychology and expositions of war's results can no doubt be made to serve an ethical as well as artistic end. But there seems little to be gained from the perpetuation of war-time hatreds by the distortion of historical incidents or the invention of 'frightfulness'."

PICTURE PROPAGANDA AND PEACE

Pictures which involve political propaganda in one form or other are always dangerous, but if labeled propaganda they would lose much of their harmful influence. Those which arouse religious or racial antagonisms are quite as bad or worse.

The German picture entitled "The Land Under the Cross," which depicts the suffering of the populace of Upper Silesia under Polish rule, to which reference has already been made, is an example of political propaganda film.

The use of such material in the national political campaign for the Presidency of the United States is already heralded and illustrated in the uncomplimentary reference originally made to one of the candidates in a prohibition film entitled "Deliverance."[56]

A German paper, the *Vossische Zeitung*, recently expressed a thoroughly sensible point of view with reference to the German picture entitled "Luther," which recently had its premier in the Ufa-Palast in Berlin.

The *New York Times*,[57] referring to this German paper as one with no particular religious bias, says that the German paper "opines that it isn't worth while to stir up sectarian strife among the people for the sake of the 'film business'."

"The reviewer of *Vorwaerts*, the leading German Socialist paper," continues the *Times*, "says that, as the reformation was 'not the work of one man and certainly not of Luther alone, a film limited to his personality must, in the nature of things give an absolutely false picture of historical events.'

---
[56] *New York Times*, June 22, 1928.
[57] March 25, 1928.

"The article continues—'*Germania*, the central organ of the Centrist (Catholic) party, has printed a sharp protest by the leading Catholic clergymen of Berlin, reading in part as follows': 'Wherever the film 'Luther' has been shown, it has produced great agitation among the Catholic population, because it injures their religious feelings most deeply, both by its tendencies and by individual scenes. In a partisan and highly exaggerated manner are shown unfortunate conditions in the Catholic church in Luther's time and historical events are distorted in a prejudiced way, and in some cases, invented. The way in which the Indulgences are treated in the film and the unworthy representation of Tetzel and other priestly persons are particularly offensive.'

"In their technical criticism most of the Berlin writers agree that the film (which runs two hours and is accompanied by music especially composed for it) while interesting and fairly well done, lacks the power to grip modern audiences for the reason that the action portrayed is 'too far in the past.'

"The proposed use of the film by the International Federation of Trade Unions in Germany, for Socialist propaganda is another illustration of the use of a film for political purposes." [58]

The picture entitled "The Moon of Israel," which depicted the Israelites under brutal Egyptian rule, is said to have occasioned serious disturbances in Delhi, India.

Moslems in the audience protested against the picture, declaring that it outraged their religious feelings and it is said that an outbreak followed and that the police arrived just in time to prevent the theatre from being wrecked by an infuriated mob.[59] The same paper added, "Censorship of American films in India is being seriously considered by the Government there, according to a Simla dispatch. The Government is doing this, it is stated, in response to a strongly expressed public opinion that American films are 'subversive of religion and morals.' The Government, when

---

[58] *Film Daily*, May 29, 1927.
[59] *New York Times*, July 6, 1927.

it last considered the problem of censorship, rejected a plan for a central board of censors and established separate boards at Bombay, Calcutta, Madras, and Rangoon, which are ports of entry for films. Other provinces complained that the work of these boards is inefficient. The Government is now considering the introduction of an official motion in the legislature for the appointment of a committee to investigate the problem."

The indirect and unintentional influence of motion pictures is further illustrated by the following comment which, while apparently trivial, nevertheless is worthy of consideration.

"German Parliamentarians believe," said the *New York Times*,[60] that "American Films are exercising too great an influence on the character of German productions. The American girl is being copied to the detriment of educational movies in the Reich. This charge is brought up in the Reichstag Committee today and Deputies were asked to concentrate their thoughts on what to do. Herr von Keudell, Minister of the Interior, believes recent regulations restricting the import of foreign films would effect the desired end, but there was evident disappointment that German stars are still trying to copy Hollywood. Just what evil influence American stage and screen stars are working on the German public was not defined by the Committee, which, however, was unanimous that the girls wielded a mystic and wicked power."

It is said that Turkey rejected the picture entitled

---

[60] *New York Times*, March 11, 1928.

"Metropolis" as communistic propaganda and that Italian authorities ordered deletions from the picture, while in China the Manchurian Government rescinded its ban against "The Big Parade" after appropriate deletions.[61]

Premier Mussolini is said to have paid high tribute to the importance of talking motion pictures after he had viewed his own image and had heard his own words recorded on the instrument known as Movietone.

"This can bring the world together; it can settle all differences; it can become the international medium, educator and adjuster; it can prevent war," the Premier is reported to have said.[62]

The importance of the introduction of sound in conjunction with the use of motion pictures, especially for propaganda, educational and musical purposes cannot be overestimated.

Some of its effectiveness may be imagined by some of the further comment contained in this article.

"If," continues *Variety*, "movietone carries Mussolini to every incorporated village of this country, which it will do if the installation cost is around $2,500, millions of Americans will suffer altered opinions of Mussolini, believed by many to be the brainiest man of this modern-day world. His face suggests great force; he looks and speaks ruggedly, and his message to the people of the United States as conveyed by the movietone is simplicity in its directness and sincerity. * * * His address is brief. He first reads it from script in Italian, repeating it in English without the script. Side views on the same reel are extremely interesting. Perhaps mostly so, the singing and running regiment of Italian soldiers, evidently Italy's crack military detachment. As these men with military precision come galloping down the great Plaza where they drill before the camera, the music is picked up as played by the band, and as that dies away in the distance, the tapping

---

[61] *Film Daily*, November 29, 1927.
[62] *Variety*, September 21, 1927.

of the trotting feet becomes a lull, like the hum of an auto engine. Another pretty picture is this same regiment grouped and singing their regimental song, probably in Italian and waving their caps upon the peak of their scabbards. * * * For politics, entertainment, propaganda or any purpose that may be made appealing, movietone seems supreme at present. Much superior to radio with its fleeting moment in the air and no substance behind that, such as the face, voice, fame and name that movietone can give."

The article concludes with the suggestion that the talking motion picture is perhaps a discovery and the perfection of an invention that may be sufficient to replace the physical presence that has been so necessary to certain types of amusement as shown upon the stage, thus permitting in substance the substitution of this mechanical device for musical comedy, or the comedy with dialogue or other similar performances.

The following article from the *New York Times* is extremely significant.

Italy's new cinema policy promises to be even more advanced than that of France.[63]

"Diplomatic circles," said the *Times*, "are watching with great interest the rapidly advancing plans of Premier Mussolini to bring the Italian film industry under his personal domination. According to those closely in touch with the developments the scheme has two main objects: First, to use the powerful propaganda of the motion picture and of the screen's latest achievement, the talking film, to insure continuation of the Fascist regime, and, second, to restore the Italian film industry to its pre-war place among the leading film-producing nations of the world.

"Aside from the political aspects, the situation is of more than passing importance to the American film industry, which dominates the Italian market and expects largely increased revenues in the next

---

[63] *New York Times*, October 2, 1928.

five years. If Signor Mussolini's ideas are carried out—and there is every reason to believe that they will succeed—a Government film monopoly will dictate the number and kind of foreign pictures to be imported into Italy and the prices they may command. Furthermore, only those foreign concerns which guarantee a wide distribution of the Italian productions will obtain the very necessary protection of the Italian Government. It will thus be seen that the Americans stand to lose heavily if the plan is fulfilled.

"It is understood that Signor Mussolini, who was one of the first important European figures to appear in a talking film, is profoundly impressed with the new phase of the art of the screen. A medium that makes it possible to be seen and heard in hundreds of places at the same time is, in the opinion of the Italian dictator, of tremendous political importance.

"The Premier has already imposed an 'Italian Film Week' upon the owners of all the Italian movie theatres. In principle none but Italian films can be shown for one week during each month, but for the present it has been found that the domestic production is not up to the requirements of such a drastic decree.

"To overcome this handicap the Duce, through his film advisers, has entered into a production agreement with the German firm of UFA, whereby the latter is to supply the technical staff and the latest equipment for speeding up Italian film making.

"Similar arrangements have been made with the largest British film producers—the British International Company—and today it is announced that a third contract has just been signed with one of the large French companies. From the French, German and British industries Premier Mussolini hopes to draw sufficient brains and equipment to make Italy once more a factor in the film world.

"Of course, the three agreements are mutual in character and in return for favors, Italy has agreed to do everything possible to advance the interests of the French, German and British pictures in the Italian markets.

"Still another step in the Italian Government's plans for taking over the film industry has been the creation of the National Film Office to supply 1,500,000 feet of film each year on topics of interest to the Italian people.

"The Fascist regime is expected to play a leading role in these productions.

Picture Propaganda and Peace

"The Government film monopoly will give ample financial support to all firms desiring to make 'national' films. Many of the leading Italian banks have agreed to underwrite the activities of the National Institute, which will be under the direct supervision of the Ministry of National Economy, and which will be closely scrutinized by Signor Mussolini himself.

"The Italian film decree, placing a 10 per cent quota on exhibitors, with a minimum rental price for domestic productions, is thus giving way to the Premier's scheme for a State-controlled industry.

"There are also well-founded reports that a Government monopoly will soon take over all the 'first-run' film theatres as a completing link in film domination.

"The real danger for the American film trade lies in the possibility that in order to continue operations in the Italian market it will be necessary to distribute a large block of Italian films annually in the United States."

The British picture entitled "Dawn," which purports to tell the story of Edith Cavell, did much to induce some clear thinking on this subject. The picture was well described in the *London Times*.[64]

---

[64] A reprint of the description from the *New York Times* of March 5, 1928, is in part as follows:

"At the start we are shown Nurse Cavell helping her first refugee to escape, without quite realizing what all of this one escape is going to imply, and then the story is developed to its inevitable dramatic conclusion. The first refugee is hidden in a cellar in her hospital in Brussels and is eventually smuggled away through Holland by means of a barge whose owner is, we understand, friendly to Nurse Cavell because his wife insists that he shall be. Other escapes follow, and it is shown how gradually the wish to rescue her fellow countrymen increases until the scenes of the cellar, which was at first a vast empty space with one solitary figure in it, becomes crowded with unfortunate allied subjects. The way in which they are smuggled out through the cellar by a concealed entrance is described, and there follow their escapes through neutral territory to their own countries. It has already been indicated in the film that some of the junior officers of the German army in Brussels are suspicious of Nurse Cavell's activities, and there is a house-to-house search from which she barely emerges without being discovered. Then an informer goes to the German authorities. In the original version this informer was a Frenchman. Now it has been decided that he shall be of no nationality. The particular junior officer involved acts on this information at once. According to the film he has

Motion Picture Problems

The obviously right point of view on this subject is that expressed so ably by Lord Birkenhead, Secretary for

already been reprimanded for his slackness in dealing with the matter of escaping refugees and it is indicated that it is in the first place a matter of military duty that he should pin what is obviously a military crime on the principal offender. The hospital of Nurse Cavell is more thoroughly searched even than before and the hiding place in the cellar is discovered. We are shown a great number of refugees escaping, and all are gone when the German soldiers start their search, but there is evidence enough and to spare and Nurse Cavell is arrested. Scenes in prison follow and her trial is shown in some detail. These scenes suggest that, while the Germans were not very likely to be impressed by her advocate, yet that the trial, from the military point of view, was a fair one. Then, when she is sentenced, she is taken back to prison, and so the film is brought to its climax with her death at the Tir National in Brussels.

"Nurse Cavell is taken into the shooting gallery by German soldiers, and there is a long episode showing her gradual approach to the spot at which she is to stand to meet her death. Placed there, the scene shifts to the firing party in charge of a young officer. This officer says, 'Firing party ready,' and when they come to this position a private in the party, who has already been indicated in a previous scene, refuses to shoot. The officer goes up to him and, after a brief expostulation, draws his revolver and levels it. The scene ends here, and the next one starts with the private's body lying on the ground in front of the firing squad. The scene then changes to Nurse Cavell, who, it is suggested, is overcome by the death of the private. She falls fainting to the ground. While she is on the ground the firing party is brought back to the 'Order.' A superior officer indicates to the officer in charge of the firing party that he must do his duty, and the scene then changes to the face of the Lutheran Chaplain, who was the only spiritual adviser allowed to be present. The expression on his face suggests that something terrible is going to happen, and the next scene shows the officer in charge pointing to his junior's revolver holster. The latter winces but draws his revolver. The scene is taken back to the recumbent figure of Nurse Cavell and back again to the officer, and with that the shooting episode ends. The next scene shows the grave of Nurse Cavell next to the grave of the shot German soldier.

"In itself, the scene is inevitably a little repellent, but it is difficult to know whether it could possibly have been made less so. Its historical accuracy is a more debatable point. Throughout Sybil Thorndike makes a dignified figure of Nurse Cavell, and an impression is always left that all the characters (except the informer) whether English, Belgian, American or German, are, in the main concerned in doing what, rightly, or wrongly, they consider to be their duty. The artistic value of the production can be more properly discussed later."

Picture Propaganda and Peace

India, in a letter to the *London Daily Telegraph*.[65]

"In the discussions which are proceeding upon the subject," said Lord Birkenhead, "it appears to me that the decisive considerations are being rather surprisingly ignored. The question is not whether the German government has any right to request a censorship over the British film. Most evidently they have no such right.

"The question is not whether our present system—such as it is—of censorship is satisfactory. Very likely it is not. The question is not whether any films heretofore exhibited in Germany have been calculated to give offense in allied countries.

"The issues (for there are two) cut far deeper.

"The first is: Is it in the interests of peace and international goodwill that we should perpetuate by public exhibition those incidents of the war which most embitter its memories? Do we desire, or do we not desire, that a new era of peace should dawn in Europe?

"Do we, or do we not, desire by every means in our power to increase that mutual good feeling which must be established in Europe unless all alike are to perish in ruin? Do we serve any useful purpose by exasperating and humiliating a government which has shown by its repudiation of the Hohenzollern dynasty its opinion of that dynasty and of its works?

"Is it really our wish that while attempting to complete the Locarno edifice, Baralong films, true or false, should be exhibited in Germany, and Nurse Cavell films in the allied countries?

"I should myself have thought it was a commonplace that every man and, still more, every woman, of good intention, who does not wish to see his son or her son involved in another war, would strive by every effort to put away the memory of these old unhappy things in the effort to establish a new and more humane relationship.

"We are told that the existence in London of a statue to the heroic and incomparable woman whom it commemorates forever, is inconsistent with these views. It is not. A dignified memorial to the immortal dead has as little relation to the incidents of a hectic film as a classical picture of the crucified Jesus to the attempt to commercialize His anguish for the purposes of Hollywood.

"The second point seems to me to be even more decisive. What

---

[65] Reprinted in *New York Times*, April 7, 1928.

would Nurse Cavell herself have said about this proposal? The true purposes of this sainted woman—her only message to the world—are engraved on her memorial:

"'Patriotism is not enough. I must have no hatred or bitterness for any one.

"Does any one suppose that the woman who, at the very moment of her agony, could speak like this would permit her death to be commercialized, with the certain result that the bitter memories associated with it would be kept alive and fertilized so as to prevent the sweet restoration of friendship and good relationship between the nations of the world?

"And what is the object of this adventure, over the frustration of which we are invited to shed tears? Is it to preach a holy message? Are the profits to be devoted to some charitable purpose? Will they establish foundation scholarships to train a new generation of women to the Nurse Cavell standards?

"Or are they intended to bring in profit to the producer and those associated with him? If this, indeed, be the purpose, is it decent so to exploit the agony and the sacrifice of the noblest woman whom the war produced? And so to exploit it in circumstances which, as I have shown, make it almost certain that nothing in the world could have seemed more horrible to that brave, proud and sensitive nature."

Sir Austen Chamberlain evidently shared substantially the same point of view.

The *New York Times* reported Sir Austen as saying, speaking as an "English gentleman," that he thought the picture "an outrage on humanity."

Sir Austen was informed by the government's technical adviser that the execution scene as filmed showed one of the firing party refusing to level his rifle and being shot on the spot, the remainder firing over Miss Cavell's head and a German officer then dispatching her while she lay fainting on the ground.

"I believe that account of the execution," Sir Austen

is reported to have said,[66] "to be wholly apocryphal and it is an outrage on a noble woman's memory to turn for purposes of commercial profit so heroic a story. It appears to be inherently incredible and I am informed that it was certainly incorrect. It was on my own responsibility that I acted and if I had to do it again, I would act in the same way."

Much indignation was expressed by the German press and the *Taegliche Rundschau,* the organ of Foreign Minister Stresemann, and a number of other papers are said to have declared that the production of a work of this kind is a blow against "the rapprochement of the nations desired by all countries." "The *Rundschau,*" says the Times,[67] "expresses the hope that the British Government will find a way to suppress the film which it alleged was only intended to rekindle the hatreds of the war period."

The same article declared that the foreign office of the German Government issued the following statement:

"The German Ambassador at London and the German Minister at Brussels are making all efforts to prevent the Nurse Cavell film being shown to the public, their standpoint being that such a film can only revive painful memories and embitter relations between the two countries."

Mr. T. P. O'Connor, the Chairman of the British Cinema Censorship Board, did his best to prevent the picture's exhibition in England. "It is quite true," he is reported to have said, "that as chief of the Board of Censors, I put the ban upon "Dawn" and that was done because the general

---
[66] *New York Times*, February 28, 1928.
[67] *New York Times*, February 9, 1928.

intelligent sentiment in England is to abstain from anything which stirs up the old animosities and hatreds which began with the World War and which would better remain buried."[68]

Later he was reported to have said: "I dare say efforts will be made to secure an exhibition of the film despite the bann, but I can unhesitatingly say I think that they won't succeed. I believe the Home Office has the same objection as the Foreign Office and ourselves. I have had only one letter criticizing the action of the Board and that was from my good friend, George Bernard Shaw, who is always wrong. The Board naturally is bound to consider the opinions of many of the most eminent statesmen of Europe and in doing so have very directly attempted to bring about a spirit of pacification in Europe which would be most helpful in preventing future wars. It was the theme we objected to, rather than the manner in which it was played."

But the picture was exhibited in England, although commercialism apparently had to divide with "charity" to accomplish it.

The decision of the British Board of Film Censors not to approve the presentation of "Dawn" was received with mixed feelings in England. It is said that many members of Parliament sought an occasion to bring the matter before the House of Commons, and that they would urge the Foreign Office immediately to indicate its policy with regard to future war films apparently upon the commercial ground that it is hardly fair to allow a British

---

[68] *New York Times*, February 29, 1928.

company to undertake expensive film productions if their work is liable to be endangered before it is shown to the public.[69]

The same article continued, "The *London Times* is inclined to question the Government's action in using pressure to have the film banned on account of its 'inexpediency.' 'Inexpedient' is a dangerous word on a censor's lips," it says. What is the nature of the inexpediency? In view of what has gone before the adjective 'political' instantly suggests itself and a political censorship, in whatever discreet feathers it be dressed, is, in England at least, a remarkably ugly bird."

In America the film apparently encountered no difficulty in obtaining admission to the country, notwithstanding the existence of ample power, strangely enough lodged with the Secretary of the Treasury, to prevent its entrance.[70]

It was passed by the New York State Censorship Commission [71] with the exception of a few sub-titles and certain scenes relating to the execution, which demonstrates that when censors have an opportunity to decide correctly, they fail to avail themselves of it.

A considerable debate and controversy at once arose with reference to the subject.

A German doctor and others in America gave their version of the incidents of the picture. And many rushed headlong into print on the burning controversial issue—

---
[69] *New York Times*, February 22, 1928.
[70] U. S. Tariff Act, 1922. Chap. X, page 135, Note 8, Par. 1453.
[71] *New York Times*, April 10, 1928.

an issue here which involved nothing more important than Mr. Selwyn's right to improve his financial position by commercializing the subject in America, at the possible risk of jeopardizing the present friendly sentiment of the people of America and Germany.

A considerable intelligent sentiment was expressed against its exhibition in America.

Mr. James W. Gerard, our distinguished war-time ambassador to Berlin, himself the author of an interesting war story, "My Four Years in Germany," from which a war picture of the same name was successfully produced, vigorously opposed its exhibition.

"Certainly it is anything but wise after the war is over," Mr. Gerard is reported to have said, "to represent incidents on the screen which may irritate other nations. I think that is specially true of this film, which is not a historical production and is one on which the emphasis is laid on unpleasant incidents. I am greatly surprised that the State Censors should have passed it.

"Motion pictures are today the most powerful means of propaganda existing. Where hundreds see a play, thousands read a book and hundreds of thousands read our newspapers, millions of persons see motion pictures, which, together with the radio, reach more people than any other methods of communication."[72]

Mr. Otto Kahn expressed the substance of the views of Lord Birkenhead and Sir Austen Chamberlain.[73]

---

[72] *New York Times*, April 12, 1928.
[73] *New York Times*, May 12, 1928.

After stating that he had not seen the film and that he had been told that the subject is reverently treated with a manifest desire to avoid the stimulation of animosities, Mr. Kahn said, "but that is not the point. The point as I see it is: Right-minded people everywhere are eager that nothing be done to keep awake or revive, and that everything be done to assuage and efface the bitter memories of the late war. They are eager that every endeavor be made to have the peoples of the world, and especially those who lately were in arms against one another, come together in a spirit of good will and fairness and enlightened cooperation, looking away from the past to the present and the future.

"To use for a sheer commercial purpose—and there is not even a pretense that the purpose of showing the Cavell film is other than to make money—the pathetic story and the tragic end of a signally noble woman is to me an utterly repellant proceeding. It is desecrating, for mere financial gain, a memory which ought to be held sacred, but the appealing eloquence of which should be mute. * * * It seems to me peculiarly incumbent upon those who, like myself, from the fateful August days of 1914 on, took their stand unequivocally with the Allied cause, to protest—because of the very spirit and sentiment which actuated their attitude—against the public exhibition of the Cavell film."

The versatile Mayor of New York is reported to have said with reference to it:

"I regard with disfavor the presentation of anything

calculated to revive war hatreds or to disturb the peaceful relations of Germany and the United States or any of the other nations."[74]

The same article reported Dr. Nicholas Murray Butler, President of Columbia University and Director of Carnegie Endowment for International Peace, as saying:

"It is my earnest hope that nothing will be undertaken, least of all for gain, that will renew the bitter memories and unhappy experiences of the Great War. It is far better now that we all bend our efforts to rebuilding the world which the War smashed to pieces and to provide for that rebuilding a firm foundation of international understanding, international sympathy and international helpfulness."

Senator Borah telegraphed: "I do not know just what the attitude of the public would be, but it should be distinctly adverse," while Mr. H. L. Mencken on the other hand declared:

"I am very strongly against trying to prevent the showing of the Cavell picture. The German Government will be very badly advised if it tries to promote friendly relations with Germany and the United States by interfering with the rights of the American people to see, say and think whatever they please.[75] I assume that the picture is

---

[74] *New York Times*, February 18, 1928.

[75] This is a curious misconception of the situation. No public would have an opportunity to have its sensibilities offended if it were not for the desire of a producer to profit by the public's willingness to be harrowed by any subject no matter how undesirable its public exhibition might be. What is the ox which is gored to do, remain passive or be gored to death by propaganda which is false in part and to which there is no adequate response?

swinish and abominable, but I am unalterably against any effort to stop its showing."

Pseudo and questionable "art" and claptrap about the freedom of the press and screen are the familiar bulwarks and safeguards of those who pander to the lowest instincts of humanity for profit. And in the confusion of thought which follows, brilliant minds like that of the incomparable Mr. Shaw, and the clever Mr. Mencken, are unconsciously led into pointless by-paths.

Thus the advertisement of the picture featured the knowing countenance of the "world's greatest literary genius" with what he was supposed to have said concerning it, as follows:[76]

"You might as well suggest that Sir George Frampton's monument should be demolished or veiled. The only question to be considered is whether the film, as a work of art, is worthy of her.

"You may take my word for it that it is.

"You have a most moving and impressive incarnation of that heroine by our greatest tragic actress whose dignity keeps the whole story on the highest plane. It has been planned and told by a young film poet who has been entirely faithful to his great theme. He has not betrayed her by a single stroke of bitterness or rancor, much less by any idle triviality of fiction.

"Both author and actress have felt, and will make us feel, that the law that Edith Cavell set above a military code and died for, is an infinitely higher law than the law of war and the conceit of patriotism.

"It rebukes us all impartially, and will edify us impartially. I hope it will take its lessons to the end of the earth."

Even the invitation to attend a private unprofessional showing of the picture in America bore the unmistakable marks of professionalism. It declared:

"As it would be as inappropriate to release 'Dawn' in a 'movie'

---

[76] *New York Times,* May 30, 1928.

Motion Picture Problems

house as it would be to celebrate Mass on Times Square, the presentation in the theatre (the Times Square Theatre, not being a movie theatre but a 'regular' theatre, whatever difference that may make) is as impressive as the play of 'Oberamergau'."

This is the same "spiritualistic" conception which induced the industry to present the "King of Kings," a life of Christ, in the "Gaiety" Theatre in New York.

Finally an attempt was made to clothe the purely commercial objective of the presentation of the picture "Dawn" in America behind the familiar screen of a division of the proceeds of exhibition with charity.

Thus Mr. Selwyn, the proprietor of the picture in America, is reported to have declared that:[77]

"It is not an effort to commercialize Edith Cavell's great sacrifice or to appeal to national prejudice and try to resurrect the feeling of bitterness between enemies who, having declared peace, seek to have it firmly cemented. The contrary is the case.

"From the commercial point of view a percentage of all the profits of the picture, no matter where shown—and it is a liberal percentage—is being diverted to the nursing homes which have been established in the memory of Edith Cavell. In London 50 percent of the receipts are being diverted to the Edith Cavell Hospital, the superintendent of which is the sister of the woman who gave her life to the cause of mankind."

Here the argument ceases with the assertion that the persistent efforts to discredit "Dawn" were obviously inspired by blind prejudice.

But more effective than all of the expressions of opinions on the subject was the refusal of the Paramount and Loew Companies to permit the picture to be shown in any

---

[77] *New York Times*, May 13, 1928.

PICTURE PROPAGANDA AND PEACE

of the houses controlled by these important companies.[78]

After all, it was not Mr. Zukor's picture nor that of Mr. Schenck. Why should it be shown in their houses?

The trade press seized upon this incident to prate about the sensitiveness of the American industry to the promotion of international "amity." And in the discussion it assumed virtues, in the industry's unwillingness to profit by this unholy film, in no way justified by its conduct in paralyzing every other cinema production industry in the world through its economic and commercial policies and practices, and in the exhibition everywhere of other pictures, to many of which reference has been made, which are quite as destructive of international amity as "Dawn."[79]

---

[78] *The New York Times* of April 23, 1928, said
"Charles C. Moskowitz, General Theatre Representative and assistant for Nicholas M. Schenck, President of Loew's Theatre said it had been the general policy to give the people what they want and in this instance it had been agreed that 'Dawn' would not meet with popular approval, but might create ill-will among persons of different nationality.

"'I think this is quite obvious from the opinions that have already been expressed by different people who are qualified to judge,' he declared.

The *New York Times* of April 25 said:
"James W. Gerard, former Ambassador to Germany, who has been active in the fight to prevent 'Dawn' from being shown in New York and other cities conferred with Adolph Zukor, President of Paramount, yesterday morning and the official announcement was sent out later in the day. Mr. Gerard declared yesterday that Mr. Zukor had expressed the opinion that 'Dawn' ought not to be presented because it seemed likely to prevent good feeling between nations."

[79] *Motion Pictures Today*, June 2, 1928, declared:
"The Producers and Distributors Association (The Hays Association) had committed itself long ago to lend its full assistance to the promotion of international amity and when the German authorities made their representation that the Cavell picture was anti-German propaganda the action was prompt and unanimous. * * * The motion picture

Motion Picture Problems

Thus from all parts of the world have come accounts of the public and governmental response to pictures which deal with these delicate, controversial, and moving subjects.

It seems particularly unfortunate that in so many instances these propaganda pictures are produced and circulated for no better ostensible purpose than to enable the film producers "to give the public what it wants," but in reality solely for the enrichment of the trade.

Is it not time that governments found effective means at least to suppress the mere commercialism of this type of subject matter, especially if and when the subject matter is untruthful and circulates misinformation or distorts the facts of history or is otherwise injurious to the public in any respect? And is it not clear that America should be the most concerned not only because most of the films, objectionable and otherwise, emanate from this country, but because the certain effect of the exhibition of films of the kind above described is seriously to injure and to impair American prestige abroad and to stimulate substantial dislike for us everywhere?

---

industry looked beyond dollars and cents in refusing to seek a cash clean-up on a sensational subject that held offense. * * * It is a matter of satisfaction to those who take pride in the motion picture industry that no one in the business touched the picture. Its presentation was under auspices not connected with pictures in any actual capacity but by a producer in the field of the spoken drama. The industry's hands are clean and it is our belief that they will remain so."

How, it may be asked, would it be possible for anyone to make a profit on any picture disapproved by the members of the Producers and Distributors Association of America? And as to the industry's sincerity, surely nothing need be added to the interminable list of seriously objectionable pictures which has already been recorded.

PICTURE PROPAGANDA AND PEACE

Is it not time that the American State Department and the Department of Commerce each changed its present policy towards this industry?

Both have blindly aided the industry to force its products, including many harmful and undesirable pictures, upon unwilling governments and audiences, overlooking, in their proper desire to aid an American industry, the far more important injury to American prestige abroad and to our friendly relations with the world which such a course involves or may involve.

Moreover, it is obviously extraordinary and improper for the State Department and the Department of Commerce, to aid abroad, industrialists here, who are charged by the Federal Trade Commission and by the Department of Justice to be engaged in one or more conspiracies to restrain or to monopolize international or interstate trade in this industry, in violation of our laws.[80]

The State Department and the Department of Commerce should say plainly and in no uncertain terms to these industrialists, "It is the duty of our Department to serve America first and thereafter to promote the interests of a particular American industry abroad. We will ren-

---

[80] See, (1) Federal Trade Commission vs. Famous Players Lasky Corporation, et al., decided against the respondents, July 9, 1927; (2) United States vs. Metro-Goldwyn-Mayer Distributing Corporation, et al., filed in the District Court of the United States for the Northern District of Illinois, Eastern Division, March, 1928, Term; (3) United States vs. Paramount Famous Lasky Corporation, et al., filed in the District Court of the United States for the Southern District of New York, in Equity, on or about May 4, 1928; (4) United States vs. First National Pictures, Inc., et al., filed at the same time and place; (5) United States vs. West Coast Theatres, Inc., et al., filed in the District Court of the United States for the Southern District of California, on or about September 28, 1928.

der no aid to any industrialists whose products are unworthy of America or whose merchandise impairs or threatens American prestige abroad or which offends the sensibilities of other governments or of other people, and until the industrialists who deal in desirable pictures, which are not harmful to the best interests of America, free themselves from charges now pending against them by the Department of Justice that they are engaged in conspiracies to violate our anti trust laws, no aid will be given to such industrialists either at home or abroad."

This would effectively coordinate the efforts and policies of these three departments, and it would tend to correct the injury abroad which this heedless trade is inflicting upon America as a whole.

(9) *The Elements Which Must Be Considered In the Formulation of the Remedy.*

It is apparent from the subject matter of the mass of propaganda films which have been reviewed, that war is at present the prevailing theme of these pictures.

Yet how incongruous it is that while publicists here and abroad, supporting the peace movement of the entire world, are exerting every effort to "scrap the war mind" and to "outlaw war," and while fifteen nations have actually signed and probably forty-five more will soon join in the great anti-war treaties, whereby each nation renounces war as a national policy, the motion picture industry in every producing country is busily engaged in producing and disseminating throughout the entire world, for exhibition to countless millions of people, pictures

PICTURE PROPAGANDA AND PEACE

which glorify war and which are in reality mere war propaganda—a propaganda persisted in not because motion picture producers or exhibitors like or want or believe in war any more than any other human beings, but because they know that the public will respond to such pictures and that a profit in their exhibition is assured to these sordid mercenaries, irrespective of the damaging and perhaps fatal results of the exhibition of such pictures.

The great anti-war treaties of August 27, 1928, which renounced war as a national policy, are a great step forward.

But all thoughtful people know that, as M. Briand is reported to have said, "it remains to organize the peace proclaimed in the Salle de l'Horloge."[81]

But how and in what manner will this Peace be organized? And what have motion pictures to do with matters of such vast importance to mankind?

The latter question is the only one within the scope of the present discussion.

Briefly, motion pictures have a tremendous relation to this subject.

In due course an international conference of government representatives will be called and held to discuss and to organize the detailed means by which the uniform national policy renouncing war may be made effective.

When that time comes, ways and means will be found to set up the adequate substitutes for the renounced policy as a means of settlement of the international disputes which constitute and are the causes of war.

---
[81] *New York Times*, August 28, 1928, quoting the Paris *Midi*.

What these causes are, are well understood by modern publicists.

Dr. Nicholas Murray Butler has dealt with them interestingly and ably on many occasions.

So has Lieutenant-Commander Kenworthy,[82] and it is not difficult to discern many of the causes from Mr. H. G. Wells' most recent book, *The Open Conspiracy.*

And it is clear to all that unless adequate means and facilities are afforded by which these causes may be eradicated with justice to all concerned, war will inevitably result notwithstanding all the treaties in the world to the contrary.

Whether these means will consist in the completion of an effective disarmament program, in a more general recourse to arbitration as a means of settlement of non-justiciable disputes, or in an enlargement of the compulsory jurisdiction of the Permanent Court of International Justice need not be considered here.

It has not been so clear until the present moment that the fancied causes of war as well as the real causes must be eliminated and that the treatment of these subjects necessarily leads to an adequate and sufficient control or regulation by appropriate and sound means of each and all of the instrumentalities through which the public mind is reached, influenced and misinformed upon these subjects which are now vital to the continued life of each nation and to the preservation of the world's peace.

Any machinery erected to aid in the preservation of international peace must include appropriate control

---
[82] Peace or War, p. 119, *et seq.*

of the means by which war is or may be stimulated or induced.

This must include particularly an adequate national and international treatment of motion pictures and probably of the other means of communication as well, with which, however, we are not now directly concerned.

Commander Kenworthy deplores the lack of peace propaganda comparable with that intentionally and unintentionally carried on in the present general glorification of war.

Publicity on the recent Anti-War Treaties[83] which agree to "outlaw war" has been extensive, but a means of co-ordinating national policies on peace propaganda, in times of peace, could be made of great value throughout the world.

Propaganda in times of peace has become increasingly important. It should be the first organized means of supporting the Anti-War Treaties. And the first of these instrumentalities to be organized should be the motion picture.

In war times it is promptly recognized as a major means of achieving victory and all of the facilities for propaganda are at once made to perform their functions with that primary objective constantly in mind.

But in times of peace the necessity for the same intensive organization and work directed to the maintenance and preservation of peace is not so apparent.

War and other propaganda pictures for public exhibi-

---

[83] Signed at Paris by 15 nations August 27, 1928.

tion, chiefly or solely for mercenary purposes, appear to be especially inexcusable.

The industry has no conviction which is supported by its pictures.

The industry merely knows the public taste for horror and panders to it for profit and, as the dealers in pornography hide behind the declaration that their pictures are educational, scientific or medical in character, so do these purveyors of the germs of war indulge in the deceitful assertion that their pictures are designed to show the horrors of war so that nations and people will not engage in it.

They also fall back upon the claim that the pictures are historical and hence educational, while in most instances, amusement pictures are, of course, nothing of the kind.

They are generally based upon romantic and fictional incidents surrounded by scenes of battle, the authenticity of which may not be relied upon with safety.

Thus they have little if any historic value in most instances and notwithstanding the absurdities of propaganda slogans such as "hateless" war films, the exhibition of war films to "prevent" and to "discourage" war, the basic fact remains that the purpose and object of the exhibition is the commercial profit of those who deal in such pictures, while the incidental effect may or may not incite the communities of two or more nations to war.

The gravity of the possible consequences of the wide dissemination and exhibition of such pictures, not unnaturally leads thoughtful people to ask why any group of in-

Picture Propaganda and Peace

dustrialists should be permitted to disseminate broadcast throughout the world their ill-considered, dangerous and harmful pictorial material solely in order that the industrialists may profit from the imbecility of the masses who are beguiled and lured, frequently by questionable methods of publicity, into paying money to see such pictures.

That governments have from time to time protested against the circulation of such harmful pictures, and the difficulties of making such protests effective beyond the territorial domains of each nation adversely affected, makes the need of an appropriate preventive and of a means of correction and suppression desirable.

Nationally if a picture offends it is comparatively easy to suppress its exhibition, although the picture industry everywhere is so adept in the skilful use of propaganda in its own behalf and the censorship officials are so stupid and so amenable or so easily misled that, what with arguments to the effect that a war film is a hateless picture, that the Edith Cavell picture is an argument against war, and displays many "noble" traits of German character, and is not intended to open the old wounds of animosity, although the Germans themselves resent it and protest against it bitterly, the officials permit many exhibitions which should obviously be suppressed.

But the task of a single nation in suppressing in other States the exhibition of pictures offensive to it is far more difficult, if not impossible, except in co-operation and by agreement among the nations.

France's ingenuity has suggested the wise requirement

that those presenting a picture for introduction into France shall supply satisfactory proof of the form in which that picture was exhibited in other countries, particularly in the country of its origin, and moreover, if it appear that the producer of the picture offered for importation into France has produced and circulated other pictures offensive to France, the privilege of importing even the inoffensive pictures may be denied until suitable amends for the exhibition of the offensive pictures have been made. This plan is effective only when adopted by countries whose prestige, and particularly, whose market, is of substantial importance.

But a country, the market of which is small or not lucrative to the importers of objectionable films, is by itself powerless to control or to prevent the circulation of these offensive pictures beyond its borders, and hence to prevent these results such nations particularly must resort to participation in the proposed cinema alliance with other nations to which reference will presently be made.

What has been said indicates that the uncontrolled dissemination of concealed motion picture propaganda which is untruthful and harmful is a menace of increasing importance to every existing government and that this instrumentality of public influence and communication is now of greater concern than ever before.

All thoughtful persons instinctively resent the possibility of governmental regulation or control of free speech, freedom of the press or freedom of action on the part of any of the other instruments of public communication, but many find themselves in the position of that humble branch of the motion picture industry in America known as the independent exhibitors who, while unanimously opposed to any governmental regulation over any branch of the industry, nevertheless prefer publicly to espouse proposed Federal regulation of the industry in America as a more desirable alternative than the continued domination of the industry by the few industrialists who now control it.

Theoretically most thoughtful people would choose governmental control of motion pictures rather than the unrestricted tyranny and control of a few private individuals whose only guide is and has been to fatten their own pocketbooks.

But powerful industries and "big business" have in the past been known to control governments and to have contributed substantially to the breakdown of law enforcement in America, which of late has been so painfully noticeable in certain fields[84] and so the alternative may under certain political administrations prove to be one and the same thing.

Internationally the control of governments by industries is far more difficult and although still possible, especially if the immense international influence and power of America is to be placed in the hands or under the direction of the representatives of the sordid motion picture industry

---

[84] Mr. Samuel Untermeyer in his able address at the College of the City of New York on July 30, 1928, reviews the subject in considerable detail.

in America, that possibility should not deter the several nations from the establishment of common facilities for the control of this important instrument of propaganda. On the contrary such a possibility should stimulate joint international action.

There is a natural desire not to question or impugn the wisdom of the ages, even when applied to conditions totally dissimilar to those with which the sages had to deal.

One may well wish to stand in all humility with Socrates, as philosopher, and say that "The sun might as easily be spared from the universe as free speech from the liberal institutions of society;" with Demosthenes, as politician, that "No greater calamity could come upon a people than the privation of free speech;" with Euripides, as dramatist, who declared "This is true liberty, when free born men, having to advise the public, may speak free;" and with Milton, as publicist, who said, "Give one the liberty to know, to utter and to argue freely according to conscience, above all liberties,"[85] aand yet desire more effective safeguards than those which exist at present in every field of modern public communication.

Unless the public has reached the stage when it is prepared to regard as cant and propaganda a great deal of the extravagant and exaggerated expressions concerning "liberty" and "freedom" by those who use these terms to afford themselves immunity while they abuse the rights of others, no practical results can be accomplished.

But it will not satisfy or serve to announce the mere

---

[85] These interesting quotations are found collected in the pamphlet entitled "The Press," by Sir Alfred Robbins.

platitude, even though it be correct, that truth is the great antidote of false propaganda as though by the prescription that only truth shall be uttered the millennium might be achieved.

For what is truth, and who possesses the courage and the virtue to speak it and how may its utterance by those congenitally and constitutionally opposed to it in every form, be induced or when necessary compelled?

The presentation of facts to the public and indeed even in private argument is and always has been a selective process in which the influence of origin, environment, circumstance, the wish and desire to believe and to substantiate one's subconscious convictions, and particularly the influence of self-interest has always played a dominating part.

Professor Hugo Munsterberg's able defense of Germany's position in the World War by showing the elusive character of the so-called facts is a masterpiece of true argument which is on the border-line of the sophistical.[86]

It leaves one clinging to the few fundamentals of belief which consoling reason tells us are unaffected by all other incidentals, whether the latter prove true or false.

He points out with telling effect that in any complex social situation different groups of ideas and moods lead to very divergent impulses and may find expressions which could hardly be understood as utterances of one central will.

"We are not aware," he continues, "of the last consequences of our own ideas. A mind is a big democracy in which a mass meeting in any

---
[86] *The Peace and America.* (D. Appleton & Co.) 35 *et seq.*

country may vote resolutions which would be hissed down in some other region. A land has not one mind, and a mind has not either. In any complex social situation we may speak and act with an inner feeling of perfect sincerity, and yet possess in the marginal regions of our mind many ideas which would demand the opposite kind of talk and action and which might in another hour push themselves into the center and take control of our behavior. La Rochefoucauld says that in every misfortune of our friends is something which we enjoy, and a hundred epigrams tell the same story of the mind's duplicity * * * Many contrasting ideas may even be in perfect equilibrium, each entirely sincere and each filling the whole mind when the situation is favoring it. * * * Hence, even if we analyze the multi-colored books of documents, we cannot find the real facts and cannot discover what this or that statesman really wanted. * * * The struggle about the true facts concerning the origin of the war usually start from psychologically wrong premises. * * * But the sins of the fact seekers go still further. They cannot help underscoring the data which fit their argument and ruling out the disturbing facts, if a point of view can be found from which they become invisible. My friend from the other side and I discuss the nationality of Alsace. I am so proud of my German Alsace, which I love, and am so delighted with its thoroughly patriotic German attitude during the war. How could it be otherwise, as every soldier from Alsace was born under the German flag? Alsace has been German as long as anyone who went with his regiment can remember it. But my friend claims Alsace is French because it was under the French regime fifty years ago, and a hundred years ago, and two hundred years ago. That is, he claims Alsace was always French. But does he not know any history? What do those two centuries under the French regime mean? Alsace was always German. When Louis XIV tore it away from the German people it had been thoroughly German since early medieval times. What did the short French rule mean compared with a thousand years of German national life? His fact is that Alsace was always French, and mine that Alsace was always German. I ignore the little episode of foreign rule which surely has not broken the thoroughly German language and tradition of the Alsacian farmer, and he ignores whatever passed before the French grasped it, because he thinks two hundred years are enough to look backward. We are both right.

"And where did this war start? The German might say, 'With the

Picture Propaganda and Peace

Russian mobilization.' The Russian would answer, 'No, before, with Austria's sharp ultimatum to Serbia.' But the Austrian would reply, 'The war began with the assassination of the Archduke.' The British would insist: 'It began much earlier with Germany's new fleet program.' The Germans date it back to King Edward's encircling policy which welded all Europe together against Germany. The French would say: 'On the contrary, it began with Bismarck's taking Lorraine.' And Germany shouts: 'Napoleon.' And Europe says: 'Frederick the Great.' And Germany trumps: 'Louis XIV.' Yet that is all superficial. Charlemagne had a most important influence on it. And if you say: 'No, the real trouble began with the great migration in the fifth century, it may be true; and yet I think the beginning was much earlier.

"Facts become facts by our selection.

"We poor newspaper readers, of course, face constant influences of this type in the big headliners and the other selective agencies of the modern press. * * * But our trust in facts has still deeper springs. No one can overcome his personal relation to the sources of information. Our feeling of confidence is essential to the very structure of our facts. The whole history of politics, of scholarship, of religion, can be explained psychologically only if we understand the tremendous importance of the personal readiness to accept or to reject the so-called facts. The faithful believer may listen to the priests of the other sect and yet his mind is deaf; he may see, and yet he is blind. If a certain statesman is the high priest of your cult, his documents are politically sacred; every doubt is inhibited in the lower brain centers before it can reach the sphere of deliberation. * * * But the fate of our facts is still more pitiful on account not only of our prejudices and beliefs, but on account of the association which has been developed in our individual life history. * * * But the influence of our mental associations colors the facts even in the most erudite minds. The papers yesterday brought out the fervent speech of the one man in the admiration of whose thorough knowledge and wisdom we men of all creeds are unanimous. Charles W. Eliot, the brave leader of the anti-neutral party, directed the attack against the Germans this time from a new side. He showed that the Germans lacked that freedom of spirit which shows itself in a nation's inventiveness. He said: 'Most of the war equipment which the Germans are now working to full capacity, including the telephone and telegraph, the wireless, electric communication of power, the aeroplane, the torpedo and the submarine were all originated, not in the Fatherland but chiefly in the Anglo Saxon countries.' Here we have expressed concrete facts, and they resound effectively in every American mind, where the same associations are held in readiness. Of course the telegraph is Morse, and the telephone is Bell, and the aeroplane is Wright, and the wireless is Marconi, and the torpedo is Whitehead, and so on. How different the same facts look when the circle of association is less influenced by American tradition. I got my physics in Germany, and therefore naturally think of the fact that the first electro-magnetic telegraph was invented and used by Gauss and Webber in Gottingen in 1833 and immediately afterward improved by Steinheil in Munich, who introduced the optical point signs. Only several years after Gauss and Webber did Morse come forward. And just as Germans had the first telegraph, they had the first telephone, which was invented by Phillip Reis in Frankfort-am-Main. As to the electric communication of power I do think that Werner Seimens was the first who, in the 70s, built electrically controlled vehicles. As to the aeroplane, I do not want to disparage the fine work of my friend Langley, but surely Lilienthal of Berlin was the first who invented the motor flying machine, which flew more than a thousand feet. The principles of the wireless transmission of ether waves was discovered by Heinrich Hertz of Bonn."

And here Dr. Munsterberg demonstrates the tremendous influence of origin, of conviction and of the other elements mentioned in the selection of facts, for he adds:

"Only the torpedoes and submarines were indeed not invented by Germans; evidently the imagination of the Germans does not run in the direction of such man-killing machines. But in every sphere of lifesaving and of life-furthering German inventiveness from the days of the first printing press to the present day appears as a most pronounced feature; and yet the leader of American thought denies its existence altogether. We say facts, and we mean will-o-the-wisps.

"But the queerest thing is," continued Dr. Munsterberg, "that not only you and I see the same facts differently, but that surely you and even I saw it yesterday so and see it today otherwise, and will see it tomorrow again quite differently. * * *

"It is not worth while to contrast the views of this season and of last, when penny-a-liners signed the proclamations on the merits of foreign lands. They simply write as the fashion commands. But it is of instructive value to see how even the strongest and the most independent thinkers change and change and always still believe firmly that they speak of facts. * * *,

"Hundreds of thousands have become convinced that there is no liberty in Germany and no morality and no sense of truth, not because they have reason to believe so, but because Charles W. Eliot has said so with emphasis and he surely can see the true facts more clearly than the crowd. Yet only a year ago in one of the most forcible speeches I ever heard from this great man, he said in New York, speaking of American students who had gone to Germany: 'They saw how two great doctrines which had sprung from the German Protestant reformation had been developed by Germans from seed then planted in Germany. The first was the doctrine of universal education developed from the Protestant conception of individual responsibility, and the second was the great doctrine of civil liberty, liberty in industry, in society, in government, liberty with order under law. These two principles took their rise in Protestant Germany and America has been the greatest beneficiary of that noble teaching."

It is not surprising that Dr. Munsterberg concluded with the following inquiries:

"Are facts only fables and fancies? Does every untruth really become a fact if it is repeated often enough? Does only the one fact stand: That there are no facts?"

Surely this illuminating discussion indicates in its application to this subject the supreme difficulty which these problems present.

Yet an effort must be made to improve the existing intolerable conditions even though their complete correction may not be possible.

The urge and pressure of competition is the supposed excuse and justification for the exploitation of the public for personal profit.

Yet if competitive conditions were made equal by law, which is and ought to be the law's function, not by a censorship of the press or of pictures or of any other instrument of public communication, but by a simple prohibitory declaration directed against a limited group of subject matter, the purveyors of communications to the public would have to assume the responsibility for their own product and conduct as they should, and if they offended, bear the consequences of their own offense.

It is not difficult to suggest the subject matter which should be proscribed.

War propaganda in time of peace, all concealed false propaganda in peace time, whatever its objective may be, the intentional or unintentional disparagement or ridicule of race, nationality or religion, the treatment of crime in an informative and attractive manner, the distortion of historical fact and the mutilation of classical literature and, indeed, whatever is deemed by duly constituted authority to contribute materially to the injury of the public, should obviously be among the prohibited subjects.

There is no liberty which should sanction or permit any group of conscienceless mercenaries to profit through the exploitation of human weaknesses.

Freedom of expression is not the only right of mankind.

In dealing with untruthful publicity and concealed propaganda, much of the controversial issue presented by the inquiry, what is truth, is dispelled by the compulsory disclosure of the persons or interests in whose behalf the publicity or propaganda is issued.

If the disclosure of personal interest be made the condition of publication and exhibition, the public as well as the duly constituted public authorities may judge of its truth or falsity whenever the issue is properly presented.

But it is essential that the public be informed and not misinformed on these subjects.

So far as pictures are concerned the effort should be to induce a species of control which will not impair or restrict the processes of thought or of freedom of legitimate expression.

The light of truthful publicity from an official channel directed to propaganda material which is concealed, false and misleading, would do much to clarify and to improve existing conditions.

Such publicity would deprive propaganda pictures of much of their injurious quality, especially if such films themselves were required to carry the official information that they are deemed by duly constituted authority to be of the kind described, since such statement would expose the vital fact of self-interest and at least apprise the intelligent of this most material circumstance.

Since propaganda is an assault upon the public mind which frequently befogs and misleads it into decisions which it alone must make, the first effort should be to formulate a program under which at least the intelligent public may be enlightened, if it wishes, without in any way impairing the legitimate freedom of action, of communication or of thought in which even the propagandist should be permitted to indulge.

When we consider the activities of the tabloid and sensational press, those of the advertisers and publicity representatives of industry, particularly the fact that motion pictures can now reach millions of people daily and by this means impregnate their minds with views of life or with ideas, which in a comparatively short time may well create a condition of mind that may turn a nation from peace to war, is it not clear that it has become and is the duty of the nations of the world, at least in the interests of the preservation of the world's peace, as well as in the interest of the preservation of the non-aggressive national ideals of each, to establish the necessary outposts to deal effectively with this subject and at least with the authority and duty to expose falsehood designed to mislead and to deceive the public to their serious detriment?

(10) *The Remedy.*

The basis of this control must be a national prescription, either legislative or executive, which will prohibit the production, distribution or exhibition within the borders of the nation, of pictures of a specified kind.

It is impossible to deal with the subject of propaganda, in detail, by legislation.

It is highly dangerous to attempt to do so, but a legislative prohibition against the use of concealed and false propaganda and the creation of a Bureau—preferably attached to the office of the Commissioner of Education in America or the Minister of Education elsewhere—authorized to formulate rules and regulations to render the statute effective is possible and is free from the dangers of detailed legislative prescription.

If unreasonable rules are adopted which impair any of the constitutional or other rights of the propagandists, the courts are open to them; and if the rules promulgated are reasonable and impair no such rights the courts will sustain the validity of the rules adopted.

It is important in this connection that among the rules adopted should be one which will require the submission of all pictures to the Bureau before their release, for inspection and tabulation for statistical purposes. This is not censorship, since there should be no power in the Bureau in America to suppress by itself pictures deemed by it to offend the law.

This is not a burden or a hardship upon the industry as is demonstrated by the fact that for years past practically all of the pictures produced in America are said to have been voluntarily presented by the producers to the National Board of Review for inspection before their release.

If, after inspection by the Bureau, the Bureau is of the opinion that a picture contains harmful, concealed or false propaganda, it should be its duty to apply to the appropriate courts for an injunction to prevent its distribution and exhibition.

Thus the rights of all concerned would be properly safeguarded and protected.

Another rule which should be adopted by the Bureau is one that will authorize the Bureau to require the distributors to place upon any films found by the Bureau to contain such propaganda the statement that the picture contains it and that it is circulated in the interests of the propagandist.

Thus the public would be informed of the vital fact of self-interest in viewing a film which contains propaganda which, while not necessarily false, should nevertheless be described as it is in reality.

The basis of international control must be an international alliance evidenced by a brief accord which would vest in a common agency accepted by these nations the powers hereinafter described.

It is useless, unwise and inexpedient to pronounce edicts against the use of propaganda.

The attempted repression might well be worse than the disease itself.

Protagonists of anything short of treason, crime, immorality and the abuse of education have a right to use propaganda if not found to be false and harmful.

It is believed that the propaganda duties and functions of such a Bureau might be made of great value.

As a basis for the intelligent exercise of its function it should establish suitable catalogues of pictures exhibited nationally and it should have general powers and duties to collect and publish statistical data and to facilitate the exchange of educational pictures with other nations.

It is important to know the character of the scenes and subject matter exhibited to the public from which data alone intelligent estimates may be made of their public effect and of the means most suitable to afford the public proper protection.

Thus its propaganda functions should properly become and be an incident of permanent and perhaps more important duties, all of which would fit into the general scheme of a gradually enforced and enforcible cultural improvement in the quality of pictorial subject matter exhibited everywhere.

CHAPTER IV

THE LEAGUE OF NATIONS AND THE INTERNATIONAL PROBLEMS

As the result of the League's activities in economic matters, an Economic Conference was held in Geneva in May, 1927, and also from October 17th to November 8th, 1927.

On this latter date a large number of nations, through their representatives, became tentative parties to an International Convention designed to abolish import and export prohibitions and restrictions.

The United States of America was represented by Mr. Hugh E. Wilson, Envoy Extraordinary and Minister Plenipotentiary to the Swiss Federal Council.

By executive decree of February 18, 1928 France declared in substance that thereafter no pictures should be imported into France or shown throughout the nation unless approved by the Minister of Public Instructions and Fine Arts, and an advisory committee of 32 members designated by him.

The brief provisions of Article 4 of this decree declared that

"The public projection of motion picture films shall be subjected to the control of the Minister of Public Instruction and Fine Arts."

and

" * * * No moving picture film may be shown to the public unless this film, including its titles and subtitles, has obtained the visa of the Minister of Public Instruction and Fine Arts. This visa can be granted only on the proper recommendation of the Commission referred to in the preceding paragraph. This visa must appear on every film exhibited.

Every foreign film submitted for a visa must be presented in the exact and integral version as it was or is projected in the country of origin, and with an exact and integral reproduction of the titles and subtitles of which a French translation must be furnished." [1]

Rules and regulations affecting the importation of motion pictures into France were promptly promulgated by the Ministry which in substance are said to have the effect of curtailing the importation of American pictures into France to the extent of about 60% of last year's total importations, and also to have established certain film quota restrictions which required that one French picture should be purchased for every seven American productions imported into France.[2]

It was the purpose of this decree to induce or to force the reciprocal exhibition of French pictures in the countries from which motion pictures were imported into France, but with this quota system there was inseparably connected the requirement that all pictures should be approved by the Commission in matters affecting public morals, reflections upon French nationals or upon French life, manners and customs and the usual subject matter generally controlled through censorship.

Thus in effect the importation and showing of motion pictures in France has become a matter of governmental and political concern, and this recognition and treatment of this instrumentality, expressed in different terminology means that France now recognizes the cinema as a new

[1] For full text of Decree see Appendix.
[2] *Variety*, May 9, 1928. See also *New York Times*, May 4, 1928.

public utility, in the sense in which that expression was used in the work entitled *The Public and the Motion Picture Industry*.

This work, published in 1926 and extensively circulated at the International Cinema Congress in Paris in the fall of that year, had clearly declared the principle that one or more nations whose markets were of substantial importance to American distributors could effect an international exploitation of their nationally produced pictures by enacting legislation designed primarily to encourage domestic production, the incidental effect of which would curtail and diminish in a substantial degree the imports of foreign pictures into such countries.

It was declared and predicted that the inevitable effect of such legislation would be to induce the execution of one or more voluntary agreements between American distributors on the one side and French or other European producers on the other, whereby in consideration of a modification of the proposed legislation the American distributors would voluntarily undertake the exploitation in America and elsewhere throughout the world of a substantial number of French or other European pictures.

It was declared that by the adoption of this principle the nations of Europe could induce a just reapportionment of the world's trade in this industry which would restore their prostrate cinema production industries, necessarily at the expense of the industry in America, since that industry now enjoys from 65% to 95% of the screen time of the theatres of the world, but on a basis free from any attitude of nationalistic reprisals against the American industry, since obviously any reapportionment which results from voluntary agreement must be less oppressive and less drastic than that which could be forced by the collective legislative action of any substantial group of nations.

This suggestion was nothing more than the application of an old and well established principle in the structure of national tariffs so frequently utilized by America in the past and so well described by the distinguished French member of the Economic Committee of the League of Nations, M. D. Serruys, in his memorandum to which reference has already been made,[3] whereby nations formulate proposed tariffs as a basis for discussion, negotiation and compromise with those adversely affected by them.

But France's cinema decree greatly simplified the solution of her cinema problems for executive action is far more effective than the more cumbersome process of legislative enactment, and the rules and regulations promptly announced and proposed by France's Minister showed a complete consciousness of the necessities of France's situation.

The public welfare aspects of the subject were given the prominence they deserve by the declaration that no pictures which disparage France, her institutions, manners or customs, or her people, would be admitted, and moreover that no other pictures made by producers who have offended in the respects stated would be admitted, and then

---

[3] Entitled *Treaties, Tariff Systems and Contractual Methods* (C. E., 1. 31).

in an effort to establish by executive decree the principle of the reciprocal exhibition of French pictures abroad, in exchange for the privilege of introducing foreign pictures into France, it was declared that for every seven pictures admitted into France one picture of French origin should be purchased or exported for exploitation abroad.

The effect of this decree and of these proposed regulations upon American imports of pictures into France was amply sufficient to induce the results which the work *The Public and the Motion Picture Industry* had predicted would inevitably follow the adoption of the legislative prescription recommended in that book.

The representative of the American industry immediately betook himself to France.

One would suppose from the newspaper accounts of the negotiations that all of the facilities of the American State Department were placed at his disposal and under his direction.

The American Ambassador to France lent his generous aid in effecting a reconciliation between the French government and the "infant" American industry.

The importance of the American cinema industry's representative was such that it apparently far outweighed that of America's distinguished Minister to Switzerland, for the latter is said to have hurried to Paris for no more important a purpose than to confer with the industry's representative and to advise him whether or not, in the opinion of the Minister, the French decree of February 18, 1928, violated the provisions of the Economic Treaty of

November 8, 1927, and constituted an unreasonable tariff barrier erected by France against American pictures.

Results were soon achieved, but what they were none but the negotiators seemed to know.

The public announcements declared that a modification of the regulations had been effected by voluntary agreements which were said to be satisfactory to all concerned.

However this may be, there are skeptics who recognize in these general platitudes the familiar earmarks of industrial propaganda and the concealment of the true facts which always leak out in due course.

Some months later a New York newspaper [4] printed the following significant news item:

> "'The Soul of France' the French war film which was known in France as 'La Grande Epreuve,'" said the *Times* "is to be distributed in the United States and Canada by Paramount Famous Lasky, it was announced yesterday by Adolph Zukor. "Paramount," declared the *Times*, "has also taken charge of the distribution of this picture in France, Belgium, Switzerland, Egypt and Holland and has the rights for its issuance in Australia, New Zealand, Dutch Indies and Brazil." The *Times* continued, "Mr. Zukor said that he considered it a striking example of the manner in which his company intends to co-operate with the French producers."

Following, as it does, so closely on the heels of the negotiations concerning the French cinema decree of February 18th and the regulations promulgated under it, this announcement is most significant.

It will be observed that whatever the terms and conditions of this agreement were they require this American

---
[4] *New York Times*, August 14, 1928.

company to distribute this French picture even in the domestic market of France, as well as in the markets of the United States and Canada and elsewhere in extremely substantial markets throughout the world.

It may be that as Mr. Zukor is reported to have said this is a striking example of the manner in which his company intends to cooperate with French producers, but it is believed that it is even a more striking illustration of the success of the French Minister of Education and France's cinema decree.

Notwithstanding the publicly declared satisfaction of the American industry with the disposition made by France of her proposed regulations under her cinema decree of February 18th, on July 7th, 1928, Mr. Wilson, America's Minister to Berne and America's representative at the Economic Conference of the League, submitted a protest against France's cinema decree as a violation of the Economic Convention of November 8, 1927.

If American industry had actually achieved success in its negotiations at Paris, Mr. Wilson would not have declared in part that [5]

"Such film interests as have dealt with the French government have aquiesced and not agreed to the procedure of the government. They have so acquiesced because they were faced with a condition in which they stood to lose heavily. They were confronted with a state of facts with which they had to deal and under force majeure, they took the best they could get in order to enable them to continue to do business temporarily.

"It obviously does not mean," continued Mr. Wilson, "that the case of the United States government is in any way prejudiced in dealing

---

[5] League of Nations, C. I. A. P., 2nd Conf., P. V. P.

with the convention which has not yet come into effect and in discussing what interpretation may be put upon that convention in the future."

In substance his contention, which was presented with great dignity and ability, was that the spirit of the Convention to abolish import prohibitions and restrictions was violated by the French decree.

The representatives of the several nations present were of the opinion that it was not competent for the conference to construe or interpret the provisions of the Convention, which view is especially sound since the Convention itself makes ample provision for the disposition of such questions in the manner provided by Article 8 thereof.

But on the merits of the subject there appears to be nothing of any substance in America's position.

Article 2 of the Convention of November 8th declared that subject to the exceptions stated later each nation undertakes to abolish in due course all import and export prohibitions or restrictions and not thereafter to impose any such provisions.

The basic exceptions are stated in Article 4 and in part are as follows:

Paragraph 1 of that Article excepts

"Prohibitions or restrictions relating to public security."

The propaganda use of motion pictures is clearly within this phrase, since it is admitted on all sides and has been sufficiently demonstrated that motion pictures may have the capacity to turn communities from peace to war, and thus endanger the public security of every nation.

Paragraph 2 excepts,

"Prohibitions or restrictions imposed on moral or humanitarian grounds."

The cinema is clearly within this exception, since it is capable of exerting an important influence upon public morals and the consequences of moral degeneracy include the whole extensive field of humanitarianism.

Paragraph 4 excepts,

"Prohibitions or restrictions imposed for the protection of public health. * * * "

Motion pictures seriously affect that part of the public health, especially of the young, described as mental hygiene.

Thus it appears that the mental subject matter conveyed to the public through the physical films which are imported are clearly within three of the basic and permanent exceptions to which the Convention is expressly declared not to be applicable.

It is only the so-called temporary exceptions which are mentioned in Article 6 to which the commodities specified in the annex to Article 6 apply and these do not specifically name motion pictures.

Indeed Section 3 of Article 6 expressly declares that

"The annex to the present Convention sets forth the exceptions coming within the provisions of *the two preceding paragraphs.*"

while these two preceding paragraphs do not affect or qualify any of the basic exceptions named in Article 4.

Article 5 of the Convention reenforces the permanent and basic exceptions, for it declares that

Motion Picture Problems

"Nothing in this Convention shall affect the right of any High Contracting Party to adopt measures prohibiting or restricting importation or exportation for the purpose of protecting, in extraordinary and abnormal circumstances, the vital interests of the country."

The interests of each country affected by the unrestricted dissemination of alien or foreign motion pictures certainly includes interests which are properly described as vital to the continued life and progress of every nation, since they include the effort to preserve each nation's culture, its art, its literature and drama, its life, manners and customs and its historic achievements, not to mention its right to preserve from counter attack through insidious intentional or unintentional propaganda or otherwise, its own ideals of race, religion, education and morality.

And so far as the existence of extraordinary and abnormal circumstances is concerned these circumstances may well be found in the extraordinary absorption of the screens of the theatres of France by the pictures of a single nation, and the practical exclusion of all French and other foreign pictures from the American market by the system now in vogue here.

Moreover, Article 7 declares that

"Should one of the High Contracting Parties be obliged to adopt any measure of prohibition or restriction against products of any foreign country, whether the Convention be applicable to that country or not, he shall frame the measure in such a way as to cause the least possible injury to the trade of the other High Contracting Parties."

This article necessarily implies the power and the right to adopt prohibitions or restrictions against the product of any foreign country so long as the measure is framed in such a way as to cause the least possible injury to the trade of other nations.

The content of motion pictures which unfortunately have emanated in such large quantities from America, as the foregoing review of propaganda pictures shows, amply justifies the French restrictions even if it be conceded that they were and are directed exclusively against such pictures.

The Protocol attached to the Convention is silent as to the exceptions contained in paragraphs 1, 2 and that part of paragraph 4 of Article 4 which relates to the public health, while paragraph 5 of the Declarations of the Conference is in keeping with the validity of the French decree. By this paragraph

"The Conference declares that the Convention affects neither the tariff systems nor the treaty-making method of the participating countries nor the measures taken to insure the application thereof, but it expresses the firm conviction that the abolition of prohibitions and restrictions should not warrant the establishment of excessive export or import duties or hindrances of any other kind which would replace those that it is the aim of the Convention to remove.

"It declares that a return to freedom of trade in the case of a particular product entails on the producing and consuming countries correlative obligations, which should take the form of an equitable regime in regard both to export and import duties, especially in cases where the latter are applicable to articles manufactured from the raw material for which free exportation is to be re-established under the Convention."

Finally it may be observed that there is nothing in any part of the Convention of November 8th which in terms or in spirit attempts to prohibit the establishment of the principle of reciprocity which is the principle upon which the French cinema decree is founded.

Some of the incidental discussion on this subject is of interest. The distinguished French member of the Economic Conference is said to have declared in substance that the question presented is not one of an economic nature, but is spiritual in character.

In reality the subject presents a mixed question in which matters affecting economics, commerce and industry are inseparably linked to those which affect public welfare, which comprise the spiritual aspects of the subject, the moral, educational, cultural and artistic phases of it.

But the subjects are inseparably linked together and may not be dealt with except as a whole and because of the inseparable nature of the subject matter any nation clearly has the right to accentuate, as it should, the primary importance of the cultural and other welfare phases of it, and to treat the economic phases as incidental to the protection of its national traditions and the cultural development of its people.

It is also interesting and significant to note that the delegates representing Germany, Austria, Italy and India rallied to the support of the position taken by France. The German delegate is said to have declared that Germany reserved the right to adopt any measures which Germany deemed necessary to safeguard her culture and traditions, while the delegate from India is said to have declared that it was India's intention to adopt resolutions similar to those of France.

Thus the subject may be left for such further action as

may be taken under the provisions of the Economic Treaty of November 8, 1927.

In view of what has been and is subsequently said concerning the interest taken in motion picture matters by the Child Welfare Committee of the League, and since the appendix includes the full and able report of Dr. Humbert on this subject, it will be sufficient to comment briefly upon the Committee's circular letter of July 10, 1925.

After studying the replies received to this circular letter, the Committee, at its third session at Geneva in May, 1927, adopted the following resolution and questionnaire:

The Child Welfare Committee has considered the resolution of the Assembly asking it to continue its enquiry into the cinema in relation to child welfare and requests the Council to ask the governments to furnish information on the lines of the questionnaire which it has drawn up:

(1) Could any arrangement usefully be made for the exchange of information between different countries in regard to films which are good or bad for children and young people?

(2) Can any facilities be given for the better international circulation of films which are especially suitable for children and young people, either for instruction or amusement?

The following excerpts from the replies of the twelve governments which had responded, to the date of the report [6] are interesting and significant.

Brazil considered that "an international information service might usefully be established for the protection of children from cinematograph films likely to have a harmful effect on them."

---
[6] C. P. E. 134, February 1, 1928.

Manitoba declared that "a universal system of classifying and stamping films * * * with reports sent detailing such classification to all censor boards and Commissions engaged in official examination of pictures" would be desirable.

Norway stated that its Censorship Board might, if necessary, be asked to furnish detailed information regarding films to an international information bureau should this be established under the auspices of the League of Nations.

Sweden declared that "an international catalogue of educational films would be of great utility."

Turkey expressed the view that "it is highly desirable that a permanent bureau should be established and placed under the supervision of the Child Welfare Committee at Geneva for the purpose of keeping the Ministries of Education of the participating States regularly informed of the appearance of films considered to be suitable for or harmful to children and young people."

The Union of South Africa was in favor of an international exchange of information in regard to films which are good or bad for children or young people and to improve the international circulation of desirable films.

The Administrator of the Transvaal suggested that "perhaps control can best be effected by the countries of origin which would be in a position to communicate information through the Council of the League of Nations to all governments."

Sweden's reply to the inquiry contained the following interesting comment:

"We are of opinion," said the communication,[7] "that although excellent in itself the idea of an international understanding between the various national bodies with a view to communicating to each other the decisions adopted by their respective countries, and that such understandings should eventually be extended by means of international agreements to prevent the circulation and use of demoralizing films, would not prove of any great advantage in practice, partly for the above-mentioned reasons (that the Swedish system of censorship which is strict operates in collaboration with the other Scandinavian States) and partly on account of the considerable divergencies in the views held on the matter, which to a certain extent appear to justify the assertion that morality is essentially a question of geographical position."

The system proposed in the succeeding chapters of this work recognizes the importance of leaving with each local community the ultimate and final decision of what may and what may not be shown in such communities, as to all pictures which survive proper national and international tests of the kind proposed.

Hence its recommendation is, national and international inspection with reports which inform and aid the local authorities to reach sound conclusions.

Sweden's view of the geographical nature of some of these questions is supported by those expressed at the League Conference convened on September 12, 1923, for the Suppression of the Traffic in Obscene Publications.

Article 1 of this Convention declared in substance the production, distribution and exhibition of obscene cinematograph films, for purposes of trade, distribution or public exhibition, to be a punishable offense.

---

[7] Stockholm, Sept. 20, 1927, League of Nations Documents, C. P. E. 134, page 7.

To advertise or to make known how and from whom such pictures can be procured, either directly or indirectly, was also prohibited.

The Convention is doubtless highly desirable so far as it goes.

But its terms are confined exclusively to the suppression of obscenity.

Its provisions fail utterly to reach any of the matters described in the Accord proposed in the later chapters of this work.

And the Conference reached the same conclusion as the Conference of 1910 had reached on this subject, that it was not possible to define the word "obscene" in terms acceptable to all States and that each must be allowed to attach to this word the signification which to each might seem suitable.[8]

The official governmental expressions cited above are clearly of sufficient weight to be accorded serious consideration and action.

The nations are very obviously groping for far more than the suggested bureau of information alone, important and desirable though that is.

A special committee of the League of Nations, of the kind advocated in this work, should of course include among its duties the type of service described in some of these communications.

In closing this brief review of the activities of the Child Welfare Committee attention is directed to the

---

[8] Final Act, Par. 2, League of Nations, C. 631. M. 237, 1923 IV C. P. O. 35, 1923.

apparent acceptance of the supposed efforts being made in America to bring about the circulation of better motion pictures in an educational, moral and cultural sense.

Both the report of the Child Welfare Committee, dated February 1, 1928 (C. P. E. 134), and the report which appears as part of the appendix of this work, include references to the National Board of Review, the National Committee for Better Films and the organization known as the Motion Picture Producers and Distributors of America, Inc., including its supposed "Formula" for the suppression of undesirable pictures, which indicate that these agencies are engaged in constructive processes designed to improve pictures in the respects stated.

As to the "Formula" the pictures themselves which have been placed in circulation since it was promulgated, are alone sufficient to demonstrate its complete absurdity and that it is mere industrial propaganda designed for popular consumption and not for industrial observance.

As to the National Board of Review and the so-called Better Films Movement, it is sufficient to direct attention to what has already been said on this subject in *The Public and the Motion Picture Industry.*

The interest and activities of the Committee on Intellectual Cooperation on the subject may now be appropriately discussed.

The forerunner of the International Cinema Congress, held in Paris in the fall of 1926, was the report which M. Julien Luchaire submitted to the International Committee on Intellectual Cooperation of the League of Nations on July 28, 1924.[9]

The International Committee on Intellectual Cooperation adopted the report and suggested that an International Motion Picture Conference be held.

In due course such a conference was organized by the French National Committee of Intellectual Cooperation.

The International Institute of Intellectual Cooperation at Paris, sometimes described as performing the executive or administrative duties of the International Committee on Intellectual Cooperation, undertook the technical organization of the Congress and conducted it in all of its details admirably and with great credit to the Director of the Institute and his associates.

The work of organization had not progressed far before there were audible rumblings concerning it in America.

Notices in the trade press in April and May, 1926, announced the purpose of the Congress to be to gather data on the industry in all its phases, social, political, educational, economic, artistic and technical,[10] and it was said that "with every nation conceding the leadership of the United States, those who come from Hollywood and New York will be the center of great interest, according to the (Paris) *Times*." [11]

It was not long, however, before the producers and distributors in America reached the conclusion that such a

---
[9] See Appendix.
[10] *Film Daily*, April 20, 1926.
[11] *Film Daily*, May 23, 1926.

congress might well prove extremely dangerous to their interests.

There were important conferences in America—conferences in which a very definite policy was formulated and adopted.

The policy was first to endeavor to induce the abandonment of the Congress altogether.

If this result could not be achieved then the policy was to belittle the Congress and its possible accomplishments through disparaging articles in the trade and other newspapers,[12] by endeavoring to confine the scope of the discussions at the Congress to the intellectual and artistic aspects of the cinema and by proposing a different plan which, if adopted, would have proved thoroughly innocuous.

Thus it was announced in the *New York Times*.[13]

"American motion picture producers have declined to enter the first International Motion Picture Congress to be held in Paris this fall. Through Will H. Hays, head of the Motion Picture Producers and Distributors Association, they have replied to the invitation that the Congress should be held a year later, so that there might be time adequately to prepare for it and that if it were held this year and the American branch of the industry participated, it would cause more harm than good by intensifying foreign resentment at the American invasion of the foreign market. 'When we were asked to take part in the Congress which was brought about by the French National Committee of Intellectual Co-operation of the League of Nations,' said F. L. Herron of the Hays office, 'we replied that we felt the Congress should be postponed for a year. America undoubtedly leads the world in motion pictures, particularly in such branches as educational pictures, but if we attempted to tell other nations that, they would want our words backed up by proof. And that would take time to prepare. In order to con-

---
[12] *Film Daily*, August 23, 1926.
[13] July 1, 1926.

tribute anything to the Congress we would have to offer something constructive out of our large experience. But even leaving that aside, we felt that the Congress at this time might easily develop into an anti-American affair if we took part in it, and as the foreign situation is none too happy at present, we did not want to complicate it.'"

These absurd utterances were followed by others of the same import.

It was stated that not only would the American trade decline to attend officially, but that its leaders would not attend even unofficially.[14]

An editorial soon appeared in one of the American trade papers.[15]

"The first International Film Congress," it was said, "sponsored by the French, will be held soon in Paris. What started off like a cyclone has developed into a delicate zephyr. England and Germany have definitely refused to participate. This country has assumed a hands-off policy. In an industry that has assumed the world-wide importance of motion pictures theory has given way to practical results born of experience. The results of the Paris gathering will be interesting."

Next day the same publication announced that Germany's attendance was then certain, but it was said,

"The 'hands-off' policy of the producers and distributors with respect to the forthcoming Paris session has not changed," Major H. L. Herron of the Hays office said yesterday. "The industry in America," he stated, "had felt the time inopportune and so is declining to attennd." [16]

Events were shaped in partial accord at least with the policies of the American producers and their agents.

It was effectively pointed out that the Congress, called at the suggestion of the Committee on Intellectual Cooper-

---

[14] *Film Daily*, August 23, 1926.
[15] *Film Daily*, September 7, 1926.
[16] *Film Daily*, September 8, 1926.

ation, organized by the French Committee devoted to the same limited sphere and conducted under the direction of the Institute, could not properly concern itself with any but intellectual and artistic problems.

The intimate relationship, and indeed the dependence of those problems upon the commercial structure and conditions in the industry, were not pointed out or, if they were, apparently they were not appreciated.

If a discussion of the economic phases of the industry were to be undertaken then, it was argued, perhaps the Economic Committee of the League would be the proper committee to give such subjects consideration and if the field of public welfare were to be included then the committee of the League on Child Welfare would appear to be interested.

And so, intellectually, the argument seemed persuasive and it prevailed.

Practically such limitations constituted a substantial assurance that there could be no results of commercial or economic importance from the Conference.

In due course the official announcements of the scope of the Congress appeared.

"The chief aims of the Congress," it was said, "are (1) to formulate the problems of international organization which present themselves in regard to the motion picture; (2) to study them systematically with a view to a future solution. Only the general interests of the motion picture will be considered and these in a strictly international spirit. The Congress will be neither industrial nor commercial. It is planned from the point of view of intellectual, artistic and educational cooperation."

Whether or not the efforts of the American trade to impose these limitations had any effect whatever, the result was nevertheless regarded in motion picture circles in America as a signal achievement by the representatives of the American producers and as a tribute to their skill in secret trade diplomacy.

But not content with this the American trade went much further.

The prospect of the creation of a permanent international organization which was known to be the main objective of the Congress was not regarded with favor by American producers and their representatives.

To counteract this objective the representatives of the American producers naively and ostensibly for the good of the nations of Europe, proposed that the League of Nations should create an international committee of "film experts" to gather information for the League and that the expenses of the committee should be borne proportionately by each nation according to the importance and standing of each in the trade.

The obvious purpose of this suggestion was to place the collection of the data and the formulation of the statement of the facts concerning the subject in the hands and under the direction of the paid representatives of the American producers.

Evidently these suggestions were too transparent to be accorded any serious consideration.

Up to the day that the Congress opened the trade press continued its unfavorable comments.

Thus, after reporting the undeniable fact of a large attendance at the Congress from many different countries, which was then assured, it was said,

" * * * But with the American industry not officially represented it is regarded as certain that the cultural angle will be sidetracked for the economic angle and organization of an offensive campaign against the American world 'monopoly' may be expected." [17]

"European producers," continued the same article, "long have decried their inability to compete effectively with American pictures and in their efforts to relieve their position they have to a certain degree the backing of statesmen who realize the tremendous economic influence pictures exert. That 'trade follows the film' is pretty generally recognized and this is one of the motivating causes of the agitation."

It was reported that the American Embassy was maintaining careful scrutiny over the Congress and it was said that an attack against American pictures and the position they held was anticipated momentarily. Col. Edward J. Lowry, representative in Europe of the Hays organization, was declared to be watching the deliberations.[18]

It may also be added that although the American Industry had announced repeatedly in the trade press that it would disregard the Congress completely and that it could be of no importance to the American industry, yet Col. Lowry was not the only representative of the Hays association in Paris anxiously watching the developments from day to day.

In due course the Congress opened on September 27, 1926, with 435 delegates representing 31 countries. Sixteen governments sent official delegates to the Congress and

---
[17] *Film Daily*, September 27, 1926.
[18] *Film Daily*, September 29, 1926.

13 international organizations, such as the International Labor Office, the Red Cross, the International Confederation of Intellectual Workers and others took part in the Congress.

But the Congress was chiefly industrial.

Before the Congress had nearly concluded its deliberations there were many unfriendly comments from the trade press in America.

"Camouflaging its motives," said one paper, "with an altruistic program and the uplift of motion pictures, the first International Motion Picture Congress is seeking to perfect a combination against the American lm 'monopoly.' " [19]

"The gentlemen conferring in Paris," said an editorial, "are much wrought up over America's domination in world markets. Any business man can understand that. Commercial envy on the part of Europe is natural. The millions in francs which those countries pay in 'tribute' to distributors here is sufficient explanation. It was not always clear why the industry here refused to participate in the deliberations. The doubt should no longer exist. France and Germany control 104 of 175 delegates and consequently the Congress." [20]

It is a relief to turn, temporarily, from these vaporings of the trade press to a consideration of the serious work of the Congress.

Its work was divided and placed in charge of eight Commissions and the resolutions which resulted bear the unmistakable mark and imprint of the intellectuals who were directing the work of the Congress and who, notwithstanding their hopeless minority in votes, nevertheless succeeded in leaving their indelible impressions upon the work of the Congress.

[19] *Film Daily*, September 30, 1926.
[20] *Ibid.*

Due to this influence and to the usual willingness of the industry everywhere to permit the adoption of numberless resolutions so long as there is no apparent method of making them effective, many of the resolutions were in every way worthy of a Congress composed primarily as this Congress should have been constituted, of statesmen, of representatives of governments, of educators and publicists, competent to discuss the problems affecting the intellectual and artistic as well as the economic and commercial phases of the subject, instead of one composed chiefly, as this Congress was, of industrialists who cared little or nothing for its intellectual aspects.

And these resolutions today constitute an irrefutable argument for the creation of a new cinema committee of the League of Nations constituted as hereinafter suggested to deal with the international phase of this important work.

Resolutions 1, 2, 3, 5, 6, 8, 10 and 13 of the First Commission, all of which appear in the Appendix, with resolutions 2, 3, 4, 8, 14, 16, 19, 21, 22, 24 and 31 of the Third Commission are also of special interest.

The work of the Fourth Commission relating to the legal status of the motion picture, to authors' rights to artistic property with regard to the film, and to conditions of work, displayed exceptional depth of reflection and ability in the conduct of its duties.

Among other excellent resolutions adopted by the Fourth Commission the following is of particular importance:

"5. That a permanent and autonomous committee should be set up, entrusted with investigation from the international point of view both of the international status of cinematographic art and industry and of the moral as well as material rights of those interested in the industry.

"The result of this inquiry will be forwarded directly to the competent bodies of the League of Nations, in the first place, to the International Institute of Intellectual Co-operation, to the International Institute of Private Law in Rome and to the United International Bureaux of Industrial, Literary and Artistic Property at Berne."

Resolutions such as these obviously were not conceived or formulated by cinema industrialists. They were unquestionably the product of the intellectual elements at the Congress.

Finally the work of the Eighth Commission, upon which depended the chief results of the Congress, was announced.

It was here that the predominance of the industrialists proved fatal.

Everyone was agreed upon the desirability of creating a permanent international organization.

There was a division as to the kind of a permanent organization which was desirable and particularly how it was to be composed and constituted.

The resolution disclosed that such an organization was deemed to be necessary for the purpose, among others, of "protecting in general the interests of the cinema industry."

The primary purpose obviously should have been to urge and if necessary to require the industry to use its best efforts everywhere to serve and to protect the interests of mankind.

Such protection as the industry required should have been subordinate to this primal purpose and to enable the industry to make that purpose effective.

Had the purpose of the resolutions of the Eighth Commission been to give effect to the resolutions of the other Commissions it would have been apparent that such results could be achieved only through an organization which in reality was a part of the League of Nations itself while reflection upon the structure of the permanent organization proposed by the Eighth Commission disclosed immediately to those who had any familiarity with the conduct of the League that there was little probability that the League would sanction or approve an organization constituted as the provisional international committee was constituted.

But the industrialists who constituted a large majority of the committee, although informed of this probability, nevertheless disregarded it.

Of approximately 16 industrialists who were members of the committee four were French and four were German and one each from England, Austria, Belgium, Holland, Hungary, Italy, Sweden and Switzerland.

The President of the International Federation of the Cinematographic Press, a representative of the International Federation of Students and of the International Literary and Artistic Association, and of the International Labor Office were to be members and other members were to be added by the committee itself to assure representation of different countries and interests, particularly of a sociations of authors, producers, technical workers, artists, members of the teaching professions and social workers.

In other words trade members and more trade members, with only such members of the teaching professions and social workers as the industrialists who composed the vast majority of the committee might see fit to elect.

Of all of the members of the committee there were but two known to be engaged in intellectual work and but one, the distinguished Director of the Institute, directly connected with the League.

There was a motion [21] in substance, to permit the League or the Committee on Intellectual Cooperation at whose suggestion the Congress was held, to create and appoint the committee and to define its duties, but it was overwhelmingly defeated and the final resolution, which spelled the apparent and temporary failure of the Congress, passed into history.

Thus a splendid effort, ably and skilfully conducted under innumerable difficulties, not the least important of which was the determined effort of the well-organized, shrewdly-manipulated and powerful industry in America which, while disseminating its usual volume of untruthful publicity, deliberately misinterpreting the purpose of the Congress and announcing its lack of interest in the subject, was in reality so much concerned in it that it was exerting all of its power, with success, to devitalize and

---

[21] Moved by the writer.

to render futile what should have been the most important work of the Congress.

The result of the Congress has been described as an apparent and temporary failure because notwithstanding the temporary success of the trade in America in devitalizing it, the intellectuals who directed its course, notably M. Julien Luchaire, the Director of the Institute,,M. Jose de Vilallonga, Rappateur of the Fourth Commission and legal advisor to the Institute, M. Louis Gallie, Secretary General of the International Confederation of Intellectual Workers and the tireless Secretary of the Congress, Mr. Fred Cornelissen, laid the foundation which demonstrates today more clearly than any other argument the urgent necessity for the present creation of a permanent and truly representative committee of the League of Nations to deal exclusively with the subjects which can be dealt with effectively only by such a committee composed and constituted as hereinafter stated.

The American trade press was prompt to record the "failure" of the Congress and, with its customary modesty, to attribute its lack of success to the official absence of the American industry.[22]

Finally in May, 1927, it was announced that the Congress to be held in Berlin in 1927 had been postponed until 1928 and it was said that the representative of the International Institute of Intellectual Cooperation had resigned from the executive committee of the body formed to create

---

[22] *Film Daily*, October 5, 1926; *Motion Pictures Today*, October 16, 1926.

the permanent organization and that the Institute's interest in the Congress had thus ceased.[23]

This was accepted in America and understood to mean the end of the so-called permanent international organization.

This was readily comprehended by those who know the industry in America.

Dr. Bausbeck, then president of the German company, Ufa, was the president of the organizing committee.

The resolution relating to the permanent organization has never been ratified or confirmed by the League or by its Committee on Intellectual Cooperation, so far as is known, and the retirement of the representative of the Institute from the committee doubtless hastened and simplified the process of its disintegration.

It is entirely conceivable that the fact that two American companies, Famous Players Lasky Corporation and Metro-Goldwyn-Mayer Corporation, were said to control two-thirds of the directorate of Ufa, of which Dr. Bausbeck was the head, may have had something to do with the postponement of a further conference until 1928, at which time the project was permitted to become entirely moribund.

The lesson which this international event, of such great possibilities, teaches is the lesson which the trade in America has consistently taught for many years. The industry's only interest in discussions of ways and means of improving the service of the trade to the public, is to

---

[23] *Film Daily*, May 17, 1927.

vitiate the discussions and by skillful publicity and by other effective means to prevent the accomplishment of any substantial results.

Periodically year after year the exhibitors' conventions in America have afforded illustrations of the same or similar import.

Thus the industry in America demonstrated again, on this occasion internationally, that oil will not mix with water, that the industry will not affiliate or cooperate in any sincere effort either with governments, with moralists, publicists or with intellectuals.

It demonstrates that what was needed then is needed now—a Congress of statesmen, the representatives of governments, of publicists and of educators to determine the course which public welfare demands that the industry everywhere shall follow and to adopt effective ways and means to require the industry to pursue it.

In the discussion which took place at the private meeting of the Committee on Intellectual Cooperation on July 26th, 1927, the following resolution was adopted.[24]

"The International Committee on Intellectual Cooperation has taken note, with interest, of the report by the Director of the Institute on the work of the Cinematograph Service, and of the important resolutions adopted by the International Cinema Congress, which are annexed to that report.

"It has also taken sympathetic note of the letter from Dr. René Sand, Chairman of the International Committee for Educational and Social Welfare Films, requesting the International Committee on In-

[24] Minutes of the 9th Session, International Committee on Intellectual Cooperation, Geneva, July 20th to 26th, 1927. C. 424. M. 157. 1927 XII page 49.

tellectual Cooperation to authorize the establishment of an International Office for Educational and Social Welfare Films.

"It recognizes the interest in the future of the establishment of an international center to serve as a connecting link between the various international and national organizations which would be concerned with educational and social welfare films.

"At the same time, it is of opinion that this question, for the very reason that it is of the greatest importance, is one upon which it can, at the moment, take no decision.

"It instructs the Institute to continue the study of this question through its Cinematograph Service, to support the work of the International Committee for Educational and Social Welfare Films, and to keep in touch with the Child Welfare Committee and other interested Sections of the League, and with such regional and national centers as are also concerned.

"It requests the Committee of Directors of the Institute to follow this question closely until the next session of the International Committee on Intellectual Cooperaton."

At this meeting M. de Reynold, Chairman of the Swiss Committee on Intellectual Cooperation, made the following interesting reference to the work of the Congress, held in the Spring of 1927 at Basle by those interested in scholastic education.[25]

"It was a small Congress," said M. de Reynold, "and had limited itself to the cinema from the point of view of education.

"The office established by the Basle Congress consisted of a permanent organization with which 11 Sections were in correspondence. Each Section carried out practical investigations on special subjects. Its library included more than 8,000 educational films. M. Rocco had informed the Committee that a Congress would be held in Rome next year.

"There would also be a Catholic Congress regarding education by means of the cinema, and Germany, which was quite in the vanguard of the movement, was also preparing important gatherings. There were numerous proofs therefore, that action on the part of the Institute ran the risk of coming too late and of overlapping with other activities.

---

[25] *Id.*, page 42.

In these circumstances," M. de Reynold thought, "it might be better for the Institute to confine itself to playing its proper part, which was to act as a source of information, while reserving the possibility of adopting a new and more restricted plan when the time came."

In addition to these activities the creation of the Educational Cinema Institute at Rome must be mentioned.

At the Third Plenary meeting of the Assembly of the League, on September 6, 1927, Count Cippico of Italy submitted a proposal for the creation of an Educational Cinema Institute at Rome, to be maintained at the expense of Italy, but under the auspices of the League of Nations.

The terms of the proposal were set forth as follows:[26]

"The Royal Italian Government, in consideration of the wishes formulated by several international congresses and meetings, encouraged by many experiments made in Italy in the use of moving pictures for the intellectual development of the nation, and its employment as an auxiliary system of teaching in every kind of public school;

"Conscious of satisfying a need which all civilized nations strongly feel, and considering that even the industrial world does not only look at the cinema with a view to speculation but with a real sense of the lofty and practical objects which it is possible to attain with this new and important form of propaganda;

"Convinced that the creation of an International Institute of the Educational Cinema, to be established in Rome, might have the most beneficed effects, not only for the governments, but also for public and private institutions and commercial enterprises, which will be able to find in it a powerful help in their business:

"Have decided to propose the creation of an International Institute of the Educational Cinema, to be established in Rome, which, according

---

[26] *League of Nations Journal of the 8th Ordinary Session of the Assembly, Geneva*, September 7, 1927, page 24. See also League of Nations, Fifty-first Session of the Council, August 30, 1928. C.5/1st Session, P. V. 1. 2235. Document C. 383, 1928. Document C. 435, 1928 XII.

to Article 24 of the Covenant, has to be placed under the direction of the League of Nations.

"For this purpose, the Royal Government offer the funds necessary for the first establishment of the Institute and for its ordinary maintenance, together with a seat in the historical palace of the 'Stamperia' in Rome.

"It will thus be possible for all nations to participate, under conditions of perfect equality and without having any pecuniary burden on them or on the budget of the League of Nations.

"The Royal Government will later state its views as to the final purposes of the Institute; but it is already possible to form an idea of its future activity.

"It is assumed that it would be a center of information for the different problems of the cinema, giving the best opportunity for a mutual interchange and diffusion of every kind of film; scholastic, hygienic, historical, archeological, artistic, and, in a general way, educational.

"I am sure that my honorable colleagues will highly appreciate the advantage of such an Institute, and I have therefore the honor to ask that the proposal of my Government should be placed on the agenda of the Assembly."

The League Journal of September 16, 1927, announced the adoption of the report of the sub-committee having the matter under consideration, which declared that the Assembly should be asked to acknowledge with gratitude the generous offer of the Italian government, the discussion as to the steps to be taken being reserved for the Council after consultation with the competent organizations, more particularly the International Committee on Intellectual Cooperation, and in agreement with the Italian government.

On September 28, 1927, the acceptance of the offer by the Council was announced by the Associated Press from Geneva.

The League of Nations and International Problems

At its meeting on September 26, 1928, the Council of the League is said to have nominated Dr. Vernon Kellogg of Washington, one of eleven persons for the governing body of the Institute, and it is said that three experts in moving picture matters will be added at the December, 1928, meeting of the Council.[27]

Highly desirable as this whole educational cinema movement is, it must nevertheless be clear that the educational phases of it are but a part of the whole great field which, like every other part of the subject, must rest entirely upon an economic, industrial and commercial basis, since even the production, the distribution and the showing of purely educational pictures involves the usual processes of trade.

Incidentally, if the channels or approaches to any of the markets for any classes of subjects are embarrassed by artificial barriers or private monopolies or restraints upon such trade, great harm is necessarily done to the natural expansion and development of the field and to desirable progress in it.

Hence, among other reasons, the need for the comprehensive organization, under the auspices of the League of Nations, advocated in this work.

But one further activity of a committee of the League may be mentioned.

On or about September 17, 1928, Mr. John Galsworthy, British author and dramatist, moved a resolution before the Committee on Arts and Letters recommending "action

---
[27] *New York Times*, September 27, 1928.

to prevent moving pictures from being used to foster ill will among nations." [28]

The Committee on Arts and Letters is a sub-committee of the Committee on Intellectual Cooperation and, while the resolution is significant as indicating the recognition by sensible people of the gravity of the situation which has been produced by the circulation throughout the world of pictures which are deemed to foster ill will among the nations, it is also important, because there are no existing means of taking effectively any action on this subject, and so this is a further proof of the need for the creation of the kind of committee or organization of the League of Nations advocated in this work.

[28] *New York Sun*, September 18, 1928.

CHAPTER V

How the Problems May Be Solved

The inquiry at this time is not what are the particular solutions of the problems, but how and in what manner they may be solved.

The power to treat the problems after they have been solved must also be carefully considered.

It has been demonstrated that these problems are not only national, but international in character and that they concern, in varying degrees of importance, the moral, intellectual, cultural and artistic quality of pictures produced in the cinema-producing nations of the world and exhibited everywhere, as well as their effect and influence broadly upon mankind.

The problems also involve the commercial and economic status of an important production industry in America, in England and in many countries of Europe, and they involve the necessity for the maintenance of an equality of opportunity in market conditions for motion pictures in all of these countries and in every other country of the world.

Obviously there is only one existing organization which has jurisdiction and power to set up and create facilities for a competent examination of such a subject and for its effective and permanent treatment.

That organization is the League of Nations.

The Right Honorable Philip Snowden, and another member of the British Parliament, Mr. A. Greenwood, recognized this fact in addressing the House of Commons on March 22d, 1927, on the subject of the British Cinematographic Films Bill.

In referring to what was described as the general agreement among all of the members of the House that it is important to do something, if possible, to prevent the exhibition of objectionable and obscene films, Mr. Snowden said, in part:[1]

"But the Bill makes no provision whatever for dealing with that matter. I think there will be agreement also that this is not a matter that can be dealt with by national action alone. If anything is to be done in regard to this subject there is only one machinery by which it can be done and that is by some international arrangement, perhaps initiated by the League of Nations."

Mr. Greenwood, at the same session of Parliament, said in part:

"Believe me, British films sin against the light as much as American films.

"There are German films, Russian films, films of all countries which may have unfortunate effect on the minds of certain peoples, and this problem can only be dealt with by friendly international understanding and I would say by means of a convention under the auspices of the League of Nations.

"This Bill," continued Mr. Greenwood, "cannot touch that great question which may prove to be one of the most important questions of our day, namely, the question of the exhibition in the East and elsewhere of undesirable films giving impressions of the life of the white peoples which can only disgust and revolt the people of the East. That may prove to be an important factor in determining our relations with the people of the East in the future. I seriously commend to the government the possibility of taking international action on those lines. * * * It ought to be regarded not merely as a manufacturing industry

[1] Official Report Parliamentary Debates, House of Commons, Vol. 204, No. 31, March 22, 1927, pages 237 to 312.

How the Problems May Be Solved

producing so many hundreds of thousands of feet of film per year, but as an industry with powers for good or evil, for making or marring the people of this and other countries. It is the moral and esthetic aspects of this industry which are all important." [2]

When President Wilson advocated the creation of a Federal Trade Commission in America to deal with unfair trade practices and methods of competition he urged it, saying, "The opinion of the country would instantly approve of such a Commission. It would not wish to see it empowered to make terms with monopoly or in any sort to assume control of business as if the government made itself responsible.

"It demands such a Commission only as an indispensable instrument of information and publicity, as a clearing house for the facts by which both the public mind and the managers of great business undertakings shall be guided and as an instrumentality for doing justice to business when the processes of the courts or the natural courses of correction outside of the courts are inadequate to adjust the remedy to the wrong in a way that will meet all the equities and circumstances of the case."[3]

The opinion of the world would now instantly approve the creation of a cinema committee of the League of Nations to deal with all phases of the subject within its jurisdiction.

What jurisdiction, it may be asked, has the League of Nations in such a matter and what can it do?

---
[2] *Ibid.*
[3] Henderson's *Federal Trade Commission*, 24.

Motion Picture Problems

The preamble of the Covenant of the League of Nations declares that the High Contracting Parties

"In order to promote international co-operation and to achieve international peace and security by the acceptance of obligations not to resort to war, by the prescription of open, just and honorable relations between nations, by the firm establishment of the understandings of international law as the actual rule of conduct among governments, and by the maintenance of justice and a scrupulous respect for all treaty obligations in the dealings of organized peoples with one another, agree to this Covenant of the League of Nations."

These obligations are recognized as imposing constructive or affirmative and not merely negative duties.[4]

It has been demonstrated that the motion picture today is exerting an influence upon mankind capable of precipitating war or of contributing substantially to the achievement and perpetuation of international peace and security.

The New York *World* in an editorial hailing the International Cinema Congress held at Paris in the fall of 1926 at the suggestion of the Committee on Intellectual Co-operation of the League of Nations, said:

"It is not an exaggeration to say that they (motion pictures) mean more than the tribunal at the Hague has ever meant. This is because they can create the state of mind that ultimately means peace or war." [5]

It has been shown that the motion picture is an instrumentality of incalculable importance in the cultivation of mutual friendships and understandings among the communities of the world, and hence that it is a primary means of cultivating and preserving the world's peace from which

---
[4] *The League of Nations—A Survey*, 1920-1926, 12.
[5] *New York World*, May 22, 1926.

How the Problems May Be Solved

it follows that all matters directly relating to the subject are necessarily within the jurisdiction of the League of Nations.

The motion picture thus becomes a subject not only worthy of consideration, but it becomes one which it is the duty of the League of Nations to consider in the manner deemed by the League to be most appropriate.

It is not intended to embark upon an extended description of the League, but sufficient must be said to explain briefly its structure to those who may not be familiar with it and to point out what the League has power to do and may do if it is so inclined.

The main organs of the League are the Assembly, the Council, and the permanent Secretariat, supplemented by the permanent Court of International Justice and the International Labor Organization.

Both the Assembly and the Council possess a large degree of independent authority and each may deal with any matter within the sphere of action of the League or affecting the peace of the world.[6]

In practice the Assembly is said to have become the general directing force of League activities.[7]

The Council, however, deals with special emergencies and with current work throughout the year and it is said to have become the League's executive organ.[8]

The Council is now composed of fourteen members, five

---
[6] *The League of Nations—A Survey*, 1920-1926, 19.
[7] *Ibid.*
[8] *Ibid.*

of whom are permanent members and nine of whom are non-permanent members, all elected by the Assembly.[9]

Although required to meet but once a year, in practice, the Council has met about four or five times a year and is summoned immediately in cases of emergency.[10]

The Secretariat is a permanent body established at the seat of the League and deals with what has been called the civil service duties of the League. It is divided into sections according to subjects and not according to nationality and is responsible to the League as a whole.[11]

The many tasks which have devolved upon the League, it is said, have necessitated the creation of various auxiliary bodies which are of two kinds.

There are technical organizations dealing with finance and economics, and there are advisory committees.

In addition to these two sets of bodies there are created, as occasion may require, various special committees for different subjects.

The technical organizations enjoy sufficient independence and flexibility to make them effective yet they remain under the general control of the Council and of the Assembly of the League.

They are modelled in principle on the League as a whole. They consist of a standing committee corresponding in part to the Council, a general conference of gov-

---

[9] *Ibid.* 20, the British Empire, France, Germany, Italy and Japan are permanent members; Canada, Chile, China, Columbia, Cuba, Finland, Holland, Poland, Roumania and Salvador are non-permanent members.
[10] *The League of Nations—Its Constitution and Organization*, 14.
[11] *The League of Nations—A Survey*, 1920-1926, 20.

ernment representatives which corresponds to the Assembly, and a Secretariat, which forms a section of the General Secretariat of the League.

The advisory committees are composed of members sometimes elected by the Council for their individual competence on any subject and sometimes by the governments officially as experts to assist the Council and the Assembly in particular matters.[12]

The so-called technical organizations are those on health, transit and communications, and the financial and economic organizations.[13]

The advisory committees include the committee on the traffic in women and children,[14] of which the Child Welfare Committee is now a part.[15] The Committee on Intellectual Cooperation is also an advisory committee.

Articles 23, 24 and 25 of the Covenant of the League of Nations, quoted at length below,[16] confer specific powers upon the League in matters of social and other activities and in the creation of international bureaus for the regulation of international matters.

---

[12] *The League of Nations—Its Constitution and Organization*, 27.
[13] *Ibid.*, 27, 28.
[14] *Ibid.*, 38.
[15] *The League of Nations—A Survey*, 1920-1926, 25.
[16] Article 23. *Social and Other Activities.*

Subject to and in accordance with the provisions of international conventions existing or hereafter to be agreed upon, the Members of the League:
    (a) will endeavor to secure and maintain fair and humane conditions of labor for men, women and children, both in their own countries and in all countries to which their commercial and industrial relations extend, and for that purpose will establish and maintain the necessary international organizations;
    (b) undertake to secure just treatment of the native inhabitants of territories under their control;

In addition to the foregoing, the International Labor Organization, or Office, as it is frequently called, is an autonomous organization with its own governing body, its own general conference and its own Secretariat, although all the state members of the League are members of it and its budget is subject to the control of the Assembly of the League.[17]

It is interesting to note that the governing body of this

(c) will entrust the League with the general supervision over the execution of agreements with regard to the traffic in women and children and the traffic in opium and other dangerous drugs;

(d) will entrust the League with the general supervision of the trade in arms and ammunition with the countries in which the control of this traffic is necessary in the common interest;

(e) will make provision to secure and maintain freedom of communications and transit and equitable treatment for the commerce of all Members of the League. In this connection, the special necessities of the regions devastated during the war of 1914-1918 shall be borne in mind;

(f) will endeavor to take steps in matters of international concern for the prevention and control of disease.

Article 24. *International Bureaus.*

1. There shall be placed under the direction of the League all international bureaus already established by general treaties, if the parties to such treaties consent. All such international bureaus and all commissions for the regulation of matters of international interest hereafter constituted shall be placed under the direction of the League.

2. In all matters of international interest which are regulated by general conventions but which are not placed under the control of international bureaus or commissions, the Secretariat of the League shall, subject to the consent of the Council and if desired by the parties, collect and distribute all relevant information and shall render any other assistance which may be necessary or desirable. * * *

Article 25. *Promotion of Red Cross and Health.*

The Members of the League agree to encourage and promote the establishment and co-operation of duly authorized voluntary national Red Cross organizations having as purposes the improvement of health, the prevention of disease and the mitigation of suffering throughout the world.

[17] *The League of Nations—Its Constitution and Organization,* 19.

organization is composed of 24 members, 12 of whom are government representatives, 6 of whom represent employers and 6 who represent the employees.[18]

While opposed to any industrial representation in any permanent organization which may be created by the League as unnecessary and undesirable, this structure of the International Labor Office is nevertheless suggestive.

Governments obviously must be represented in any organization created by the League in the cinema field. So must the interests of the public through competent publicists. The economic and commercial aspects of the subject can best be dealt with by economists rather than by members of the particular industry in question. An organization composed and controlled half by government representatives, one-quarter by publicists and one-quarter by economists and general trade experts, in the opinion of the writer, would be ideal.

The League of Nations is maintained financially by the member states and a share of expenses is allocated among them on a carefully adjusted basis.

The annual budget is under the control of the Assembly and the total authorized League budget for the years 1921 to 1924, inclusive, give an average of 22,757,769 gold francs a year, equivalent to $4,391,187 American dollars or about £902,370 sterling at par.[19]

The budget in 1926 was £980,494.[20] The 1927 budget was $4,888,244.

---

[18] *Reconstruction* by Maurice Fanshawe, 64.
[19] *The League of Nations, Its Constitution and Organization*, 46.
[20] *Geneva, 1926*, by H. Wilson Harris, 56.

The International Labor Office, the Health Organization in so far as it deals with mental hygiene, and four existing committees of the League, namely, the Committee on Economics, the Committee on Child Welfare, the Committee on Transit and Communications, and the Committee on Intellectual Cooperation, are, or ought to be, interested in the phases of the motion picture which affect their work. The League Health Organization, which owes its existence to Articles 23, 24 and 25 of the Covenant of the League of Nations, ought to be deeply concerned in the subject because it involves that branch of international health which relates to mental hygiene.[21]

The Committee on Intellectual Cooperation has already given the intellectual phases of the subject consideration and as has been shown directed and supervised the International Cinema Congress at Paris in 1926, but as already indicated the only subjects properly before that body were those which affected its intellectual and artistic phases and that Congress was unable to and did not attempt to deal with any of the other problems presented by this intricate subject.

So it is with the Committee on Child Welfare.

Cinema questions have in the past come before this committee and in May, 1926, full and important reports[22] were submitted to the committee on the effects of the cinematograph on the mental and moral well-being of children, and resolutions were adopted which constitute further evidence

---

[21] Fanshawe's *Reconstruction*, p. 161.
[22] See Appendix.

How the Problems May Be Solved

of the need for a cinema committee of the League of Nations to deal with the whole subject.

These resolutions[23] are as follows:

"The Committee recognizes, on the one hand, the attraction and importance of the cinematograph in certain circumstances from the point of view of the healthy recreation, instruction and education of children and young people, but it is convinced, on the other hand, that the abuse of the cinema has definitely harmful effects upon the minds of children and young people and, according to certain medical authorities, upon their nervous system and physical health.

"The Committee, appreciating the interest felt by the International Institute of Intellectual Co-operation in the question of the cinematograph, desires to assure it of the importance which the Committee itself attaches to the question from the point of view of the moral and intellectual development of children and young people, and requests it to devote special attention to the co-operation of all concerned in the production, circulation and utilization of good films.

"The Committee recommends:

"1. That, in each State, offices for control or preliminary censorship should be established, whose decisions would be enforced by fixed penalties, with a view to preventing the exhibition of demoralizing films; the views of educationalists and parents should, so far as possible, be represented in these offices.

"2. That all possible means should be employed to encourage the exhibition and the international exchange of films calculated to promote the intellectual, moral and physical education of children and young people.

"3. That an international understanding should be entered into by the various national offices with a view to communicating to each other the decisions adopted and the penalties imposed in their respective countries, and that such understanding should eventually be extended by means of international argreements to prevent the circulation and use of demoralizing films.

---

[23] C. 264, M. 103, 1926, IV, pages 144, 145.

"4. That each State should prescribe the necessary measures of hygiene and security in connection with the ventilation, the cubic capacity, the exits and emergency exits of cinema theatres, and should take steps as soon as possible to prohibit the exhibition of inflammable films."

As will be shown presently, a plan which would be effective could be developed with the aid of a cinema committee of the League of Nations supplemented with national cinema committees, particularly in the cinema-producing countries of the world.

This suggestion presupposes an international cinema alliance and the execution of the international accord presently described by a substantial group of nations.

The cinema problems have not yet reached the League's Health Organization, the committee on Transit and Communications or the Committee on Economics, so far as is known.[24]

But it is apparent from what has been said that the subject cannot be dealt with piecemeal.

The public welfare phases of it, particularly its mental hygiene, child welfare and its intellectual aspects, are inseparably linked and interwoven with the economic and commercial questions involved, including questions of interest to the International Labor Office and to the Committee on Transit and Communications.

The questions overlap each other at every turn and no existing committee or other organization of the League

---

[24] Except that on July 7, 1928, the United States Minister to Switzerland claimed before the economic conference of the League that the French cinema decree of February 18, 1928, violated the treaty against the creation of artificial trade barriers.

How the Problems May Be Solved

is qualified to examine every phase of the many problems within the League's jurisdiction which the whole intricate and extremely important subject presents.

The work of any new committee or organization created must in the nature of things be financed by the League. But if the League will create and bring into existence the proper facilities and dignify the subject with its direction, responsibility and control, it is entirely conceivable that some of the work which could readily be entrusted to one or more sub-committees might well be financed in America, not by the industry, as the adroit representative of the trade there suggested, but by private sources interested in the public welfare aspects of the subject.

The American public is concerned and deeply concerned in this matter and quite as vitally as other communities of the world. It is, to a substantial degree, America's problem and if given the opportunity the American public will surely respond and respond generously to the prosecution of work under such auspices as those proposed.

And by way of precedent it may be added that the Council of the League, on July 7, 1923, approved the principle of a proposal to appoint a committee of experts to investigate on the spot, in various countries, the exact extent of the traffic in women and children and the effectiveness of measures theretofore adopted for its supervision, and chose a small committee to carry out this inquiry. The expenses of this committee "are defrayed from private sources in

America, a sum of $75,000 being contributed by the American Bureau of Social Hygiene. * * *"[25]

Indeed, the whole question of finance is answered and presents no difficulty whatever if the nations will agree to require all films, before entrance into the country, to be presented for inspection to the films import inspectors designated by the League committee in the country of the film's origin.

Fees would, of course, have to be imposed and paid for this service.

The service, as will presently appear, could be made to play so important a part in rendering the work of the cinema committee and the several national committees effective, particularly in improving the quality of pictures at the source of production and not by ineffective deletions at the places of exhibition, that most of the expense of the international committee and of the national committees, if not all of it, could and should be met by this means. And since the pictures made in America are now those chiefly exported from that country and imported into the nations which may sign the proposed accord by far the largest portion of the expense of maintaining the committees would necessarily fall in the first instance upon the producers and distributors in America.

Expenses of this nature, like all tariff charges, are invariably passed on by the producers to the distributors and by them on to the ultimate consumers, the public, throughout the world.

---

[25] Fanshawe, *Reconstruction*, 203.

How the Problems May Be Solved

It is apparent from what has been said that a new technical organization or a new committee or a new international commission for the solution and treatment of the problems of international interest and importance in this field should be created by and placed under the direction of the League of Nations.

CHAPTER VI

THE BROKEN REEDS—CENSORSHIP AND THE INDUSTRY

As a preface to the discussion which is to follow it may be useful to deal briefly with the subject of censorship chiefly for the purpose of demonstrating the practical unanimity of opinion in all nations and states upon the subject matter which should be, but which is not, excluded from the pictures which are exhibited publicly everywhere.

The discussion is useful also as a demonstration of the ineffectiveness of censorship as now administered.

The different application of the same principle in many places, after the pictures have been produced and frequently have passed beyond the control of their makers is a convincing argument in favor of the abolition of censorship and the substitution in its place of inspection, at the source or origin of production, which inspection can be made effective in the manner hereinafter discussed.

The preliminary expression of the views of inspectors, before the product is finished and ready for circulation, and while it is still the subject of effective and inexpensive alteration and correction, will prove a double benefit to the producers and to the nations of the world which need, at their several ports of entry the data and information which the reports of the inspectors at the place of origin would supply as a sound basis for final decision concerning the admission or rejection of these subjects.

Censorship and the industry itself, are both broken reeds upon which to lean in the effort to improve the moral tone and cultural quality of pictures.

Censorship may prevent the exhibition of some of the grossest pictures, but other methods of prevention would in most such instances be equally or more effective.

As has already been demonstrated, the industry itself, in America, is hopeless so far as the internal correction of any lucrative practice in which it wishes to engage is concerned.

A review of the censorship regulations in force in some of the States in America, and the censorship regulations of certain nations shows quite clearly the kind of pictures which the censorship States of America, and indeed all States, wish to discourage.

For that reason, and as a basis for the proposed international accord, it is desirable to examine some of the existing restrictions, for the public is well aware that notwithstanding these censorship prohibitions pictures are still produced and exhibited in unfortunately large quantities which continue to display many of the undesirable elements which it has been the purpose of these censorship restrictions to eliminate.

Thus the censorship standards prescribed by the Board of Censors of the State of Maryland cover a wide field of indelicate and obviously undesirable pictures, many of which would not necessarily fall within the prohibition of the usual statutes against indecency.[1]

---
[1] 1926 *Film Year Book*, 436; see Appendix.

The standards [2] of the Ohio State Board of Censors, one of the first created in America, are less specific but quite clearly classify the pictures which it is obviously undesirable to exhibit publicly.

The standards of the Board of Censors of the State of Pennsylvania are in substantial accord with the others.[3]

Abroad most nations have censorship standards of varying degrees of strictness.

Thus the British Board of Film Censors in London have a long and detailed list of subjects deemed by them to be offensive.[4]

On April 19, 1921, the Minister of Justice of Belgium issued a circular letter interpreting the law of Belgium and announcing the standards of interpretation to be followed.

It was said: [4a]

"1. The law of September 1, 1920, is not a censorship law. The commission has not to judge concerning the political, philosophical or religious tendencies of the films presented for authorization.

"2. The commission must only consider measures for the protection of children.

"Therefore, the following films must be prohibited for family or juvenile presentation:

"(a) Films showing scenes of theft, inasmuch as they may induce young people to imitate them.

"(b) Films showing acts of roughness or cruelty; murder, suicide, executions, torture, etc.

"(c) Films liable to awaken prematurely in minds of minors improper sensibilities even when such films are not precisely immoral.

Nevertheless in this case the censors will avoid an excess of puritanism in order not to lose public approval.

---

2 See Appendix.
3 *1926 Film Year Book*, p. 437.
4 *Ibid.*, p. 815.
4a *Ibid.*, p. 815.

"Must also be prohibited for children and family representations films showing violent practices, terrifying surgical operations under pretense of scientific documentation or anything able to impress violently children's minds and injure their moral health."

The prohibitions of France are somewhat more specific [5] while those of India,[6] Italy [7] and Japan [8] present the respective views of those countries.

Thus it appears that the whole subject is more a matter of taste, opinion and judgment involving the natural desire of all governments to improve the moral tone and cultural quality of pictures exhibited to their nationals, than to prevent the exhibition of the grossest pictures, the exhibition of which would doubtless fall within other criminal laws in every country, without specific prohibitions in laws relating to the censorship of pictures.

It is believed that even the most ardent opponents of censorship, of which the writer is one, recognize the obvious desirability and necessity of governmental action usually designated as censorship, from a political standpoint, subject, nevertheless to the extremely wise declaration of the Belgium Minister of Justice that the censors "have not to judge concerning the political, philosophical or religious tendencies of the films presented."

Yet even this must be subject to some limitations— freedom of speech and of pictorial representation is obviously desirable. It should not be curtailed because of mere

---
[5] 1926 *Film Year Book*, 817; see Appendix. See also cinema decree of February 18, 1928 and regulations adopted thereunder.
see Appendix.
see Appendix.
see Appendix.

differences of opinion; but no government worthy of the name would or should permit the exhibition within its borders of pictures which incite the public to violence or to unwarranted attack upon the government itself or upon other peoples or which debase the public taste or morals. Self-preservation as the first law of nature is applicable to governments as well as to individuals.

And so, even here, the matter is one of degree and of judgment and opinion largely, which should and must rest finally in the hands of the government.

What is needed everywhere are legislative prohibitions in much broader terms than have heretofore been in general use—prohibitions against the production, distribution and exhibition of motion pictures which are injurious in any respect to the public welfare, whether in matters of morals or education, or which tend to ridicule religion or to incite race or national prejudices, and a more effective enforcement of existing laws which attempt to afford adequate relief in some of these matters.

With such statutes, each nation would be equipped to interpret its own policies and moral and educational standards without any censorship laws, except such of a political character, or for purposes of import inspection as are deemed to be necessary, and the interpretation of the laws would rest where this important function belongs, with the existing judicial branch of the government, and justice would be administered by the individual judges in accord with their interpretation of the public policy of the nation and of the standards recognized in their respective communities.

Any State legislative body can readily define what pictures are to be prohibited. There is no difficulty in the prescription. The difficulty is in the administration and application of whatever the prescription is.

This depends largely upon the mental, moral and cultural equipment of those whose duty it is to enforce the prescription.

Poorly paid, poorly educated public officials, especially those who act as administratives only, are wholly unfit to meet the necessities of the situation.

As will presently be shown, extremely important results could be obtained if a group of nations would agree upon the prescription to be applied to all pictures imported into these countries and would request the League of Nations to create an international cinema committee with supplementary national committees, particularly in all motion picture producing countries, authorized to set up and designate one or more film import inspectors to inspect, at the source of production, all films intended for import into any one of the group of nations in question.

This film import inspection at the source or origin of production, which incidentally is not censorship, would result in preliminary import certificates in the nature of reports which would apprise each nation of the facts concerning each subject inspected.

It would directly and immediately affect and improve the quality of pictures made in America for purposes of import into the countries establishing the system.

It would in time lead to improvement in the quality

of pictures made in America and designed for American consumption.

But fundamental improvement in quality in the respects under discussion, can only come with the reconstruction of commercial conditions, particularly in America, which will free the industry of its present monopolistic control, to the end that those who are prepared and who desire to make pictures of higher moral tone and better cultural quality than those now prevalent may at least not be excluded from the markets of the world by the artificial trade conditions which now exist quite generally everywhere.

This can be effected not only by the enforcement of the Anti-Trust Laws in America, but it may be effected by the co-operation of the governments of Europe in entering into the International Accord presently described, and by the adoption of decrees, similar to that of France, until a just and voluntary reapportionment of the world's trade is accomplished.

Obviously no one can guarantee that a restoration of competition or of commercial freedom in this field will, of itself, immediately induce the production and exhibition of pictures of the kind described. And so the proposed commercial reconstruction must be supplemented with appropriate safeguards to assure this result.

But judging the future by the past the conduct of the industry in America today guarantees that there will be no change in the moral, intellectual and cultural quality of pictures, as Mr. Terry Ramsaye says, "for a generation or more."

And so some of those who do not propose to sit idly by until the three or four men who, Mr. Ramsaye correctly says, control the destinies of the cinema industries throughout the world, decide that the time has come for them to give to the public of the world pictures which are wholesome and beneficial instead of those which are not, prefer to place themselves behind the only movement which can bring improvement in the industry and to the public as well. That movement was initiated by the book, *The Public and the Motion Picture Industry,* the declared purpose of which was to initiate and to render articulate an international movement to fix and establish the status of the motion picture in every nation as a new public utility and to require the industry, without diminishing the popularity of its entertainments to consecrate its service to the cultivation and preservation of the world's peace and the moral, intellectual and cultural development of mankind.

It is the purpose of the present volume to stimulate that movement and, as its preface indicates, to induce the Council of the League of Nations to create a cinema committee of the League to deal with the whole subject as the most and only effective means of achieving the desirable international results under discussion.

CHAPTER VII

THE PROPOSED INTERNATIONAL CINEMA ALLIANCE AND THE PROPOSED ACCORD

A group of nations should define the pictures to be prohibited from entrance and from exhibition in each nation comprising the group.

Each such nation should agree not to admit such pictures or any pictures until they have been inspected in the country of their origin by inspectors designated by or in behalf of all.

The League of Nations should be requested to create a cinema committee, or other appropriate organization, to supervise the execution of this agreement, to establish national committees and film import inspectors in the motion picture producing countries, to inspect and report on pictures intended for import into any such nations, to make a complete world survey of the subject and later to make such recommendations as it deems proper; and also to initiate such of the activities recommended in the resolutions of the International Motion Picture Congress held in Paris in 1926 under the auspices of the International Institute of Intellectual Co-operation, as may be desirable.

The certificates or reports of the film import inspectors should be advisory only. They should be similar to the visa on a passport and each nation should of course reserve to itself the right to determine whether a particular subject did or did not fall within the accepted definition of prohibited pictures.

The proposed cinema committee of the League of Nations could thus render a great service not only to its members, but to the public and to the industry everywhere, in the two major divisions of this subject.

A sensible application of the definition by the film import inspectors would soon immeasurably improve the quality of motion pictures exhibited everywhere by the elimination of the type of subject matter which tends to stimulate unfriendliness among different races and nationalities and of subject matter which is injurious to the public in many other respects.

This is the public welfare branch of the subject.

The data which would result from the world survey which should be made, would give the nations the needed material on which to base a sound, international, economic, as well as public welfare, policy under which the cinema producing industries, notably of England, France and Italy, could be restored to a prosperous condition, and under which the cinema industries of Germany and of the Scandinavian countries could more nearly attain the position to which the merit of their product entitles them, without undue nationalistic reprisals against the industry in America.

This involves the economic, industrial and commercial branch of the subject upon which every other consideration necessarily depends.

It is believed that before the suggested world survey could be completed, one or more agreements affecting international trade between British and European producers on

Proposed International Alliance and Proposed Accord

one side and distributors in America on the other, would inevitably result, the practical effect of which would be to bring about a voluntary reapportionment of the world trade in this industry, which would effectively prevent and forestall the enactment of legislation or the promulgation of executive decrees which will be more prejudicial to the interests of the industry in America and less beneficial to the cinema producing industries of other nations than the voluntary agreements of the kind proposed would be.

The Accord should be substantially as follows:

"To assure to its nationals an equality of opportunity in the cinematographic trade and to induce and encourage the exhibition within its borders of motion pictures which, without diminishing the popularity of their entertainment will promote the public welfare, peace and friendly relations between the communities of the world, the undersigned agree:

"1. That from and after the date upon which this Convention is effective, each will prohibit and prevent the production, distribution, importation and exhibition within its borders of motion pictures and advertisements thereof, which tend to expose to contempt, ridicule, prejudice or disparagement any race, nationality or religion, or which tend to stimulate class, racial, national or religious hatred, or which tend to foment social or political unrest, discontent or unfriendliness on the part of or towards the people of any nation or community, or which tend to encourage or promote war, or which are unpatriotic or which improperly display the flag or other emblem of this or any other government, nation or state; or which distort or untruthfully depict the facts of history as interpreted in the place of exhibition, the works of literature or the drama, or which tend to circulate misinformation in matters of an educational nature, or which misrepresent, from the standpoint of the nation in which the exhibition occurs, the life, manners, characteristics or customs, of these or any other nations, or which present crime or immorality in an informative or attractive manner, or which are detrimental to the public health, mental or physical, or which are immoral or which tend to debase or which intentionally disseminate concealed false propaganda or which are injurious to the public or any part thereof in any respect.

"2. That no motion picture films or advertisements thereof, of foreign origin, shall be imported into any nation which is a party hereto, until such films and advertisements have been inspected in the country of origin thereof, by inspectors, designated by or in behalf of the parties hereto, and unless and until the certificate and report of such inspectors has been attached to each such film or advertisement.

"3. Each party hereto requests the League of Nations to create a permanent cinema committee or organization, in such form as it deems proper, to supervise the execution of this agreement and to formulate recommendations for adoption by all nations relative to motion pictures; to conduct a world survey and examination of the subject of motion pictures in every branch of the cinematographic industry; to appoint and designate, particularly in each nation in which motion pictures are produced in substantial quantities, national committees or other suitable representatives to perform such functions within its jurisdiction as it may prescribe, including the inspection, upon receipt of inspection fees prescribed by it of all motion picture films and advertisements thereof, presented to such inspectors for inspection prior to importation thereof, into any of the nations which are parties hereto, and to deal with all phases of the subject of motion pictures within the jurisdiction of the League of Nations.

"4. Each party hereto reserves to itself, nevertheless, the exclusive right to adjudge and determine, in the manner adopted by each, the question as to whether a particular film or any advertisement thereof, does or does not violate any of the foregoing provisions, or any of its national or local laws, and the certificates or reports of the film import inspectors, designated pursuant hereto, shall be deemed to be advisory only, and shall not be conclusive upon any such party.

"5. This convention shall become operative and effective as to each signatory ninety (90) days from and after the date of the execution thereof by such party."

Nations which are parties to this Accord will adopt national statutes or, when appropriate, executive decrees to give effect to the prohibitions which the Accord contains.

Other states and nations not parties to this international accord may see fit to adopt the national program which is here suggested.

Every State needs a simple prohibition of the kind proposed.

These prohibitions should be supplemented with a provision conferring power upon a designated administrative official to make rules and regulations and to perform the research and statistical function suggested in the chapter on Propaganda and, either by statute or by decree or by these rules, those releasing any pictures for public exhibition within any State should be required to submit them to the administrative official specified, for inspection, *prior* to release.

Obviously, nations which are not opposed to the exercise of the function of censorship by administrative officials will authorize this official to discharge this function after he has inspected the pictures.

But in America and in Great Britain and in her Dominions and Colonies, where many believe that these repressive measures should be exercised only after judicial intervention, the safer and perhaps the better course is to confine the administrative official's authority strictly to inspection and to require him and to permit any citizen if he fails to perform his duty, to apply to the courts to suppress pictures which violate the prohibitions.

It must be remembered that we are not dealing with a physical subject matter like meat, impure physical foods, drugs or the use of alcohol for beverage purposes in all of which the physical content does or does not meet requirements capable not only of specific and exact statement and definition, but capable of accurate ascertainment.

We are dealing with a subject which defies exact identification because, whether a given picture is or is not the kind easily defined and prohibited, is necessarily, in most instances, a matter of opinion, taste and individual judgment as to which there is a wide variety of legitimate difference and disagreement.

But whose individual opinion, taste and judgment shall determine whether the public is or is not to be outraged or harmed by a particular subject matter?

Shall it be the producer who produces and exhibits his wares for profit, or shall it be the sober minded judiciary of each State? The choice is a simple one.

It is for the reasons stated that the final determination of the question of what may and what may not be publicly shown should be made a judicial and not an administrative question.

The enactment of the prohibitions suggested supplies an adequate justiciable basis for every claim that a specified picture violates one or more of such prohibitions.[1]

---

[1] The following form of law, or, when appropriate, executive decree, is suitable for adoption in any state or nation with such supplementary additions, particularly as to form which local or domestic law may make necessary or desirable:

"To assure an equality of opportunity in the cinematographic trade and to encourage the exhibition within the borders of the State of motion pictures which, without diminishing the popularity of their entertainment, will promote the public welfare, peace and friendly relations between the communities of the world, be it enacted:

"1. That from and after the date upon which this law takes effect, the production, distribution, importation and exhibition within the borders of the State of motion pictures and advertisements thereof, which tend to expose to contempt, ridicule, prejudice or disparagement any

It is obviously desirable to protect all religions not from legitimate discussion or debate but from ridicule, disparagement or contemptuous treatment.

We need not pause to dissect the emotion of patriotism to ascertain under what circumstances it is a "conceit," as suggested by Mr. Shaw; when it becomes "the last refuge of a scoundrel," as declared by Dr. Samuel Johnson, and whether it is only aggressive or imperialistic patriotism or all patriotism which Mr. H. G. Wells and his followers in internationalism scorn, or whether Mr. Drinkwater's old-fashioned devotion to the emotion is still compatible with our modern existence.

---

race, nationality or religion, or which tend to stimulate class, racial, national or religious hatred, or which tend to foment social or political unrest, discontent or unfriendliness on the part of or towards the people of any nation or community, or which tend to encourage or promote war, or which are unpatriotic or which improperly display the flag or emblem of this or any other government, nation or State, or which distort or untruthfully depict the facts of history as interpreted in the place of exhibition, the works of literature or the drama, or which tend to circulate misinformation in matters of an educational nature, or which misrepresent from the standpoint of the State in which the exhibition occurs, the life, manners, characteristics or customs of such State or of any other nations, or which present crime or immorality in an informative or attractive manner, or which are detrimental to the public health, mental or physical, or which are immoral or which tend to debase or which intentionally disseminate harmful, concealed false propaganda, or which are injurious to the public or any part thereof in any respect.

"2. Full and complete power is hereby vested in (an appropriate administrative officer or commissioner) to make and to enforce rules and regulations for the abolition of all unfair methods of competition and unfair practices harmful to the development of the trade and to make the foregoing enactment effective, including the power to require all those proposing to release any motion pictures for public exhibition within the State, to submit such pictures to said official for inspection prior to the release thereof.

"3. It shall be the duty of said official to apply to a court of competent jurisdiction for an injunction to restrain and enjoin the exhibition of any motion picture or the use of any advertisements thereof,

The proposed prohibitions are not drastic nor do they impose any serious burden upon the industry.

So far as the mechanics of the work involved is concerned the inspectors or inspection committee would perform effectively the service so long performed ineffectively by the National Board of Review in New York, or by any one of the existing censorship boards in America or elsewhere throughout the world.

There are, therefore, no practical objections to the successful operation of the plan.

The proposed prohibitions are in substance a brief but comprehensive resume of the existing censorship provisions throughout the world and they are less specific and less exacting than the prescriptions which the industry in America has ostensibly and ostentatiously written for itself, first in 1921,[2] and again at the trade conference in

---

deemed by him to violate any of the foregoing provisions, and in the event that said official fails in due course to apply for such injunction as to any picture or advertisement thereof, deemed by any person in the public's behalf to violate any of the provisions thereof, such person or persons shall have the right to apply to a court of competent jurisdiction for an injunction to restrain the distribution and exhibition of any such picture or advertisement."

[2] The following resolutions were unanimously adopted on March 5, 1921, by the National Association of the Motion Picture Industry in New York City and are quoted from the Cathechism on Motion Pictures in Interstate Commerce by the Rev. William Sheafe Chase, D.D., president of the New York Civic League and published by that organization, 452 Broadway, Albany, N. Y.

"RESOLVED, that the National Association of the Motion Picture Industry reaffirms its emphatic protests against the production, distribution and exhibition of all motion pictures which are obscene, salacious, indecent and immoral; and be it further

"RESOLVED, that while the creators of the art of the motion picture must in no way be hampered or prohibited from depicting honestly and clearly life as it is, to the end that this art may not be hindered in its movement toward the dignity of other arts, the motion picture should not be prostituted to a use or as a means toward arousing bawdy

Proposed International Alliance and Proposed Accord

emotions or pandering to a salacious curiosity, or in any other manner injurious to public welfare; and be it further

RESOLVED, to the end that the motion picture be held in that high plane which it has already attained, that the producers of motion pictures refrain from producing motion pictures

"1. (a) which emphasize and exaggerate sex appeal or depict scenes therein exploiting interest in sex in an improper or suggestive form or manner.

"2. (b) based upon white slavery or commercialized vice, or scenes showing the procurement of women or any of the activities attendant upon this traffic.

"3. (c) thematically making prominent an illicit love affair which tends to make virtue odious and vice attractive.

"4. (d) with scenes which exhibit nakedness or persons scantily dressed, particularly suggestive bedroom or bathroom scenes and scenes of inciting dances.

"5. (e) with scenes which unnecessarily prolong expressions or demonstrations of passionate love.

"6. (f) predominantly concerned with the underworld or vice and crime, and like scenes, unless the scenes are part of an essential conflict between good and evil.

"7. (g) of stories which make drunkenness and gambling attractive, or with scenes which show the use of narcotics or unnatural practices dangerous to social morality.

"8. (h) of stories and scenes which may instruct the morally feeble in methods of committing crime, or by cumulative processes emphasize crime and the commission of crime.

"9. (i) of stories or scenes which ridicule or deprecate public officials, officers of the law, the United States Army, the United States Navy, or other governmental authority, or which tend to weaken the authority of the law.

"10. (j) of stories or scenes or incidents which offend the religious belief of any persons, creed or sect, or ridicule ministers, priests, rabbis or recognized religious leaders of any religious sect, and also which are disrespectful to objects or symbols used in connection with any religion.

"11. (k) of stories or with scenes which unduly emphasize bloodshed and violence without justification in the structure of the story.

"12. (l) of stories or with scenes which are vulgar and portray improper gestures, posturing and attitudes.

"13. (m) with salacious titles and subtitles in connection with their presentation or exhibition and the use of salacious advertising matter, photographs and lithographs in connection therewith, and it is further

"RESOLVED, that this association record its intention to aid and assist the properly constituted authorities in the criminal prosecution of any producer, distributor or exhibitor of motion pictures who shall produce, distribute or exhibit any obscene, salacious or immoral motion picture in violation of the law, to the end that the recognized public good accomplished by the motion picture shall be preserved and advanced, and be it further

Motion Picture Problems

New York between October 10th and 15th, 1927.[3]

"RESOLVED, that any member of this association wilfully refusing to carry into effect these resolutions shall be subject to expulsion as a member of this association, and, further, subject to such other penalties as the association may fix, and be it further

"RESOLVED, that all exhibitors, producers and distributors of motion pictures, not members of this association, be urged to co-operate to carry into full effect these resolutions."

These resolutions with one additional paragraph were known in the industry at the time of their adoption as the industry's "Fourteen Points."

The "catechism" declares that the National Association of the Motion Picture Industry then represented approximately 95% of the producers of motion pictures exhibited in the United States and that the following producing and distributing members whose slightly changed names indicate that they are the predecessors of some of the important distributors today, included the following: Associated First National Pictures, Inc. (now First National Pictures, Inc.), Educational Film Exchanges, Inc., Famous Players Lasky Corporation, Fox Film Corporation; Goldwyn Pictures Corporation, Metro Pictures Corporation (now combined as Metro-Goldwyn-Mayer Corporation); Pathe Exchange, Inc., Universal Film Manufacturing Company, United Artists Corporation.

[3] Many if not all of the foregoing companies which still exist found it necessary or desirable to subscribe to the so-called Producers' Resolution No. 2 adopted at the trade conference in New York between October 10th and 15th, 1927, in the following peculiarly and unnecessarily offensive language:

"Whereas, for the purpose of further establishing and maintaining the highest possible moral and artistic standards in motion pictures, the following companies, members of Motion Picture Producers and Distributors of America, Inc., to-wit: (including Cecil B. DeMille Pictures Corporation, Educational Film Exchanges, Inc., F. B. O. Pictures Corporation, First National Pictures, Inc., Fox Film Corporation, Metro-Goldwyn-Mayer Distributing Corporation, Paramount Famous Lasky Corporation, Pathe Exchange, Inc., United Artists Corporation, Universal Pictures Corporation, Vitagraph, Inc., Warner Brothers Pictures, Inc.) and the following members of the Association of Motion Picture Producers, Inc., of California, to-wit: (Cecil B. DeMille Pictures Corporation, F. B. O. Pictures Corporation, First National Productions Corporation, William Fox Vaudeville Company, Metro-Goldwyn-Mayer Corporation, Paramount Famous Lasky Corporation, United Artists Studio Corporation, Universal Pictures Corporation, Warner Brothers Pictures, Inc.) have adopted the following formula with reference to the selection and rejection of certain story material for picturization:

"RESOLVED, that these things which are included in the following list shall not appear in pictures produced by the members of this association, irrespective of the manner in which they are treated: (1)

Proposed International Alliance and Proposed Accord

These industrial declarations are pregnant with the admission of the character of the pictures which were prevalent in the trade before the declarations were made, and

pointed profanity—by either title or lip—this includes the words, God, Lord, Jesus Christ (unless they be used reverently in connection with proper religious ceremonies) Hell, damn, gawd and every other profane and vulgar expression, however it may be spelled; (2) any licentious or suggestive nudity—in fact or in silhouette; and any lecherous and licentious notice thereof by other characters in the picture; (3) the illegal traffic in drugs; (4) any inference of sex perversion; (5) white slavery; (6) miscegenation (sex relationships between the white and black races); (7) sex hygiene and venereal diseases; (8) scenes of actual child birth—in fact or in silhouette; (9) children's sex organs; (10) ridicule of the clergy; (11) wilful offense to any nation, race or creed; and

"BE IT FURTHER RESOLVED, that special care be exercised in the manner in which the following subjects are treated, to the end that vulgarity and suggestiveness may be eliminated and that good taste may be emphasized: (1) the use of the Flag; (2) international relations (avoiding picturizing in an unfavorable light another country's religion, history, institutions, prominent people and citizenry); (4) arson; (5) the use of fire arms; (6) theft, robbery, safe cracking and dynamiting of trains, mines, buildings, etc. (having in mind the effect which a too detailed description of these may have upon the moron; (7) brutality and possible gruesomeness; (8) technique of committing murder by whatever method; (9) methods of smuggling; (10) third degree methods; (11) actual hangings or electrocutions as legal punishments for crime; (12) sympathy for criminals; (13) attitude toward public characters and institutions; (14) sedition; (15) apparent cruelty to children and animals; (16) branding of people or animals; (17) the sale of women or of a woman selling her virtue; (18) rape or attempted rape; (19) first night scenes; (20) man and woman in bed together; (21) deliberate seduction of girls; (22) the institution of marriage; (23) surgical operations; (24) the use of drugs; (25) titles or scenes having to do with law enforcement or law enforcement officers; (26) excessive or lustful kissing, particularly when one character or the other is a heavy.

"RESOLVED, that the execution of the purposes of this resolution is a fair trade practice."

The foregoing resolutions constitute what became known in the industry as the 11 so-called "don'ts" and 26 "be carefuls" with which the sophisticates in the trade in America amuse themselves, and to which the producers and distributors pay no attention whatever except as their public exploitation contributes to deluding the public to believe that the resolutions were to be performed by the industry.

yet the last pronouncement was made as recently as October, 1927.

The pictures themselves from 1921 and even after October, 1927, indicate a substantial disregard of many of the resolutions which justifies the impression that the resolutions were passed for public consumption rather than for industrial observance.

How can the trade now complain if States and nations take the industry at its own word and adopt, in the form of enforcible enactments substantially the same prescriptions to which the industry has itself unanimously subscribed?

If these self-imposed restrictions had been observed even in substantial part it might be said that there is no occasion for an international treatment of the subject which supplies the means to enforce the observance of the principles which are involved.

But the pictures of today and their advertisements are more eloquent than the loud protestations of purity of purpose which have emanated from the industry.

The fact that although the industry made its declaration first in 1921 and deemed it to be desirable to reiterate it in 1927 is alone significant, but the pictures show that even before the ink was dry on the paper upon which the resolutions of 1927 were inscribed and before the reverberations of the protestations of sanctity had died away, the industry was in active violation of the precepts which they had declared they would follow in the future.

No one with any knowledge of the subject attaches the slightest importance to these or similar trade declarations.

They are recognized as mere industrial propaganda, intended only for public consumption.

While the industry in America would first doubtless oppose the creation of a cinema committee of the League such opposition is and will be quite misguided, and in time will probably give way to a more enlightened policy born of the conviction that such a committee may well afford a considerable conciliatory measure of protection to the American industry against unwise nationalistic action designed solely to injure the industry in this country.

In 1927 the United States of America, notwithstanding its own unique tariff policy was tentatively signatory to the convention at Geneva against the passage of unreasonable tariff barriers, and in July, 1928, the American Minister to Berne presented at Geneva, without success, the contention of the American industry and of the American State Department that the French cinema decree of February 18, 1928, violated the same treaty to which France also was a party. This is important here as showing that America and the American industry are not above seeking the protection which in a proper and meritorious case the League of Nations is capable of affording both to America and the American industry.

It would be far better for the American industry to join or to help to form an effective international cinema cartel and to facilitate the creation of a League cinema committee rather than to oppose and to resist the inevitable reapportionment of the world's trade which the conciliatory offices of the League Committee might well tend to ameliorate and to make more palatable to the industrialists in America.

And so, for all of the reasons stated, it will be found that the formation of an international cinema alliance by the execution of the proposed accord, with the request upon the League of Nations to take the necessary action to supervise its execution and to render it effective, is the best means of establishing and maintaining the facilities for an essential international control over the subject, which within a brief period of time will induce and result in a better quality of subject matter and supply the foundations upon which sound, economic national and international policies may be formulated and carried out.

CHAPTER VIII

THE PROPOSED CINEMA COMMITTEE OF THE LEAGUE OF NATIONS

Since the problems involve considerations of public welfare, and of an economic and commercial nature, it is appropriate that the committee or commission be composed in part of members of the existing organizations and committees of the League which have to deal with these subjects.

It should also include representatives from the International Labor Office and representatives of such governments as may wish to be represented on it and such additional educators, economists and publicists, and such experts, outside of the motion picture industry, either as members of the committee or attached to it, as the Council or the committee may deem to be necessary or desirable.

It should not include any representative of the cinema trade of any nation.

Knowledge of the industry is one thing. Financial interest in it is another. It is axiomatic that a man cannot faithfully serve two masters. The interests of the public are not necessarily those of the industry. If there be anyone in the motion picture industry otherwise competent to serve upon such committee, let him either surrender all financial interest in it or else forego the distinction of service upon such committee.

The world has now had sufficient demonstration of the futility of endeavoring to induce bodies composed in part of statesmen or publicists or both and members of the trade, to decide mixed questions relating to public welfare and to the motion picture trade.

The failure to obtain much-needed results at the International Cinema Congress at Paris in 1926, the conferences of the British Trade Committee prior to the passage of the British Films Bill and even the activities of the Mixed French Committees which preceded the promulgation of France's cinema decree of February 18, 1928, sufficiently establishes the inevitable futility of such efforts.

It is believed that if it had not been for the exceptional strength, courage and ability of France's Minister of Education, M. Herriot, the industrial members of the French Committee would have rendered that Committee's efforts fruitless.

It is confidently believed that the Minister brought his project to a successful conclusion notwithstanding the views of some of the industrial members of that Committee.

Such data as may be needed can be obtained from experts without making any representative of the trade a member of such committee.

Notwithstanding the foregoing illustrations, a somewhat similar experiment is about to be made.

It is announced [1] that the International Chamber of Commerce will begin at Paris on November 14, 1928, "to explore the possibility of 'regularizing' all existing motion picture restrictions."

---

[1] *New York Times*, September 27, 1928.

Proposed Cinema Committee of the League of Nations

The intervention of this body might, conceivably, serve a useful purpose, but since the problems presented by the effort "to regularize" tariffs, quota and other motion picture restrictions, especially the censorship restrictions, are primarily governmental, the League of Nations is clearly better qualified to deal with these problems than any commercial or industrial agency.

Indeed, the League of Nations is the only organization which is capable of formulating a sound structure and of executing an effective program not only for the benefit of the trade but for public welfare everywhere.

The subjects are inseparable and the persistent effort to separate them leads only to further confusion.

The International Chamber of Commerce is interested only in trade and is not qualified to deal with the public welfare phases of the subject, and hence it could not, in the nature of things, achieve a complete or successful result.

It is believed that the particular form of the organization, that is to say, whether it is established by the League as a technical organization, or as an advisory committee or as a commission under Article 24 of the Covenant, can best be determined by those whose experience qualifies them to decide this question wisely after they have had an opportunity to study and to understand the facts and the implications which they involve.

Questions concerning the powers of such a body and what its functions should be are most important and should also, in large part, be decided by the Council of the League.

That the League will not exceed its jurisdiction in such

an undertaking is certain even under the natural pressure and desire to undertake the correction of all the evils "the heartache and the thousand natural shocks that flesh is heir to."

There was a resolution moved from the platform of the 1926 Assembly of the League by Lord Cecil urging the appointment of a committee to examine League activities present and prospective and to decide which are strictly international and therefore within the League's sphere of activity, and which are not.[2]

"This," said Mr. Harris, "was thought to be aimed primarily at some of the enterprises falling within the purview of the Fifth Commission, the more so since Lord Cecil took as one of his illustrations of work the League ought not to do, a resolution regarding swimming baths which had been before the League's Child Welfare Committee."

Sir Austen Chamberlain also sounded an appropriate note of warning and cauation:[3]

"There is but one danger," he said, "that I see in this endeavor; it is that we should allow our zeal for good causes to outrun our discretion, and should be tempted to overlook the limitations inherent in our constitution, and so to meddle with matters which lie wholly within the scope and authority of the individual national governments and are not dependent for their solution on international agreement. We must remember when deciding what work the League should undertake and what to decline, that it is an international and not a supernational body —an association of equal and sovereign States and not a super State with an independent and overriding authority of its own.

"But this is not all. Since the League is not a super State but an association of States, its Council is not a super-government but an association of governments. Since it works by persuasion and conciliation it can only work by agreement."

---

[2] *Geneva, 1926*, by H. Wilson Harris, 42.
[3] *The League*, by Sir Austen Chamberlain, 21, December, 1926.

Again he said in the same speech:

"It follows that the League must work in the main not by force, but by persuasion. Its policy must be one of conciliation, not coercion. It must seek its main support in the willing co-operation of its members, in public opinion, and in the moral force which it derives from its representative character."

The importance of the work which the League has done in other fields and is capable of doing in connection with the motion picture—particularly by securing the voluntary consent of several nations to the adoption of a definite policy formulated by the League which would be productive of good results to all concerned is thus accentuated.

In the creation of the proposed body it is important that the fullest power should be conferred. The use of such power is a matter for subsequent consideration.

Power should be conferred in broad, simple terms to deal with all phases of the motion picture and the problems which it presents, within the jurisdiction of the League of Nations.

As a prototype of structure it would be difficult to surpass that of the Committee on Intellectual Cooperation.

Originally composed of but twelve distinguished scholars, later increased to fourteen, this splendid committee established national committees in 35 or more countries to co-operate with it in its work, thus creating an effective world wide organization which is exactly what is needed in the motion picture field.

The work of this committee was greatly aided by the generous offer of France to endow, with 2,000,000 francs a year, an International Institute of Intellectual Cooperation at Paris under the direction of that committee.

The gift was accepted, commodious quarters were supplied in the Palais Royal, erected originally for Cardinal Richelieu between 1625 and 1634, and the work of the Institute began.

The Institute now functions as the executive or administrative part of the Committee on Intellectual Co-operation.

The work of the committee and of the Institute is necessarily intellectual in character and does not relate to trade or commerce in any of its branches.

The motion picture, as already indicated, includes both the intellectual field and the field of commerce.

As a prototype of the kind of work which must be undertaken in the motion picture field, an examination of the creation and activities of the so-called Opium Committee of the League is full of helpful and suggestive material.

It may be pointed out that many believe with the unofficial writer of a recent article in the *Osservatore Romano*, the official organ of the Vatican, that the pictures which unfortunately emanate in such large part from America, contain what was described as a "lethal poison."

Pictures, however, are not wholly bad and they have immense beneficient potentialities.

The same thing may be said of opium—medicine and science would be seriously handicapped without it.

Pictures are produced in comparatively few countries. They are disseminated and broadcast throughout the world.

America is the largest producer and the largest consumer of pictures, but the consumption of pictures throughout the world is extensive and is rapidly increasing.

China, on the other hand, produces considerably over half of the world's opium,[4] and is a large user of opium for smoking purposes.

India is said to be one of the largest growers [5] but "the morphia content of opium produced in India and China is too low to be profitably manufactured into any of the drugs with which the western world is afflicted. Opium with a high morphia content is produced chiefly in Turkey, Persia and Jugoslavia." [6] Thus, the centers of production are exposed—America, the chief producer of pictures; Turkey, Persia, Jugoslavia, China and India the producers of opium.

Before the war the world-wide movement against opium had begun with the offer of the British government to reduce Indian production and to control its export to China.

In 1909 there was an international conference at the invitation of the United States of America, a non-producer

---

[4] *Reconstruction*, by Maurice Fanshawe, 191.

[5] *Ibid.*, 183.

[6] *Ibid.*, 189. However, D. W. MacCormack, a member of the Persian Commission, was reported to have said that while opium is said to constitute 1-5 of Persia's export trade it produces only 1-2 of 1% of the world opium supply and is of relatively low narcotic content. World production was said to be not less than 5,000 tons while medicinal requirements are said to be from 200 to 400 tons.
More than 3-4 of the world's supply was said to come from Turkey and 6% each from Macedonia, Greece, India and Europe.
New York Times, August 24, 1927.

of the drug, 1,000,000 of whose nationals were said to be addicted to its use.[7]

The conference was attended by 13 States and the general lines of the campaign against opium were laid down and subsequently formed the basis of a definite international opium convention drawn up at the Hague in 1912.[8]

"It aimed," said Mr. Fanshawe, "at controlling the distribution of raw opium which is used for smoking purposes, and gradually suppressing prepared opium from which derivitive drugs such as morphine and heroin are obtained. As regards international control of the traffic entry was to be prohibited and export controlled to countries which restricted import."

Mr. Fanshawe points out that ratification of this convention was important and that the whole situation was upset by the war, which induced a large increase in the use and demand for drugs of all kinds.

Mr. Fanshawe describes the activities of the League in this connection and says that the first Assembly of the League in 1920 established an advisory committee on the traffic in opium and other dangerous drugs, and that in the following year the Council appointed representatives from all of the countries chiefly concerned, except America, who at that time was avoiding any direct connection with the work of the League.

He points out that the committee utilized the existing machinery for the solution of the problem and devised new machinery.

Its efforts induced a large number of nations to become signatories to The Hague Convention of 1912, statistics

---
[7] *Geneva, 1928*, by H. Wilson Harris, 55.
[8] *Reconstruction* by Maurice Fanshawe, 184.

which in effect were a census of the world's drugs were compiled, and the committee became a clearing house of information on the subject and suggestions were made to the governments concerning penalties for the internal traffic in and consumption of drugs, many of which were adopted. Special questions of transport were referred to the committee on communications and transit. But, as Mr. Fanshawe said, "viewing the problem as a whole the advisory committee soon saw that enforcement of the 1912 convention was in any case not enough. Control of illicit traffic in drugs, in fact, could not be carried out *as long as there was a vast production of the raw products from which the drugs are manufactured. Vast production inevitably meant vast smuggling.*" And so the committee prepared a program for limiting the production of raw materials.

It became necessary, therefore, to ascertain the annual requirements of the world in the use of this drug for medicinal and scientific purposes. These steps in their application to motion pictures are most suggestive.

While this work was in progress an official American delegation headed by Mr. Stephen G. Porter, chairman of the Foreign Relations Committee of the House of Representatives, attended the Fifth Session of the Advisory Committee in May, 1923, and proposed that to give effect to the Hague Convention it was desirable that it be recognized that the use of opium and its products for other than medicinal and scientific purposes be regarded as an abuse and not legitimate and that in order to prevent the abuse of these products it is necessary to exercise control over the production of raw opium in such a manner that there will be no surplus available for non-medicinal and non-scientific purposes.[9]

Here, then, was a proposal to the League to find ways and means to curtail and to regulate the production of a merchantable commodity, necessarily a question of internal national policy but, because of the baneful effects which that product when produced was exerting generally upon the welfare of humanity, an international question of grave importance.

India, it was said, wished and asserted the right to use opium in its edible form, claiming that it had always been so used as a household remedy by millions beyond the reach of any medical aid.

But after full discussion the advisory committee unanimously reached a practical compromise, accepted the suggested American plan to which effect was to be given by calling a conference of producing and manufacturing states to settle the final basis of distribution.[10]

The conference lasted from November, 1924, to February, 1925, and unfortunately the American and Chinese delegations withdrew from the conference before its completion.

A convention was, however, finally signed on February 11, 1925, by Great Britain, India, France, Japan, Holland, Portugal and Siam which declared the importation,

---
[9] *Reconstruction* by Maurice Fanshawe, 189.
[10] *Reconstruction* by Maurice Fanshawe, 190

sale and preparation of opium for sale to be a government *monopoly not to be leased to private individuals.*[11]

Mr. Fanshawe gives a summary of the results which is interesting and important.

> "The retirement, however, of the American delegations," said Mr. Fanshawe, "did not mean that the conference was unable to produce any definite results. It completed its work by unanimously adopting a convention * * * Thus, as far as general results go, it may be said there is no question that reduction of production of drugs everywhere to the scientific and medical needs of the world is still the objective that must be continually kept in view. But its immediate realization cannot yet be counted upon in view of existing political conditions in China as well as in Persia and in Turkey. As far, however, as the manufacture of drugs is concerned, which is the problem in which western countries are more closely interested, a system of control has been started by the League and gradually developed to a point where it can be made effective. *The creation of a permanent board of control at Geneva is of great importance. For the first time a central international organization will be able to know the origin and destination of all drugs, and be empowered to bring pressure by means of public opinion on any country which is producing or dealing in dangerous amounts of drugs.*" [12]

The significance of these results, as illustrative of what the League has done and with appropriate modifications and adaptations, what it may do in connection with a subject which is far more than a mere commercial pursuit and which exerts an important influence upon the mentality, the morality and hence the general health and welfare of mankind appears to justify the digression from the direct consideration of the subject under discussion.

In its specific application to motion pictures the League has an immense field within its jurisdiction.

---

[11] *Reconstruction* by Maurice Fanshawe, 191.
[12] *Ibid.*, 193.

MOTION PICTURE PROBLEMS

Internationally the work involves two major divisions.

Public welfare, which embraces (1) the affirmative encouragement and promotion of the world's peace through improvement in the quality of motion pictures and the development of mankind by similar means (2) intellectually, (3) morally, (4) culturally and (5) artistically, and (6) negatively by the suppression and elimination, by international convention and other appropriate means, of pictures which incite to war or which stimulate racial, national or religious hatreds or prejudices, or which are unhealthy or otherwise harmful to the public in any respect.

In the economic field the assurance of equality of opportunity everywhere to all producers of wholesome desirable pictures is of chief importance.

This is of international consequence, and hence the policies which will most certainly afford such assurance must be examined, formulated and recommended to the several nations in the form of appropriate conventions and proposed national legislative or executive decrees for separate adoption.

A cinema committee of the League could call conferences of government representatives and present to them one or more conventions or agreements under which each government could pledge itself to adopt specific legislative or executive measures, as nearly uniform as varying conditions would permit, to render effective principles affecting both of the major divisions to which reference has been made.

The committee could formulate and recommend to the

several states which did not participate in the convention, such policies as may be found to be desirable for adoption.

Nationally, the matter of first importance will be found to be that of public welfare as heretofore described.

The matter of secondary importance is the economic, industrial and commercial aspects of the subject both from the standpoint of domestic and foreign trade.

The matter of third importance is that of government revenue to be derived from the trade both domestic and foreign.

It will be desirable to make recommendations of particular methods, which a careful international study indicates would give the best results, with the least inconvenience to the trade.

It is believed that after full examination of the subject the most appropriate recommendations will be found to include the following:

(1) That each state fix, establish and declare the status of the motion picture within its borders, in the abstract, to be a public utility.

(2) That each enact a broad statute, substantially in the form proposed in the suggested accord and prohibiting in simple terms the production, distribution and exhibition of pictures which are injurious to the public in any respect.

(3) That each authorize and request the cinema committee of the League of Nations to establish national committees wherever deemed desirable but particularly in the cinema producing states, and that no film shall be imported into any of the nations so agreeing unless and until it has

been submitted to the cinema import inspector or inspectors so designated by the cinema committees to serve as such in the country of the film's origin and authorizing such inspectors to grant preliminary preferential and such other film import certificates as may be agreed upon.

(4) Economic and commercial reconstruction can best be achieved by one of three methods.

(a) In countries not opposed to complete governmental regulation or control, a simple declaration that complete power to deal with the whole subject is vested and placed in the hands of a single administrative official, preferably the Minister of Education, with power to make appropriate rules and regulations to this end, will prove to be the most effective method. This may even include and embrace the state monopolization and operation of the function of distribution or of one or more other branches of the industry.

(b) In other countries which are opposed in principle to state control or regulation of the kind suggested and hence to all state monopolies, there must be a re-establishment of fair competition in every branch of the trade. This can best be achieved by the national enactment heretofore suggested, by the prohibition of all unfair methods of competition and by expressly including within that term and by prohibiting, or at least greatly modifying the use of exclusive exhibition contracts which induce and make possible the private monopolistic control of the industry.

(c) The proposed adoption of either method by any nation or by a group of nations constituting an important part of the world's market from a lucrative point of view, will inevitably lead to the negotiation of international trade agreements between groups of producers on the one side and one or more distributors of motion pictures in America on the other, by means of which the existing monopolization of the screens of the world by pictures emanating from but one nation may be substantially modified and reduced and the cinema production industries of the producing nations of the world revived and restored to a profitable condition. Thus a reapportionment of the world's trade in this pursuit becomes not only possible but inevitable.

Many of the resolutions adopted at the International Cinema Congress show in detail other important work which should be performed by a permanent organization of the kind described.

It should, among other things, also begin to collect the facts and data on all phases of the subject from all parts of the world, and it should perform the service which the representatives of Norway, Brazil, Manitoba, Sweden, Turkey, The Union of South Africa and the Administrator of The Transvaal recommended to the Child Welfare Committee of the League, as heretofore indicated.

This should include a regular service which would supply advanced information from the country of origin of all pictures to every censorship board in the world and to every port of entry, presenting suitable data upon the pictures about to be offered for importation into each one of the countries to which such data should be sent.

It should particularly create national committees in every country to aid it in its work. It should formulate a system of preferential import certificates or licenses as suggested in the perfection of which the national committees would prove invaluable.

It should consider and determine the extent to which it may be desirable to recommend to State Members the adoption of principles and policies involving a governmental unity of purpose in matters of a moral, educational and economic nature.

It should extend its conciliatory offices and permit its facilities to be used in the negotiation of trade agreements between the states and between individuals or groups of individuals as occasion may require.

Such a committee should endeavor to conclude an international film copyright convention in accord with the extremely well considered recommendations of the Fourth Commission of the International Cinema Congress. Such a result would prove of great value to the industry everywhere.

So, also, if the proposed League Committee would take up and determine which of the trade practices prevent progress and desirable development and declare them to be unfair methods of competition and recommend that they be so declared and forbidden by the several nations, a further important service would have been performed.

Such a committee could help the nations and the communities of the world to help themselves.

And after the status of the industry is established everywhere as one impressed with substantial public duties and responsibilities, after the several nations of the world have prescribed simply that pictures which are injurious to the public for any reason shall not be publicly exhibited, and after the governments have prohibited unfair methods of competition and have restored fair competition within their borders and developed the system of preferential import certificates to which reference has been made, pictures which are better in the moral, educational and cultural sense than those now prevalent will surely result and the production industries of the world will prosper once more.

CHAPTER IX

THE PROPOSED NATIONAL COMMITTEES

Each national committee should be composed of elements similar to those which should constitute the International Cinema Committee of the League of Nations.

The powers and functions of such committees should be such as may be prescribed from time to time by the International Committee.

They should include the duty to collect and present to the International Committee facts and data with the recommendations of the committee concerning all phases of the cinema from the national point of view.

Each should act as an appropriate channel through which those in any country desiring to present data or material or problems to the International Committee for consideration may present such matters first to the national committee in order that the International Committee may have the benefit of the recommendations of the national committee concerning such matters as are brought to its attention in this manner.

Together these national committes functioning on matters of common concern through the International Committee will constitute a great world organization through which the problems described could and would be solved primarily in the interests of the public of the world and secondarily with justice to the trade.

There is one matter which these national committees could undertake which would soon make the system which would be built around the International Committee and its national committees immensely effective.

The importance of dealing with the opium problem and the regulation of production to meet medicinal and scientific needs has already been shown.

This is similar in some respects to the increasing importance of ascertaining each country's need for imported pictures.

Many nations will inevitably soon expressly limit the number of pictures which may be imported into such countries.

Germany led the way in this respect as of January 1, 1928, and was soon followed by France. Each has fixed a specific quota of pictures which may be imported within a specified period of time and each has left a wide degree of discretion in the hands of the administrative officials whose business it is to deal with this subject.

These governmental expressions and declarations of policy are the obvious forerunners of the reapportionment of the world's trade in this industry on a basis which it is to be hoped will be scientific in its relation to world consumption and just to all concerned.

The importance of regulating the content of pictures when and as produced and not after the undesirable pictures have been despatched for exhibition everywhere throughout the world, often beyond recall, cannot be overestimated.

The problem, without the aid of the League of Nations, is more difficult than that relating to the control of opium at the source of production or that relating to the enforcement of prohibition in America.

Yet these are not reasons for the abandonment of the problems.

They can be solved by the efficient aid of the League of Nations.

Legalized or other censorship is neither desirable nor practical.

But film inspection, at the source of production, of the kind presently described, is highly desirable and extremely practical.

Inspection is not censorship.

A film censor is one who examines a film and whose permission is necessary for its exhibition.

An inspector is one who merely inspects and examines and reports the result of his inspection to some higher or ultimate authority.

If, as the result of the inspection, the inspector certifies that a film meets the specified requirements adopted by a group of nations, as entitling a film to a preferential right to enter each country which subscribes to such an agreement, a preferential film import certificate would be attached to the film and it would proceed on its way.

This certificate should carry the same implication as the visa on a passport issued by a government to its own citizens to visit some other country with the latter's approval.

The visa guarantees nothing. It certifies certain facts. If the person whose passport has been duly visaed develops in transit a contagious disease or if the authorities at the port of destination learn facts not previously known which show that the holder of the passport, even though visaed, is not entitled to entry, he is dealt with accordingly and, if necessary, the visa is cancelled.

So it should be as to films.

If on inspection of the film in the country of its origin it is found not to be of the character specified and required by the standards which must be adopted by the nations, the film inspectors would classify it in accord with such powers as the government wished to confer upon them and they would so report the facts to the committee which by appropriate routine should report to the existing officers in the ports of entry of each of the countries signatory to the agreement. The report should at least include a statement of the fact of inspection, the identity of the film and the classification to which it was assigned with such comments as the inspectors deemed to be desirable.

Thus no government would surrender the right to accept or reject any film at any of its ports of entry. But film inspection at the place of origin of the film would supply most desirable advance information concerning the contents of each picture which would enable each government to determine for itself the doubtful and borderline cases.

The effect which this system would in time exert upon the quality of pictures would be very great, especially if the findings of the inspectors are given due publicity in the country of origin and elsewhere.

The Proposed National Committees

A set of principles would in due course be evolved just as they have been formulated as the result of experience by the various censorship boards throughout the world.[1]

The proper application of these principles is more important and far more difficult than their formulation, and they doubtless could be applied more successfully and advantageously by inspectors or by a board of inspectors designated by the cinema committee of the League than they could be if designated separately by each government.

Thus governments would have little difficulty in agreeing among themselves that pictures which are immoral, which are inaccurate in matters of history or education, or which mutilate or distort works of literature, or which contain elements which are affirmatively harmful to the maintenance of friendly international relations, as for example those pictures which stimulate racial and national or religious prejudices or which tend to incite people to violence, to hatred of one another and ultimately to war, certainly should not be entitled to a preferential film import certificate.

Indeed, such pictures should only receive the certificate of condemnation which they deserve with a brief statement of facts which would constitute a warning to all port authorities in order that their entrance into any nation could be prevented.

But whether a film is of the kind described is, of course, except in the plainest and grossest cases a matter of opinion, and so final decision of the right to entry should be

---
[1] See Standards of Censorship Boards, Appendix.

reserved by and should rest with the several governments at their ports of entry.

But all of such officials should be presented and equipped with the complete information and data which this system would enable the national committees to supply.

If it be said that the work is not practical, not work which designated members of such a national committee could or would be willing to perform, the answer is that the boards of censorship have performed inquisitorial functions involved in this work and are performing them today in many places throughout the world, rather than at the comparatively few sources of production.

Not so long ago Dr. Nicholas Murray Butler said,

"I am sure the time is coming when a board of educators in morals and manners and authentic past and present customs will be a feature of the big producing organiations." [2]

Following that suggestion and subsequent conferences between Dr. Butler and the producers in America, a committee was appointed composed in part of Columbia University professors and in part of those from the industry for the ostensible purpose of facilitating collaboration in matters of the kind proposed, but without any element of definite and demonstrable value attached to the act of inspection and its consequences, nothing but absurdity can or will result.

If the governments make a substantial difference between the terms upon which a film bearing a preferential

---

[2] Reprint in *Motion Pictures Today*, October 16, 1926.

import certificate and those which do not may enter each country, that certificate would become of value and all producers would endeavor to conform to the fixed requirements which would entitle their films to receive it.

If the inspector or board of inspectors are poorly paid men and women of little education, or persons whose concepts of morality, education and culture are no higher than those now reflected in the pictures of the present day, or if they are subsidized or corrupted by the industry, no material change will result from the system proposed, or from any conceivable system; but if the work of inspection is entrusted to educators willing to serve the League of Nations, men and women who are competent to deal with such matters, an immense influence could thus be exerted upon the quality of motion pictures, especially as the opportunity to designate these special inspectors will permit of a most desirable interchange of nationals, Europeans serving in America, and, conceivably, Americans serving abroad.

If for example a producer knew in advance of completing his production that if he interpolated certain scenes in his picture it would be denied admission and hence exhibition in perhaps ten countries which contribute perhaps a very large proportion of the world's revenues to be derived from the exhibition of such picture throughout the world, then, as a matter of business, those scenes would be deleted voluntarily, and not as they sometimes are today by many different censorship boards throughout the world but at or near the producer's studio.

The principle is susceptible of great development, and

could be made of incalculable value to Great Britain in her situation in the Far East where so much damage has already been done, by the ill-considered pictorial rubbish produced here and exhibited there and elsewhere.

The system is not at all designed as and is not a barrier to embarrass or impede the entry of films into the countries which subscribe to the suggested convention.

Quite the contrary.

The sources of picture production are infinitely fewer than the ports of entry. To concentrate inspection at the source of production would prove to be a great benefit to the industry everywhere. It would be distinctly helpful. If a picture is to be rejected by a country or by ten nations it is better for the producer to know it at or near the studio than at the innumerable ports of ten different countries after transportation and other charges have been multiplied and added to the cost of production.

Those who oppose censorship and governmental regulation of the industry by commissions say that pictures cannot be made better by law and that the only hope of improvement in quality lies in educating the public taste for pictures which are better in an intellectual, moral or cultural sense.

No one disputes the desirability of public education. But how may the public's taste for better pictures be cultivated when under the present regime mercenary producers and their literary vandals are and for years have been engaged in deliberately contributing with complete success to the development of an appalling state of "universal morinity" and to the deterioration of the public taste and morals.

The instrument of greatest power in this respect is the motion picture. Those who now control it will not change their practices or improve the quality of their pictures until it becomes more profitable to do so. If the governments of the world or even some of them would adopt the course suggested it would be more profitable.

In practical operation and effect the international cinema committee after a thorough study of the subject would formulate the principles to which the governments could appropriately subscribe and present them to the governments for adoption.

The committee would designate the inspectors in each of the producing countries, fix the fees to be charged; the compensation to be paid and in all other respects perform this invaluable service in behalf of a group of governments which service it is now quite impossible for any nation to perform for itself.

The committee could and should exert a large influence in the administration of the duties of the inspectors.

It would not be long before efforts at affirmative improvement supplementing negative repression could be developed with success.

Thus the *producers* could and would be educated by this system at the source of production and through them with this indispensable aid the public taste could and would be improved.

If England and a group of ten or more European

nations joined perhaps by a group of progressive Latin-American countries, subscribed to the system which has been described a desirable change for the better in the quality of picture production could be effected within a remarkably short time.

The producers in America could not afford to disregard and would make their pictures conform to the import requirements of such an array of governments which control the entrance to markets of such immense financial importance to these producers, and if they did not conform to them, what an impetus would be given to British and European and to Latin production, for obviously each country must and will have pictures to exhibit and if for any cause those pictures cease to come from America that moment would be seized upon by every other producing nation to increase and improve its own domestic production.

Thus, in spite of the producers of the present day, pictures can be made fit for exhibition everywhere and, as in the opium problem, where only after years of study it was realized that the point at which to focus attention is the source of production, so in pictures, at this late day, the same thing is shown to be true.

What has been said demonstrates the tremendously important work capable of being done by the proposed national cinema committees of the League of Nations if a substantial number of governments see fit to enter into agreements with one another of the kind described.

APPENDIX

APPENDIX 1

M. Luchaire's Report of July 28th, 1924, to Committee On Intellectual Cooperation

RELATIONS OF THE CINEMATOGRAPH TO INTELLECTUAL LIFE.

Memorandum by M. Julien Luchaire, submitted to the Committee, and Resolutions adopted by the Committee, on July 28th, 1924.

I. THE DEVELOPMENT OF THE CINEMATOGRAPH.

The development of the cinematograph is one of the most important movements in the history of intellectual life during the last twenty years. In that short space of time the conditions which stimulate and nourish the imagination, feeling and thought of the masses in every country have been transformed by this new invention; the influence exercised by the cinema on the populace can only find a parallel in that of the theatre in the cities of ancient Greece and that of the daily Press in modern nations since the nineteenth century.

According to approximate estimates which probably fall short of the truth, there are now at least 50,000 cinema halls in the world. Taking the average number of spectators in each cinema to be 300, and remembering that each picture is usually repeated ten times, a film which goes all over the world, as many do, is seen in a relatively short space of time by 150 million persons.

Appendix

Never at any time has any product of human thought enjoyed so widespread and rapid a circulation.

Undoubtedly the impression made upon this enormous public is superficial compared with the influence of certain books which have taken years or centuries to impress themselves on a part of the human race—certain sacred books, for instance—and which have profoundly affected its thought, but it is a striking fact that only the Bible and the Koran have an indisputably larger circulation than that of the latest film from Los Angeles.

Moreover, while it is true that the success even of the best films is as short-lived as it is immense, the productions of the cinema, taken as a whole, exercise a constant influence. The mass of the public has a veritable passion for the cinema. The favourite literature of these classes of the populace, i.e., serials or novels in instalments, is in process of being transferred to the cinema; after having for a time provided the basis for a large proportion of cinematographic production, the popular novel has now become the servant of the film, for which it acts as advertisement and explanation.

To-day the lower classes derive from the cinema show (whether or not they have previously read the serial) a large part of the emotions and thoughts which make up their mental life. In many countries nowadays, apart from the hours devoted to work, meals and sleep, nearly all the leisure time of immense numbers of people belonging to the middle and lower classes in the towns are spent at football matches or at the cinema.

APPENDIX

Shows have always had a profound appeal for the masses. The spectacle provided by the cinema, which gives a vivid reproduction of life, and the rapid and often feverish action staged upon an immense scene in a garish light while the spectators are plunged in darkness, produce a kind of hallucination. The actors in the drama, their emotions and their actions carry conviction greater than in any other form of entertainment. The great actors, the "stars" of the cinema, receive innumerable letters from unknown admirers—a proof of the charm which emanates from their personalities, and, what is more to our purpose, from the characters they represent.

We cannot question, therefore, that the cinema is a powerful medium for the diffusion of moral, social and even political ideas or modes of thought. During the war the cinema was widely used for patriotic propaganda. It has also been adapted to religious propaganda in certain countries; in the United States, it is estimated that about twenty-five thousand churches use the screen as an adjunct to the pulpit. In many countries schools employ it as an aid to education, and it is used in science not only for demonstration but for experiments.

There is a further reason why the Committee on Intellectual Co-operation should include the cinema within the scope of its activities; this new and extraordinarily efficient instrument of intellectual action is intrinsically international.

Differences of language, which form a barrier between men, do not exist for the cinema. Moreover, conditions in the cinema trade are such that, if a film is to pay, it must

Appendix

be saleable in every country, or at least in a very large number of countries. Authors and producers are thus obliged to compose their works in a form that will enable them to be understood and appreciated by spectators of the most varied races and countries. The consequence is that the national character of films is reduced almost to nothing, or is confined to the picturesque element; the simplest motives, and those which have the most universal appeal, are most in favor.

These motives may be the basest or the loftiest; and therein lies the most important problem of the cinema. Is it to have the high education value and the elevating and ennobling influence which the theatre seems to have had on the masses in ancient Greece? Or is it to have the debasing influence of vulgar music-hall shows or of cheap novels? Doubtless, its influence will be in both directions, for so vast and varied a mass of production must inevitably contain some admixture of evil with the good. No man can attempt to control the colossal cinematographic industry of our times any more than he could endeavor to control the vast activities of the printing-press. Nevertheless, in the former as in the latter case, good influence acting in harmony, and the intervention of high authorities, may be of some avail in increasing the proportion of good and diminishing that of evil. An attempt can be made to draw up a programme of international action in this sphere; we will endeavor in a moment to sketch the salient points of such a programme.

First, however, we must settle a question to which critics of great authority have for a long time past given

APPENDIX

the most pessimistic replies. Is not the cinema, by its nature and purpose, condemned to vulgarity, except in its scientific or educational aspects? No: after what has been achieved during the last few years in the principal producing countries we are bound to recognise that the cinema can and should be a great art while at the same time remaining a popular art. This is now an incontestable fact, and opens up one of the most hopeful prospects ever revealed in the intellectual history of mankind. Apart from a very few poems, only the great masterpieces of architecture have been able to combine perfect beauty with that simplicity which alone can gain the comprehension and love of the humblest intelligence; and both these forms of art are so far restricted by their local character as to be inaccessible to a large section of the human race. The mere possibility that the cinema might become a great new *universal art should* earn it the attention of all who have the intellectual future of humanity at heart.

The invention of the cinematograph is only thirty years old; it was led up to by less than half a century of experiment, the importance of which was purely mechanical. It was not until the opening years of the twentieth century that the invention of the machine for unrolling perforated films heralded the advent of a new art. It would be unjust to reproach this art for its infantile incoherence; we may rather congratulate ourselves on its quick development. Indeed, its extraordinary success has obliged it to outgrow its strength;; a limited organisation has now to cope with an immense production, as the public demands new films every week; and it is, of course,

Appendix

inevitable that a production which can reach millions of spectators in a single week cannot remain on the programme for long. This excessive strain on cinema producers has unfortunate effects on the standard of plot and production and on that of the actors themselves, who have to be hastily recruited without having time to gain experience which could be acquired in normal circumstances.

The art of the cinema involves the most complicated processes. A considerable movement of capital is caused by every undertaking, whether old or new; it is estimated that in the United States, where the cinema is already the third national industry in financial importance, from four to six new companies spring up daily. Statistics, dating back some time, show that in the course of 12 months the capital invested in new cinema enterprises exceeded the following figures:

United States	$26,000,000
Sweden	35,000,000 crowns
England	£2,000,000
France	20,000,000 francs
Italy	35,000,000 lire

(company undertakings only, excluding a very large number of private enterprises).

At present, even in France, where the available capital is very limited, it is not unusual for from 3 to 4 millions to be spent on the production of a single film. Few are the enterprises, even theatrical, in which similar sums are involved. Nor does there seem to be any limit to the favor with which capitalists regard the cinema. Whatever difficulties this industry may encounter in certain directions, to which we will refer below, it is supported by the favor of the public, which grows from year to year, and the movement of capital in the industry cannot therefore fail to increase. The total takings of cinema theatres in the United States rose from about 75 million dollars in 1919-20 to over 90 millions in 1920-21, an increase of more than 20 per cent in one year.

An immense reserve of capital is therefore at the disposal of an industry whose influence on the intellectual life of mankind is already great and may become still greater.

If we consider the cinema as a pictorial art and a factor in the artistic education of the public, we shall find that it gives earnest of progress in several directions. It has transformed the scenic representation of architectural subjects and interiors. As its resources are not limited like those of the theatre proper, it is able to obtain much vaster, bolder and more complete effects. Instead of painted perspective, a whole street or square, in three dimensions, is set up in the studio; art has at its service almost the whole realm of reality and a much wider scope for imagination. Moreover, as the scenery has only to be erected once, the scene can be changed indefinitely; the number of different views placed before the public in two or three hours of entertainment is therefore increased ten, twenty, or even a hundredfold as compared with the theatre. It may even be thought that film authors are nowadays excessively liberal in this respect, but it must be recognised that they provide their public with a feast of the eye which must have a profound effect in forming their visual taste; they undoubtedly enrich it, and awaken this taste in many people who rarely go to the theatre.

Moreover, the cinema makes use of actual reality, which the theatre was never able to do. It employs it in its commonest as in its rarest aspects. It arouses the curiosity of the public by presenting strange and distant scenes; and it educates their taste by showing them the beauty of everyday scenes, which they had not always realized; a skilfully chosen point of view or a clever arrangement of lights may reveal an unsuspected grandeur in the scenes of ordinary life.

The fact of appearing on the screen and of taking part in a play transforms and idealises the most common objects; and this constitutes an artistic lesson for the lower classes, who rarely have an opportunity of seeing real works of art, and very often cannot understand them when they do. Modern literature and drama have attempted to achieve such transfigurations, but how contemptible are their efforts compared with the possibilities of the camera!

One of the chief resources of the cinema in influencing the visual artistic sense is its power of successively presenting images of quite different sizes: distant horizons followed abruptly by highly magnified details. This is not always done with proper moderation; wisely used, however, it is one of the most powerful instruments ever put into the hands of Art.

The hundreds of varied scenes which a single well-constructed film places before us are living scenes: flowing rivers, leaves fluttering in the breeze, clouds sailing across the sky—all form the background for the clash of human emotions. The reproduction of reality is almost perfect; it will soon be absolutely perfect, since the application of color photography to the cinema is now merely a matter of adjustment; moreover, in the present state of the technique of lighting the representation of reality in black and white scarcely disturbs the imagination. Both the illusion and the effect are overwhelming.

It has been said that they are *too* overwhelming, and that this marvelous power is just what prevents cinematography from being a great art. The object of this argument is to bring cinematograph into the same contempt as that from which photography has never quite escaped. But there can be no comparison between the resources or difficulties of animated photography and that of static photography. Even the latter produces works of real art: the choice of a subject and the manner in which the photographer sees and conceives it are true artistic processes. In the latter part of the last century, photography formed the artistic education of many people.

Cinematography, however, makes much greater demands on the artistic sense. The planning of so many scenes requires from the author an effort of the imagination in the process of which he may attain greatness. Then, in order to construct a scene, whether it requires a set piece or a selected spot, the producer has a most complex task; he must view the scene as a whole like a decorative painter, attend to detail like a painter of *genre,* control and move crowds much greater than any theatrical

APPENDIX

stage-manager has ever handled, and regulate attitudes and facial expressions with the minute attention to detail rendered necessary by "close-ups." The actors themselves, though no longer bound by the spoken word, must develop the mimetic art to its utmost limits; and the widely varied conditions in which they are called upon to act demand immense versatility. Apart from these main factors, there are the draughtsmen, the decorators, the specialists in furniture, draperies, costumes, posters and even titles and sub-titles, to say nothing of the lighting specialists; in short, the cinema theatre involves a great collective effort for the creation of a complex work of art in which extreme realism must be combined with extreme imaginative effort.

This is not the place to consider what are the rules of the cinema regarded as a dramatic art. The critics usually agree in saying they must be very different from those of the traditional theatre, and that they are not yet definitely established. It would appear that the "plastic" aspect of this adolescent art has made more rapid progress than its "dramatic" aspect. The chief point to note is that the screen also has great possibilities in connection with the presentation of human actions, passions and even thoughts. For the life of mankind can be represented on the screen in many aspects that the old theatre could not attempt to reproduce; both comedy and tragedy have already taken on new forms, but in this sphere the era of discoveries has scarcely begun.

It is hardly venturesome to assume that when color-photography and the synchronisation of the cinema with

APPENDIX

the phonograph have been accomplished, as they undoubtedly will be, the cinema will tend in a large degree to replace the old theatre, and will certainly outstrip it in variety and scope. It will be *par excellence* the theatre of the masses; it will have penetrated into the remotest regions of the globe and into the smallest village, and will thus arouse the mirth and emotion of the whole human race.

It is essential, therefore, to consider without delay what can be done to ensure that its influence will at the same time be moral and instructive. It is quite clear that at present the choice of subjects and the spirit in which they are treated are not wholly satisfactory from this point of view. But here we must make a distinction. The cinema shows of today (for the moment we are not speaking of educational and scientific films) are generally instructive for ignorant people. They see countries and habits of life of which they had never heard, and historical reconstructions which, even if not wholly accurate, are at least suggestive; they see a thousand aspects of human activity which, in the narrow circle of their daily life, had not come within their purview; in the news films they witness important events all over the world.

Morally, also, the cinema of today contains both good and evil. The modern film is hardly ever immoral as music-hall shows are immoral; it is rarely indecent. This is saying a great deal; but films full of silly sentimentality or of fantastic adventures occupy too great a place in the annual output of the principal companies. Stories of "crooks" are also much too frequently shown. In short, the cinema, while far removed from the music-hall, bears too great a similarity to the popular melodrama and to the theatre of the suburban and plebeian quarters of the large towns. The cinema has no big central theatres reserved for high-lass productions; picture palaces situated in the centre of large towns have appreciably the same programme as will subsequently be shown in more remote cinemas. This will probably always be the case, as the film must have a public running into millions. But it is to be hoped that films of real æsthetic value will become more numerous; the art of the cinema can reconcile its desire to please the crowd with the ambition to maintain a certain intellectual standard. If the best methods have not yet been found, the search for them should be encouraged. The object of what has been said above is to demonstrate the necessity of providing such encouragement in certain forms—a matter with which we shall deal more fully below.

II. Use of the Screen in Education.

The Committee is particularly interested in the scientific and educational use of the cinematograph. Here again we realize that this new art is still very young. In the field of scientific research it is clear that there are great prospects for an instrument which can show biological phenomena in full activity. But to adapt it to each separate branch of science is a difficult business, involving extended and costly experiments. The screen has already been turned to good account, particularly in astronomy and biology; Dr. Commandon's experiments in France are

Appendix

well-known. No methodical research seems, however, to have been undertaken with a view to extending the use of animated pictures to every branch of science in which they could be employed. In the last section of this report we shall advert to some proposals which have been made for the creation of cinematograph *conservatoires* or *institutes.*

It is safe to assert that cinematograph apparatus will soon have become one of the most valuable adjuncts to zoology, ethnology and geography; nor can history do without a perpetual evidence of the aspect of contemporary events and a permanent record of the most dramatic moments in the lives of nations. Here again, it is desirable that historians should agree upon a method of selecting and preserving those pictures which will be of the greatest historical value.

We shall dwell at greater length on the school cinema, which might develop very rapidly if the Governments or institutions concerned would take the proper steps; and we shall see that, on *certain points, an international agreement might* be contemplated to secure this object.

The French Government, among others, has given attention to the problems raised by the educational use of the cinema; and in 1915 it appointed an "Extra-Parliamentary Committee to inquire into the means of extending the use of the cinematograph in all branches of education." The members of this Committee were recognised authorities in science, education and the cinema industry. It concluded its work in 1920 with a report, the main passages of which are annexed. The report deals with the question in all its principal aspects, and may form a use-

APPENDIX

ful basis for discussion and for the drawing-up of the proposals. Certain of its conclusions may be briefly examined here.

In the first place, the report advocates, in principle, the use of the screen at every stage of education. It is quite true that moving pictures may be as valuable in demonstrating the most delicate scientific processes as in the most elementary teaching. A child can learn from the film to distinguish the appearance and behaviour of different kinds of animals, so that he can remember what they look like when alive. The movements of the most complicated surgical operation can be gone through time after time before a medical student, until he can repeat them unhesitatingly and without possibility of error. It must, however, be realised that the screen is not to be used in the same way in every branch of education—a point which is perhaps insufficiently emphasised in the French report. That "the cinema must not displace personal teaching, but must be an adjunct to it, and purely cinematograph classes must not be held" is a truism, but the importance of the screen as an adjunct may vary, and it may be used in widely different ways for the teaching of different subjects.

We put forward a few suggestions which might indicate the proper course of the development of the school cinema, or, at least, provide a useful basis for discussion.

(1) First of all, "the Cinema in Schools" is not the correct expression to use. We should rather say "the Screen in Schools," because in very many cases it is essential for the picture to remain static before the pupil's

eyes. In point of fact, the best school apparatus now gives an ingenious combination of fixed and moving pictures; but in the school films in use the two kinds of picture are not always judiciously proportioned. There seems to be a pre-conceived idea that moving pictures are preferable to, and better than, the fixed kind. This is by no means true, particularly in education.

(2) All objects and scenes which the pupil is intended to watch and remember in movement should be shown in movement, now that it is possible to do so. Illustrations in text books representing objects and scenes which ought to be seen in movement should be absolutely banned, as giving a distorted impression of the actual facts.

(3) Generally speaking, the tendency should be to substitute the cinema picture for the picture on paper, because the latter is always imperfect and often difficult to understand, particularly for small children. Accordingly, the series of pictures to be shown at each lesson should be connected as closely as possible with the book used for the lesson. Though the screen cannot take the place of the teacher, it can to some extent displace the book, and should, at all events, be used in combination with it.

(4) Consequently, the use of the screen at special lessons entirely devoted to a species of cinematograph show is to be discouraged, as being educationally a mistake. The screen should be used in combination with teaching, and it should be possible to use it in the place where teaching is ordinarily given, whenever it may be of

Appendix

advantage—if necessary for a very short time. It should also be possible to go back to the beginning of the picture several times over.

(5) The screen cannot be worked on these lines unless inexpensive apparatus and films are used in elementary and secondary schools, so that every class in every school can soon have its own cinematograph. The easiest apparatus to handle will be the best for schools, and at the same time there must be no risk of fire. If it is to do its proper work the apparatus must quickly become a thing in daily use, like the book or the blackboard, and the pupils must be able to handle it as easily as the teacher.

(6) The mode of using the cinema in schools must be improved, having regard to the fact that it can act upon the mind of the spectator:

    (*a*) By absolutely faithful presentation of the subject;

    (*b*) By the representation of the subject simplified;

    (*c*) By the representation of the subject in sections;

    (*d*) By the representation of the subject intensified (magnified, represented, speeded up, slowed down, built up by degrees, or superimposed).

These different methods must be employed according to a logical scheme, taking into account the subject to be dealt with and the age of the pupils.

Appendix

(7) It must be more particularly realised that the screen is not merely an improved method of demonstrating and explaining, but is also a valuable means of suggestion. It will be so used at all stages of education, whenever it is desired to accustom the pupil to certain movements, or rapidly to instil certain forms of knowledge which do not require deep thought. Generally speaking, the screen will be used as a time-saver—often a valuable one—in the teaching of all subjects which depend largely on visual memory.

(8) In order to economise effort and save expense in making films, and to derive the maximum profit from them, it is advisable to decide definitely to what extent photographs of life and photographs of representations (animated or fixed, maps, plans and diagrams) are respectively to be used.

The principles which govern methods being settled, an agreement must be reached on certain principles of organisation, and, in particular, the best form for an international arrangement must be found. On this point the "International Committee on Cinematographic Teaching in Universities," appointed by the Swiss Students' Federation, has, in connection with scientific educational films, made some valuable suggestions (see letter from the Chairman of the League of Nations Committee on Intellectual Co-operation dated July 1st, 1924). It points out:

> "That the number of really scientific films on the market is very small, and that some of them are very expensive;

APPENDIX

"That most of the valuable films were made by professors for their own research work or lectures, so that there is often only one copy in the collection of some university institute, and in case of fire such films would be lost forever;

"That there is in no case any official proof of authors' rights and priority rights in these films, or any check on the fulfillment of the conditions imposed by the author for their being shown;

"That work may be wasted on re-making a film which already exists, though its existence is not known owing to the absence of any register giving descriptions of the existing scientific films;

"That, as scientific films are generally very expensive to produce and have a limited public, the production of such films should be encouraged by all possible means."

In view of these considerations, the International Committee on Cinematographic Teaching in Universities puts forward the following proposals:

1. That an International Bureau for Cinematographic Teaching in Universities be established.

2. That an international catalogue of scientific films be compiled. It would contain the following particulars: length of film, date on which taken, name of author, name of institute or firm by which taken, together with a short description by the author and details as to possibilities of purchase, hire or exchange. This catalogue would follow the Brussels

system of decimal bibliographical classification, in the form of a card index.

3. That the catalogue be published and placed on sale.

4. That periodical reports be issued to inform subscribers of all additions and alternations to the catalogue.

5. The International Bureau will publish periodical reports on all questions connected with the manufacture and distribution of scientific films, and also on its own work.

6. The International Bureau will take all possible steps to encourage relations between university bodies making films for purely scientific purposes (not on a commercial basis) and wishing to exchange such films.

7. The International Bureau may, if requested to do so, give technical advice to institutions making university films.

8. The International Bureau will enforce the fulfillment of any conditions which the author may lay down for the presentation of his films. When the International Bureau has justified its existence and demonstrated its advantages, it might extend its field of work in the following directions:

9. It would acquire films which should, if possible, be sold or hired at cost price to the various university institutions.

10. It will take action in all questions connected with films which are required by universities, etc., but

APPENDIX

which were made as commercial propositions. It will endeavour to secure these films on the most advantageous terms.

11. The administrative expenses of the International Bureau will be met by members' subscriptions and by donations.

12. The Bureau will encourage the formation of national and local committees for cinematograph teaching in universities, and will support all endeavours to obtain national or local funds for the manufacture of scientific films.

It will in all cases give advice upon the choice of films, the purchase of apparatus, and all other questions connected with cinematographic teaching in universities.

This appears to be an excellent scheme. We would only point out that the expenses of the Bureau would be considerable, and under present circumstances it might be difficult to meet them. Meanwhile, proposal No. 2 (international catalogue of scientific films) could be carried out at once. The Committee on Intellectual Co-operation might authorise the International Committee on Cinematographic Teaching in Universities to approach all the institutions concerned on its behalf with a view to obtaining the information required; and the first catalogue might be issued as an annex to the *International Bulletin of University Information*. This would undoubtedly have excellent results.

In the case of films for elementary and secondary education, the problem is somewhat different. While scientific films might, in order to save time and money, be produced at and distributed from an international centre, this could not be done with instruments which are to be used for the education of the young and the adolescent, and which must therefore be adapted to the special conditions of each country. There are, however, certain steps of an international character which might be taken to encourage the development of the cinema in schools.

In the first place the Governments and institutions concerned might be informed of the observations and recommendations of the Committee on Intellectual Co-operation on this question, and the National Committees on Intellectual Co-operation might be invited to discuss them.

Secondly, the Committee on Intellectual Co-operation might arrange, as early as possible for an international exhibition of school films in the simplest form, and might appoint a special committee to report upon it.

An international library of school films might be contemplated as a later development.

III. SCHEMES FOR AN INTERNATIONAL ORGANISATION.

It is not, of course, desirable that the Committee should confine its interest and its efforts to problems connected with the cinema in schools. As the resolution on the cinematograph adopted by the University Sub-Committee on April 30th, 1924, puts it, it would be well "to examine the means whereby, thanks to a better international *entente,* the cinematograph might exercise a fruitful influence on the development of culture."

Appendix

Moreover, the cinema industry itself has realised what an advantage a good international organisation would be for the cinematograph. Of course, the interests of the representatives of the industry and those of the Committee on Intellectual Co-operation might not always coincide. There is, however, much that is of value in the suggestions embodied in the resolutions of the last "International Cinema Congress," although they are concerned much more with the protection and development of the art of the cinema than with its improvement, whereas the Committee's business is just as much with the means of improving cinema productions as with the means of increasing their number.

Apart from this, however, we may observe that the representatives of the cinema industry are specifically interested in the following points:

(1) The protection of the property rights of authors and publishers of films. On this point the Congress adopted the following recommendations:

> "That the groups affiliated to the International Congress should inquire into the possibility of inducing their respective countries to place a national mark on every film published, and should endeavor to find legal means of obtaining international protection for films. With this object the Congress decides to establish an international legal bureau for the film industry, which will study all problems in any way connected with the protection and exploitation of films.

APPENDIX

"That, as is done in England, authors and publishers should take concerted measures to reduce the excessive length of films, and to eliminate repetitions of scenes and unnecessary captions, which make programs unduly long and result in their being presented much too rapidly.

"In pursuance of this decision, authors and publishers should produce several versions of a film, but it must be understood that managers may not alter films in any way whatever without reference to the authors. It is agreed, however, that the different versions of a film will in all cases constitute only a single production."

It should be noted that this resolution does not deal with all the property problems connected with the cinematograph. The essence of the important question of the respective rights of authors and publishers is not considered, though it is at present causing much litigation; moreover, it involves the much more serious problem of the relations between artistic and commercial interests in this industry.

(2) The question of taxation, i.e., that of the relation between artistic and commercial interests on the one hand and the public exchequer on the other. Complaints are made in cinema circles that the industry is in many cases extremely heavily taxed on the ground that it is very lucrative.

This point was dealt with by the Paris Congress in the following resolution:

Appendix

"The International Congress of Cinematograph Managers, in session in Paris on October 23rd, 24th, 25th, and 26th, protests against all entertainment taxes as unfair, and recommends that every country should initiate a campaign for their abolition, on the following grounds:

"(*a*) The cinema has become an absolutely necessary means of recreation and amusement for the people. In times of political or economic crisis it is their one moral safeguard. In times of peace it is an unequalled medium for the diffusion of scientific knowledge and artistic taste.

"(*b*) Notwithstanding the statements of the public authorities, the tax is borne by the cinema proprietor and not by the public; it falls on the turnover and not on the profits.

"(*c*) Cinema proprietors are subject not only to all the duties and taxes imposed on the industry in their country but also to an exceptional additional tax in the form of the entertainment tax.

Subsidiary Resolution.

"(*d*) Having regard to the financial difficulties of certain countries, the Paris Congress recommends that, where Governments necessitate a temporary tax, it should be a single tax and should take account of the artistic value of the production."

It should be noted that paragraph (*a*) of this resolution assumes as a fact something which is still open to debate, namely, that the cinematograph in its present phase is an admirable instrument for intellectual and moral education. As, however, the Committee is concerned to improve cinema productions in these two aspects, it may quite properly consider how to protect the cinema against extortionate taxation.

(3) The censorship. This is the question of the relations between the cinema and the political—and, to a less extent, the moral—authorities. It is a serious and a delicate question, and the Paris Congress postponed its thorough consideration to a later meeting. It did, however, recommend that in every country there should be one central censorship, and that the presentation of the film should not be conditional upon fresh authorization from the local authorities in every town.

(4) The creation of a permanent international organization. In the minutes of the Paris Congress we find the following resolution on this point:

"The Congress decides to establish an International Cinema Federation.

"All countries will be invited to join this Federation, including Germany, which, owing to existing circumstances, has not been able to attend the Congress.

"A draft constitution has been submitted by the French Managers' Syndicate. It will be amended and approved by the International Committee, which requests the French Syndicate to add the final touches and to forward the draft to all foreign organisations.

"A provisional committee is appointed.

Appendix

"After consulting the Technical Committee, the Congress recommends that there should be appointed a permanent technical committee of the International Federation with the following objects:

"(1) to obtain the adoption of the standardised schedule of spare parts for the different kinds of cinematograph apparatus;

"(2) to organise international competitions in order to stimulate research and invention in connection with the cinematograph industry and the preservation of films;

"(3) to study all questions of interest in connection with the cinematograph industry.

"The Congress considers that it is highly important to create as soon as possible a central organisation to act as intermediary between the different nations, to collect the reports sent in regarding the progress accomplished and the results attained, and to communicate them to the persons interested.

"The Congress unanimously decides to postpone the consideration of the creation of an international organisation until the Federation at present being planned shall be in working order.

"The Congress recommends that an appeal should be made to the representatives of the Press throughout the world, inviting them to give their attention to the efforts to secure not only the abolition of an unjust system of taxation but also the recognition of the cinema as an instrument of unequalled value for the education and edification of the masses."

APPENDIX

It is clear from these declarations, and from information subsequently received, that, although a permanent international organisation is desired, it is not yet in existence. Moreover, the Paris Congress did not represent all the powers in the cinematograph world; the provisional committee of the International Federation included no member from America, Italy or Germany. It would appear that a fresh stimulus is required.

Will the Committee on Intellectual Co-operation give this stimulus? We think that it ought to do so. Indeed, considerable as may be the material interests involved, the intellectual aspect is even more important, and must be emphasised in any international discussion or undertaking connected with cinematography. This is desirable even in the material interests of the cinema world. At the opening of this report we attempted to show to what a pitch of development, to what almost unlimited influence the cinema can attain; but it can only do so if its quality improves and if it justifies the public confidence. Yet signs of a certain lassitude on the part of the public have not of late been wanting.

The Committee clearly cannot itself control the interests of cinematography—even its higher interests. But it can do a great deal to see that they are placed in good hands and that the complicated problems connected with the development of this great art are considered and settled in the best possible way. It can emphatically urge that the question must be considered, and can bring about as soon as possible a meeting of the persons most competent to study it. An international cinematograph con-

APPENDIX

gress, which should meet at the Committee's invitation and under its auspices, would bring together representatives of promoters, producers, authors, artists, critics and directors.

The program of this congress could be drawn up by a committee which might be approached by the International Cinematograph Federation, and on which the Committee on Intellectual Co-operation should be represented. This program should include all questions connected with the development and improvement of cinema production.[1]

RESOLUTIONS PROPOSED BY M. LUCHAIRE AND ADOPTED BY
THE SUB-COMMITTEE FOR UNIVERSITY RELATIONS
ON JULY 22ND, 1924.

(1) "The Committee is of opinion that the publication of an international catalogue of scientific films would serve a useful purpose. It instructs the International University Information Office to come to an understanding with the Swiss Federation of Students regarding the drawing-up of this catalogue."

(2) "The Committee would welcome with pleasure the meeting of an international congress of cinematography in the program of which the scientific artists and educa-

---

[1] In a letter to the Secretary-General of the League dated June 4th, 1924, Dr. Francis S. Onderdonk, Jr., proposed the establishment of an "International Clearing-house," for the exchange of information as to the best films available, by the "Better Film Societies" of the various countries and similar organizations in England, France, Italy, Switzerland, U.S.A., Germany, Austria and Sweden. He has approached these associations and thinks that an organization of this kind is practicable.

APPENDIX

tional interests affected by the development of cinematography would be the first question to be examined. A member of the Directing Board of the International Office might attend such a congress."

(3) "The Committee recommends the organisation of an international exhibition of scientific pictures and pictures for other educational purposes, both fixed and moving."

136. THE CINEMATOGRAPH IN ITS RELATION TO INTELLECTUAL LIFE: REPORT BY M. LUCHAIRE.

M. LUCHAIRE submitted a report, consisting of three parts, namely, the development of the cinematograph, the use of the magic lantern in education, and plans for international organisation (Annex 4).

The report ended with the three following resolutions, which had already been adopted by the Sub-Committee on Inter-University Relations on July 22nd, 1924:

"(1) The Committee is of opinion that the publication of an international catalogue of scientific films would serve a useful purpose. It instructs the International University Information Office to come to an understanding with the Swiss Federation of Students regarding the drawing-up of this catalogue."

"(2) The Committee would welcome with pleasure the meeting of an international congress of cinematography in the programme of which the scientific, artistic and educational interests affected by the development of cinematography would be the first

Appendix

question to be examined. A member of the Directing Board of the International Office might attend such a congress.

"(3) The Committee recommends the organization of an international exhibition of scientific pictures and pictures for other educational purposes, both fixed and moving."

On the proposal of the CHAIRMAN, supported by M. DESTREE, the Committee congratulated M. Luchaire on having taken the initiative in drawing up so interesting a report on such an important subject.

The three resolutions were adopted.

M. DE CASTRO emphasized the advisability of publishing an international catalogue of scientific films. He had occasion to concern himself with the relations between the cinematograph and education, above all, medical education, and possessed some three hundred films. Scientific films enabled an explanation to be made of a surgical operation and showed the course of nervous or rare diseases. They were permanent documents of the first order. Unfortunately, these films were very expensive, and it would be advisable to take steps to approach the cinematograph companies with a view to obtaining reductions in price.

The Committee decided to bear this suggestion in mind, which might be considered later.

APPENDIX 2

Dr. Humbert's Report to Child Welfare Committee, Geneva, May, 1926.[1]

14. EFFECT OF THE CINEMATOGRAPH ON THE MENTAL AND MORAL WELL-BEING OF CHILDREN.

On the invitation of the CHAIRMAN, Dr. Longeuil, delegate of the International Institute for Intellectual Co-operation, took his seat at the Committee table.

The CHAIRMAN welcomed Dr. Longeuil and opened the discussion on the report before the Committee (Annex 5) and on Dr. Humbert's draft resolution, which read as follows:

"The Committee, having studied the question of the influence of the cinematograph on the mental, physical and moral condition of children, recognizes, on the one hand, the attraction of films and the important part which they may play *in specific circumstances* in the healthy recreation, instruction and education of young people, but is convinced, on the other hand, that the abuse of cinema shows has an undoubtedly harmful effect on the minds, nervous systems and physical health of young people.

---

[1] League of Nations, C. 264 M. 103, 1926 V, C. P. E., 2nd Session P. V., Geneva, May 1926. Advisory Commission for the Protection and Welfare of Children and Young People. Child Welfare Committee Minutes of the Second Session held at Geneva from Thursday, March 25th to Thursday, April 1st, 1926.

"In order to remedy these drawbacks of cinema shows:

"1. The Committee pronounces in favor of the exercise of general supervision over films shown to young people up to as advanced an age as possible, according to the laws and customs of each country, it being mentioned that certain legislations have found it desirable to exercise supervision up to the age of eighteen years. The Committee considers that a minimum age for admission to cinema halls (*e.g.*, six years) should be fixed by all legislations.

"2. The Committee recommends supervision in the form of a preventive censorship exercised by a board including educational experts and making a distinction between two categories of films: those intended for adults and those suitable for young people.

"3. The Committee expresses the opinion that any film censorship should draw up special rules different from those of any kind of censorship, taking into full account the special effect of the film, particularly on young people, and recommends the creation of a board of supervision of this kind in countries not yet possessing one, such board to act in conformity with the legislation of the country and its decisions to be enforced by judicial or administrative measures.

"The Committee proposes that the possibility of concluding a convention between the boards already in existence or which may be created in future should be studied, such convention to provide that these boards should communicate to each other all the de-

APPENDIX

cisions taken and penalties imposed by them in their respective countries. This convention might subsequently be extended in the form of more detailed agreements with regard to the censorship, seizure or destruction of immoral films.

"4. Censorship should also apply to photographs, figures, posters and texts used as advertisements outside cinema halls.

"5. The administrative competence of the board of censors should be such as to allow of the institution of an *administrative* committee for the purpose of supervising the execution of the proposed measures of censorship, the admission to halls and the material conditions of displays.

"6. The restrictions imposed with regard to the admittance of minors to cinema shows should also be enforced when the minor is accompanied by parents or any other adults.

"Furthermore, minors (the term being understood according to the definition given in the respective national legislations) should only be admitted to shows specially described as exclusively reserved for young people.

"7. The Committee, knowing the interest displayed by the International Institute for Intellectual Co-operation in the question of the cinematograph, wishes to inform this Bureau of the importance which it attaches to this question from the point of view of the moral and physical protection of children and requests

Appendix

it to devote special attention to securing the co-operation of all parties concerned in either the production or display of good films capable of eliminating gradually all cinematographic productions harmful to children."

Dr. Humbert explained that his draft resolution was in reality only a summary of the suggestions or conclusions derived from certain documents he had studied. It would be for the Committee, after a brief discussion, to decide whether this draft should not be referred to a Sub-Committee inasmuch as it mentioned the possibility of a convention. He wished to thank the Secretariat for the very numerous and interesting documents it had collected, and particularly the series of legislative texts, which had been of great use to him in his researches. He regretted that, for reasons beyond his control, his own report had not been handed to the Secretariat in time for distribution to the members of the Committee, and he asked for permission to summarize this report (Annex 5 *a*).

Last year, the Italian delegation had submitted an illuminating report on the question. He himself had dealt with it less from the point of view of prohibition than from the more positive point of view of propaganda in favor of films suitable for being shown to popular audiences and even school children. With the help of the Junior Red Cross, he had been able to draw up a report, with the collaboration of teaching circles, and, having learnt the previous year that the Secretariat was undertaking an enquiry on the question, he had thought it would be interesting to

APPENDIX

sum up the views of pedagogic and school circles on the cinema. His report should not, therefore, be regarded as an expression of his personal opinion. He had been struck by the concordance of views expressed by countries as far apart and different as Belgium and Australia, for example, which led to the same practically unanimous conclusions and were embodied in the present draft resolution.

The report dealt with the harmful effects and the abuse of the cinema theatre not only on the minds of young people but also on their nervous system and physical health. In this connection, the documents supplied by the Secretariat only contained one legislative text, emanating from Japan, which took into account the physical effect on children. In Appendix 1 to Annex 5 the following passage occurred: " . . . the result is equally harmful from the educational and the hygienic points of view."

It was thought desirable not to begin the draft resolution with a wholesale condemnation of the cinema. On the contrary, the utility of the film *in specific circumstances* was recognised. This remark was in concordance with certain views mentioned in his report, particularly those of Mme. Janvier in connection with Belgium. Moreover, it appeared from investigations made in Germany that the film attracted children more perhaps by its process than by its contents; children thought by associations of ideas that were principally visual. There was, however, no denying the harmful effect of certain cinema melodramas.

Was it necessary to undertake an enquiry with regard to the influence of the cinema on children? Statistics

Appendix

showed that, out of 1,056 boys and girls questioned, 98 per cent of the boys and 89 per cent of the girls frequented the cinema and nearly half of them went every week. A Polish enquiry on the kinds of films specially appreciated by children showed that boys preferred scenes of violence and girls sentimental themes.

Nearly all those consulted pronounced in favour of educational, historical, etc., films and against the cinema theatre. A German neurologist, having analysed 250 cinema films, had found 97 murders, 51 cases of adultery, 19 seductions, 22 abductions and 43 suicides. Among the principal protagonists were 176 thieves, 25 prostitutes, 35 drunkards, etc. Even if the end of the film was a happy one, the effect on children of this representation of persons in conflict with society and good morals remained the same. The Committee would no doubt agree that children ought not to be allowed to visit this kind of thing once a week.

The report dealt successively with the harmful effects of the abuse of the cinema theatre on: (1) the morals of the child; (2) his nervous system; and (3) his physical health; and contained numerous facts on each of these three categories which constituted valuable material for study.

Dr. Humbert then went on to comment on his draft resolution. In connection with the possibility of a convention between boards of censors, he said that it was not for the Committee to prepare such a convention, but if agreements of this kind were to be drawn up, the Committee ought to be called upon to give its opinion in connection with the protection of children. The proposals submitted

APPENDIX

did not aim at attacking cinema production—far from it; but the considerable sums spent on immoral films would be put to better use in producing beautiful films on travels, historical events, the working of certain industries, etc.

Collaboration with the International Institute for Intellectual Co-operation and the voluntary associations, as proposed in the draft resolution, would make it possible to influence public opinion in order that good films might be well attended and melodrama neglected.

Dr. LONGEUIL said that, in the course of a long stay at Hollywood, he had had occasion to converse with film producers and had been told that melodramas were remunerative but that producers who wished to produce educational films were ruined. Would it not be possible to arrange by means of mutual co-operation for the production of films of value to children? If the general public could be persuaded to take an interest in good films, it was probable that the work of reform undertaken would secure the support of the majority of producers.

The speaker approved Dr. Humbert's resolution. Measures must be taken for the selection of films to be shown to children, and an age-limit for children must be fixed. Above this age there were no other limits but the control exercised by public opinion itself and by the administrative censorship. Care must also be taken to prevent children witnessing films unsuitable for their age, in contravention of the intention of the law, on the ground that they were accompanied by their parents. It was difficult to see what difference this made in the effect produced on the child. Super-

APPENDIX

vision should also be exercised over advertisements of cinema theatres. There could be no doubt that in large towns where cinema halls were numerous the abundance of flamboyant posters in certain streets had an effect on the child's mind. Furthermore, it should not be sufficient to say that certain films were forbidden or allowed for children; the public should be warned by means of more detailed notices. Lastly, it would perhaps be better to replace the word "censorship" by the word "supervision," which was less controversial.

The International Institute for Intellectual Cooperation had a special section which dealt with the cinematograph and drew up a repertory of films suitable for children. Although one might be skeptical as to the so-called educational value of the cinema at school, there could be no doubt that educational films (geography, scientific or industrial processes) were of real value.

The International Institute for Intellectual Co-operation would endeavour to get into touch with film producers and help certain of them to put their products on the market. From the point of view of children, the problem had two aspects: the films children should see and those they should not see. It was possible to take action in these two directions, and the Institute for Intellectual Co-operation would be glad to avail itself of any useful suggestions which the League of Nations might make.

M. AMADOR (Spain) congratulated Dr. Humbert on his statement. The facts observed were sufficiently numerous to justify urgent measures being taken and to cause the

APPENDIX

Committee to deal with the problem. Reports drawn up by magistrates of children's courts in Spain showed that films were directly or indirectly responsible for many crimes committed by children. These might be regarded, however, as only personal opinions, and it would be desirable for all the members of the Committee who were acquainted with facts similar to those mentioned by Dr. Humbert to make them known so that a kind of statistical compilation might be made.

Several of the questions dealt with in the draft resolution had already been considered by a large number of States. A draft decree of the Children's Protection Board of Madrid laid down the principle of censorship, with regard to which two ministerial ordinances had been promulgated in 1912 and 1913. This draft, without going as far as Dr. Humbert's recommendations, contained stipulations regarding lanterns used for projecting films, the focussing of films, changes of light, etc.

The problem was so vast that, after a brief discussion, it could be referred to a Sub-Committee, which might submit a report at a subsequent session. It was important that the League of Nations should deal with it in order to encourage States to strengthen their regulations in this connection and to induce the powerful cinematographic enterprises to follow the recommendations made.

Alluding to one of Dr. Longeuil's remarks, M. Amador thought it was better to keep the word "censorship" and avoid the word "supervision," which might be liable to give rise to difficulties if conventions were drawn up.

Appendix

Dr. ESTRID HEIN (Denmark) said that, before leaving her country, she had had a conversation with the head of the Danish Board of Censorship with regard to the experience acquired during the thirteen years that the system of censorship had been in operation. The situation appeared to be satisfactory. There were three censors: one school teacher, one former theatre manager and one representative of the Ministry for Justice. The chief censor thought it important that his colleagues should not be limited in their functions as censors but should remain in daily contact with practical life. They should see to it that films should be fit to be witnessed by anyone, even by children under sixteen. This would be in the interests of the film agents themselves, for a film lost two-thirds of its value if it could not be seen by children. According to Danish legislation, it was only possible completely to prohibit a film or to prohibit it for children but not to make cuts in it. The unpractical aspect of this state of affairs had been realized, and the film agents themselves, before hiring a film, consulted the censors so as not to run a needless risk. The censor might then suggest to them certain cuts and the film could be officially passed.

About 5 per cent of the films were prohibited for children, and the fact that the proportion was so small was due partly to the cuts mentioned and partly to the fact that Denmark, being a small country, only used a small proportion of the films produced and could afford to disregard bad ones.

The Danish delegate could not express any opinion on

APPENDIX

Dr. Humbert's draft resolution, as she had not had time to study it.

She thought, however, that a great many of the opinions set forth in his interesting report were slightly exaggerated. Personally, as an oculist, she considered that the development of certain eye troubles in children was due more to too much school work and to defective hygienic conditions than to the cinema. If the reasonable elements among young people were consulted, they would probably be against excessive intervention in this domain. As the head of the Danish Board of Censorship had said, the present generation would never appreciate the cinema as much as the coming generation.

There was one question which, although not directly related to the present problem, was of great importance, and that was the censorship of broadcasting. This was undoubtedly an international question, as, in this domain, there were no frontiers. Questioned on this subject, a Danish censor had said that items not suitable for the ears of children were placed on the programme after eight o'clock at night. This measure seemed hardly satisfactory unless combined with a system of selection of some severity.

As the report on the cinematograph distributed to the Committee seemed to indicate that the countries which had met with the least difficulties were those in which the censorship had been established at the very beginning of the cinematograph industry, the Danish delegate had thought it well to draw her colleagues' attention to the question of wireless telephony in its relation to children.

APPENDIX

M. BOURGOIS (France) asked if there was a cinematograph industry in Denmark. This was a factor which greatly complicated the question.

Dr. Estrid HEIN (Denmark) replied that the industry was very undeveloped in her country.

M. POSNER (Poland) considered that Dr. Humbert's report, interesting and full of information though it was, contained several exaggerations. As Poland did not figure among the countries mentioned in the report, he thought it well to recall the fact that his country had established a film censorship at the Press Bureau of the Ministry for the Interior. It consisted of three censors, who were men of letters. A committee of experts composed of school teachers was consulted in the case of all films which the censor judged pernicious to children. In 1924, out of 948 films examined by the censors, 287, or hardly a quarter, were authorised for young people. According to the law of 1919, admittance to cinema halls and theatres was prohibited for young people under 17 years of age. In spite of this rule, official reports had to admit that children under 17 years frequented cinema halls by means of ruses, such as wearing students' caps. In reality, the exercise of the censorship was very difficult. Literary works of the most unexceptionable character could be converted into more or less reprehensible films. It was also necessary to consider the influence of the capital interests involved. Furthermore, the accusations levelled against the cinema were sometimes exaggerated. Crime among children existed before the cinema, and one might as well accuse the adven-

APPENDIX

ture stories which children had always read. It was true that the cinema undoubtedly could exercise a harmful influence on young imaginations. The drawback of documentary or educational films was that they were liable to be dull.

The first factor which had to be taken into account was that of the enormous capital invested in cinematograph enterprises. The second was the public itself, for the education of which nothing had been done for twenty years. A film was bad not because it showed acts of brigandage but because it was ugly. Beauty could not be dangerous. If an international movement were created for the education of the public in this direction, a certain measure of success might be achieved, but too much must not be expected. To sum up, Dr. Humbert's report and his conclusions, apart from exaggerations, constituted a good beginning for the movement which must be set on foot to safeguard and promote the physical and moral health of the coming generation.

M. SUGIMURA (Japan) considered that the Committee should approve Dr. Humbert's report. This was a sphere in which the Committee should take a strong line. It was important, however, not to attach too much importance to the form of the various legislations but to consider the circumstances in which they were to be applied. In Japan, in which few films were produced that were not historical or educational, censorship was exercised chiefly on imported films, as these sometimes tended to destroy the good elements in Japan's traditional customs. The Japanese

Appendix

censorship treated adults on the same plane as minors. Its tendency was to be too severe, so that at the moment the Government was inclined to slacken the present regime. What was important was not so much the law as its application. Dr. Humbert's report constituted a good beginning in the work of international co-operation and showed that here was a task with which the present Committee must deal.

On the proposal of Marquis DE CALBOLI (Italy), the *continuation of the discussion was postponed to the next meeting.*

The CHAIRMAN suggested that it might be worth recommending propaganda through the film in favor of the League of Nations, particularly in the humanitarian sphere.

M. POSNER (Poland) ventured to recall the fact that the question of propaganda was entered on the agenda of the next session of the Traffic in Women Committee.

SIXTH MEETING
held on Monday, March 29th, 1926, at 9 a. m.

Chairman: Don Pedro SANGRO Y ROS DE OLANO

Present: All the members of the Committee and the Assessors, with the exception of Mme. Luisi, Miss Abbott, Mr. Bascom Johnson and M. Valdes Valdes.

15. EFFECT OF THE CINEMATOGAPH ON THE MENTAL AND MORAL WELL-BEING OF CHILDREN

(continuation of the discussion).

M. ROLLET said that the magistrates who sat on the children's courts in Paris had always realized the pernicious influence of certain films on a large number of crimes. Thus, before the introduction of the censorship in 1919, the police-court of the Seine had condemned a band of young thieves who called themselves "La Main qui etreint," a name taken from a film which was being shown at that moment. It was, of course, true that a censorship, even if strictly exercised, did not prevent a certain number of crimes being represented on the screen. He himself had assisted some time ago in prohibiting a film which showed the holding-up of a train. In spite of the exotic character of the costumes and the acrobatic feats of horsemanship, he thought it preferable not to show children that it was possible to hold up a train by means of certain signals. This prohibition had not prevented a mysterious affair of the holding-up and robbery of a train which had occurred two months ago. It was for the parents and for the schools to supervise children, and he thought it would be useful to provide that children below a certain age should not be admitted to the cinema unless accompanied by their parents or someone representing the scholastic authority or a guardian.

Though he did not admit that the effect of the cinema on the physical health or the eyesight of children was as serious as some of his colleagues believed, he nevertheless agreed with Dr. Humbert in thinking that under a fairly low age—six or seven years, for example—entry to the cinema should be refused to children, even if they were accompanied. Finally, he agreed with Dr. Hein and M.

Appendix

Sugimura in thinking that the censorship should be general, as things that were bad for children less than 18 years old were also bad for young people of from 20 to 25 years of age.

Marquis DE' CALBOLI (Italy) proposed to close the discussion by putting to the vote the draft resolution of Dr. Humbert. The effects of the cinema on the nervous system of the child had been somewhat exaggerated and, under the advice of a specialist, he had himself been led to insist on this point in his report more than was perhaps warranted by the facts. Nevertheless, it would be well to draw attention in the resolution to the effect of the cinema on the health and, according to certain medical authorities, on the nervous system and eyesight of children. There should also be added a reference to the hours at which films were shown and a provision for the admission of a mother of a family into the supervisory organ to be instituted in each country. It would also be well to contemplate international co-operation and to insist that preventive measures should be taken. Finally, he proposed to maintain the restrictions on the admission of minors even if accompanied.

M. BOURGOIS (France) pointed out that the part to be played by the International Central Office would be to collect the various laws governing the film industry and the information as to censored films. The importance of good films must not be overlooked, nor the desirability of raising the quality of such spectacles. Distinguished persons had taken steps in this direction in France, and the Societe de l'Etoile at Lyons had obtained excellent results.

APPENDIX

It would be well if international associations of this kind might come to an understanding in regard to the purchase of films; they might constitute purchasing trusts which would make their requirements felt in the market.

M. CIUNTU (Roumania) thought that it was advisable to insist on the two aspects of the problem—the danger of the film, on the one hand, and its educative value, on the other.

He was prepared to admit all the difficulties of the various aspects of the question, but exaggeration must be avoided. It must be admitted that there were numerous factors to explain the wearing of spectacles by children.

In Roumania, where four-fifths of the population were farmers, the danger was inconsiderable, all the more so as there was a censorship and as the admission to the cinema of children and scholars was prohibited. The problem which arose was the extension of the cinema into the country districts. A plan of education by means of the film was in course of preparation at the Ministry for Public Instruction. Owing to the special importance of visual memory, a good film was a remarkable method of education. It enabled teachers to impress upon the mind geographical, historical and artistic truths, to enrich the knowledge of their pupils, and to educate the taste and the imagination. Children were enabled to become better acquainted with the countries of the world, and sentiments of a wider brotherhood were strengthened. It was well to be severe, but it was better to act in a positive direction, and he would wish this preoccupation to take precedence in the resolution of Dr. Humbert.

Miss WHITTON said that her country had already accomplished the task which the Committee proposed to undertake in the international field. Censorship had been established in eight provinces, and the co-operation of the various bureaus had been organized. At present 90 per cent of the films were subject to censorship, and Canada had adopted a uniform standard for admitting or rejecting films. Women played an important part in the body which controlled not only films but the material conditions under which they were shown. She would observe, in passing, that the proceeds of this work brought to the Treasury sums which were not negligible.

On the strength of this experience, she would warn the Committee of certain dangers. For example, the Committee should refrain from recommending that the various States should communicate to one another their standard of censorship. The majority of the countries, for example, would be amazed by the standard in force in certain provinces of Canada, where films were rejected in which a woman was represented as smoking. In practice, it would be seen that the establishment of the censorship was not everything in itself, and that what finally mattered was public opinion. It was not the repression of the evil which would yield happy results, but the impulse given to the forces of enlightenment. A newspaper illustrated this idea by showing on the one side of a street a cinema giving an educational film the entrance to which was absolutely deserted, whereas, on the other side of the street, two policemen could scarcely control the crowd at the entrance to a cinema where there was a bill of "The Admirable Crichton" under the title of "Male and Female," with a note to the effect that it had been condemned by the censorship.

Canada had endeavored to develop public welfare in a positive direction. Thus, a white list had been drawn up containing more than fifty comic films and fifty educational films recommended as good for all spectators. The film industry co-operated in this work by circulating this list to all cinemas, so that the parents and teachers assuming responsibility—which, after all, lay in the first instance with them—had only to consult this list. The Government itself had produced more than 150 films on history, geography and industry and was producing a film on the welfare of children. Reference should be made, in passing, to the considerable value, from the economic point of view, of this kind of representation. Thus, as the result of a film on the clothing industry where the machines used for sewing were exhibited, the local agency had been obliged on the following day to order a large consignment of sewing machines from the factory in order to meet the orders which it immediately received.

If the intention of the resolution of Dr. Humbert were to emphasize all these favorable possibilities, she was prepared to accept it. Nevertheless, parents must not be relieved of their responsibility, but, on the contrary, the exercise of this responsibility must be imposed on them. For this reason, she would ask that an absolute minimum age should not be determined for the admission of children unaccompanied. In the workers' quarters it was usual to see the father of the family with his wife at the cinema with their children on their knees. This was the only distraction which was within their reach, and it was preferable that they should bring their children there than that the father should go to a public-house or the children be shut up without supervision in an apartment. In conclusion, she accepted the proposal of Dr. Humbert subject to the amendment to which she had referred, and she would ask the Committee to remember that censorship, like patriotism, was not sufficient in itself.

M. MARTIN (France) spoke as follows:

Like every other member of the Committee, I have applauded the remarkable report which Dr. Humbert has submitted on the question of the effect of the cinema on the mental and moral well-being of children, and I should have nothing to add to the report and to the very wise observations of several of our colleagues on this question if I did not think it well to examine the same subject from the double aspect of the health and the security of children in the cinemas and of the protection of children employed in enterprises for the production of films or for establishing certain scenarios, mindful of the fact that, if the moral health of children is of importance, their physical health and security are equally so.

I would remind you briefly of the disadvantages already enumerated, namely, excessive fatigue of the eyes and the irritation of the nervous system of the children present at

APPENDIX

cinema representations and, I would add, the danger to their general health from staying several hours in a close atmosphere, subject to a high temperature, where tuberculosis infection is particularly to be feared. I note that this consideration has not been lost sight of in the document submitted on the question by the Government of Japan, where it is indicated, with reference to the colony of Kwangtung, paragraphs 2, 3, 4 and 5, that the following steps have been taken in dealing with cinema-halls:

2. If the film takes more than an hour to show, there must be an interval of ten minutes for recreation, and during this interval all windows will be opened and the rooms aired.

3. To prevent overcrowding, the number present should be fixed beforehand, according to the dimensions of the room.

4. As far as possible, rooms should be ventilated, even when films are being shown.

5. Should it be impossible to open all the windows on account of the cold, every person present must leave the room during the interval for recreation. The room will then be aired by opening all the windows and, ten minutes later, the spectators will return.

The aspect of security must be considered. I might quote several examples of accidents which have happened in cinemas, but I will confine myself to mentioning only one characteristic incident, which happened about five years ago in France at Valence, capital of the Department of the Drome, which was a veritable catastrophe.

Appendix

The bishop of the town had organized a holiday cinema matinee for children. During the representation the film caught fire. The fire was rapidly extinguished, but the children were seized with panic and rushed towards the exit. Those who were in the balconies hastily descended the staircase and they were not able to leave the hall sufficiently quickly. The crowd was such that the children were thrown down, trodden underfoot and suffocated. More than a hundred children were killed in this accident. There should always be numerous emergency exits leading to the open air which would make possible a quick evacuation of the cinema-halls by the spectators.

The majority of films used are made of celluloid, a substance which is particularly inflammable. It would seem to be necessary to prohibit, within a period which should be fixed but which should be reduced to the minimum strictly necessary, the use of such films. Important companies have for a long time been using non-inflammable films made of acetate of cellulose, which have been thoroughly tested. Although the price of these films is at present somewhat higher than the films made of celluloid, there should be no hesitation in taking steps which are calculated to safeguard the lives of the spectators and the operators.

It would also seem to be necessary to protect children employed in companies in which films are taken for representation or in which specific scenarios are established.

The French Government has already been considering this question, and the Chamber of Deputies adopted on

Appendix

December 30th, 1925, a Bill modifying in particular Articles 58, 59 and 60 of Section III of Chapter V of the first part of Book II of the Labor Code. According to this bill:

> *Article* 58: Children of either sex less than 15 years of age shall not be employed as actors, supernumeraries, etc., in theatres, cafes, and other entertainment establishments, *nor in companies for the production of films.*
>
> *Article* 59: The Minister for Public Education and Fine Arts of Paris and the Prefects in the Departments may, as an exceptional measure, authorize the employment of one or several children in theatres and by companies for the production of films or the establishment of specific scenarios.

The Ministry for Labor and the Ministry for Public Education have submitted this Bill for the approval of the Senate.

The employment of children in theatres and music-halls is already subject to regulation in France, but only for public representations and for children from 13 years old. In principle, authorizations are not given for children less than nine years old, nor are they given if the pieces in which they are to appear are of a character likely to injure their morals or their health.

These wise measures of protection will be extended to children below fifteen years employed in companies for the production of films. In regard to these children, anxiety is felt not only owing to the moral risks but also to the injury which may result to the nervous system in general,

Appendix

and particularly to the eyesight, from the intensive system of lighting necessary to ensure the clearness of the negatives.

The supervision of the public authorities in France is extended also to children and women occupied or employed in industrial and commercial establishments, since under Article 12 of the Decree of March 21st, 1914, children less than eighteen years of age and women may not be employed either in the production, manipulation or sale of writings, printed matter, bills, drawings, engravings, paintings, emblems, images, or other objects the sale, offering, exhibition, posting, or distribution of which is repressed by the penal laws as contrary to public morality. It is also prohibited to employ children less than sixteen years of age and women less than twenty-one years of age in any kind of work in places where writings, printed matter, posters, engravings, pictures, emblems, images or other objects are manufactured, prepared or sold, even though the objects do not come under the penal laws but are of a character calculated to offend the moral sense.

In conclusion, I would point out that, if the Committee, as a result of this important and interesting discussion, thinks it necessary to adopt resolutions, these resolutions should be brief but very explicit and should embody the following principles:

> An obligatory censorship for films and songs sometimes given in the cinemas.
>
> The absolute prohibition of immoral films, it being

laid down that films should, above all, be educational, instructive, artistic and wholesomely entertaining.

Measures necessary for health and security should also be prescribed in regard to the airing, cubic capacity, exits and emergency exits of cinema-halls.

It is also necessary to prohibit within a maximum period of five years the use of inflammable films.

If these necessary measures are adopted, they will be beneficial for children and for adults. They will encourage film companies to produce and to foster films which are really educational and instructive. Far from damaging their important business, such steps cannot fail to encourage it.

Here, however, as in other fields, it is not sufficient to legislate. It is also necessary to supervise the carrying-out of the steps legally imposed.

The SECRETARY proposed that Miss Whitton, M. Ciuntu and M. Martin should submit their suggestions to the Sub-Committee in order that a draft resolution might be drawn up which the Committee would examine at a later meeting.

This proposal was adopted.

EFFECTS OF THE CINEMATOGRAPH ON THE MENTAL AND MORAL WELL-BEING OF CHILDREN

Report by the Secretariat submitted to the Committee on March 27th, 1926.

1. GENERAL SITUATION

The Advisory Commission for the Protection and Welfare of Children and Young People adopted the following

Appendix

recommendation at its Fourth Session, which was held at Geneva from May 20th to 27th, 1925:

> *"The Effect of the Cinematograph on the Mental and Moral Well-being of Children.*—The Committee appreciates the importance of this question, as to which it has received evidence from the Italian delegate. It proposes to place this subject on its agenda for discussion next session, and it would be glad if the Secretariat would collect such information as is available, including the steps taken in different countries to exercise supervision over the character of the pictures shown to children."

The Council of the League of Nations approved the recommendation of the Advisory Commission at its meeting on June 9th, 1925, and the Secretary-General accordingly requested all the Governments to inform him whether measures had been adopted in the different countries with a view to exercising supervision over films shown to children, and, if they replied in the affirmative, to forward copies of the laws, decrees and regulations at present in force in each of the countries concerned.

The following Governments have up to date replied to the Secretary-General's enquiry:

AUSTRIA	CZECHOSLOVAKIA
BELGIUM	DANZIG
BRITISH COLONIES:	DENMARK
FEDERATED MALAY STATES	EGYPT
CANADA	ESTHONIA
CUBA	FRANCE

APPENDIX

FRENCH PROTECTORATES:
  MOROCCO
  TUNIS
GERMANY
GREAT BRITAIN
HUNGARY
INDIA
ITALY
JAPAN
JAPANESE COLONIES:
  FORMOSA
  KWANGTUNG
  SAKHALIN
LATVIA
MONACO
NETHERLANDS
NEW ZEALAND
NORWAY
ROUMANIA
SALVADOR
SPAIN
SWEDEN
SWITZERLAND
UNION OF SOUTH AFRICA
UNITED STATES OF AMERICA
URUGUAY
VENEZUELA

2. ADMISSION OF MINORS TO CINEMATOGRAPH PERFORMANCES

A. COUNTRIES IN WHICH ADMISSION IS CONTROLLED BY REGULATIONS.

(a) *Partial Prohibition.*

AUSTRIA.—Decree of the Ministry of the Interior dated September 18th, 1912:

Article 23.—"Children and persons under sixteen may only be admitted to a performance if the programme has been passed for exhibition to children and minors in accordance with paragraph 2, art. 18[1], and provided that it ends before 8 P. M."

---

[1] The authorization must mention whether the film in question may be shown to children or to minors (paragraph 2, art. 18).

APPENDIX

BELGIUM.—Law of September 1st, 1920, prohibiting minors who have not turned sixteen attending cinema exhibitions:

Article 1.—"Minors of either sex who have not reached the age of sixteen shall not be allowed to be present at any public cinema performance."

Article 2.—"The prohibition contained in the preceding article shall not apply to cinema-halls where only those films are exhibited which shall have been licensed by a Commission the organization and duties of which are to be laid down by a Royal Decree."

CANADA.—Rules regulating theatres and cinematograph establishments are matters within the jurisdiction of each province.

Alberta.—The only restriction in force is that no person under fifteen years of age is allowed to attend moving-picture shows during school hours unless accompanied by parents or guardians.

British Columbia.—No person in charge of a moving-picture theatre, and, in the case of a company or society, no manager or other person in charge of the establishment, shall receive in anyway or permit to attend at any show therein any child less than fourteen years old unless such child is accompanied by an adult.

This section shall not, unless the Lieutenant-Governor in Council by regulation otherwise provides, apply to children received or permitted to attend such show between the hours of 3.30 o'clock and 6 o'clock in the afternoon on days upon which the public schools are open in the place

APPENDIX

where such moving-picture theatre is situated, or before 6 o'clock in the afternoon of any other day.

In case of any proceedings charging an offence against any of the provisions of this section, in the absence of other evidence to prove the age of a child, or by way of corroboration of other evidence, the justice of the peace, magistrate or judge before whom the charge is heard may infer the age from the appearance of the child. (Moving-Pictures Act, 1914, sec. 11, as amended 1915.)

Nova Scotia.—Children under the age of ten years unaccompanied by an adult shall not be permitted to attend any theatre or place of amusement at which an admission fee is charged. Children, apparently under the age of sixteen years unaccompanied by an adult, shall not be permitted to attend by night any theatre or place of amusement at which an admission fee is charged.

Children apparently under the age of sixteen years shall not be permitted to attend during their school hours any theatres or places of amusement. (The Theatres, Cinematographs and Amusements Act, and Regulations thereunder, Consolidated 1922.)

Ontario.—A child under the age of fifteen years unaccompanied by an adult shall not be permitted to attend any exhibition by cinematograph, moving-picture machine, or other similar apparatus for admission to which a fee is charged, except on Saturday of each week and on public and legal holidays, between the hours of 9 a. m. and 6 p. m., during which hours a matron to be remunerated by the exhibitor shall be engaged in each theatre, whose duty it shall

APPENDIX

be to supervise the conduct of such children and of adults toward them while in such theatre. (The Theatres and Cinematographs Act, sec. 10.)

Quebec.—No person or persons in charge of a hall for moving pictures where shows are given by means of cinematograph, and, in the case of a company or society, no manager or other person in charge of the establishment shall receive, in any way, at such shows, any child less than sixteen years old, unless such child is accompanied by his or her father, mother, tutor or teacher or by a guardian specially authorized by the father or mother.

Notwithstanding the above provision, children less than sixteen years old may attend exhibitions of moving pictures without being so accompanied when the advertisement of the exhibition announces a program only of pictures authorized for children by the Board of Censors of moving pictures according to the provisions of Article 3713 (*a*), and of no other pictures. (1 Geo. V., 2nd Session, ch. 34, sec. 1, amended by 9 Geo. V., ch. 48, sec. 1.)

Saskatchewan.—Children under the age of fourteen years shall not, if unaccompanied by a parent or responsible person, be permitted to attend any exhibition by cinematograph, moving-picture machine or similar apparatus after the hour of 8 o'clock in the evening. (R. S. S. 1920, ch. 181, sec. 18, Theatres and Cinematograph Act.)

CZECHOSLOVAKIA.—Extracts from a communication from the Ministry of Foreign Affairs:

"Under the regulation promulgated by a Decree of the Ministry of the Interior dated October 18th, 1912

APPENDIX

(No. 191 of the Collection of Decrees), and under the similar regulations promulgated in Slovakia and Sub-Carpathian Russia after the war, application for permission to give public cinematograph performances open to children and persons under sixteen years of age may be refused by the Advisory Committee set up in the Ministry of the Interior to decide how far the films may have a prejudical effect on young people from a moral and intellectual point of view."

DANZIG.—Law on the Cinematograph, December 1st, 1925:

Article 3, Paragraph 1.—"Films which may be exhibited to children under sixteen shall be subject to special authorization. . . ."

Paragraph 2.—"At the request of the Child Welfare Office of the commune or communal group, or an application from the school authorities, the commune or communal group, after consulting the representatives of the Child Welfare Organizations responsible for health and morals, may take other measures with regard to the admission of young people to cinema performances, and those responsible for these performances shall be required to conform thereto, subject to the right of appeal to the competent authority."

Paragraph 4.—"Children under twelve may not be admitted to performances after 7 p. m."

DENMARK.—Extract from a report of September 18th, 1922, addressed to the Ministry of Justice by the Censors of Films:

"The Decree promulgated on July 5th, 1913, by the Minister of Justice empowers the censors to forbid the performance of certain films before children under the age of sixteen, but the method in which these powers are to be exercised is left to the discretion of the censors themselves."

GERMANY.—Law on Cinema Performances, dated May 12th, 1920:

Article 3.—"Films to the performance of which young persons under eighteen years of age are admitted require special permission . . .

". . . On the proposal of the children's department of the commune or district or, in the absence of a children's department, on that of the school authorities, the commune or a communal association, after hearing the representatives of children's organizations, and without prejudice to any more stringent measures which may be laid down by the provincial laws, may take further measures in the interests of health and morality with regard to the admission of children, and the proprietors of cinemas shall be obliged to comply with these measures. The latter may, however, appeal against these measures to the competent authorities."

HUNGARY.—Extracts from the regulations of the Royal Ministry of the Interior (page 5, paragraph 13):

"Young persons under eighteen years of age shall not be permitted to attend cinematographic displays the subject-matter or method of presentation of which or of any parts of which are likely prejudically to affect the character of adolescents or their mental or moral development or unduly to excite their imagination."

Page 7, chapter 3 (paragraph 20):

"Young persons who have not completed their eighteenth year shall only be permitted to attend cinematographic displays the films in respect of which have been certified by the National Film Censorship Commission to be suitable for exhibition to the young. The age of the young persons shall be determined approximately."

INDIA.—Extract from a copy of a leter from the Secretary to the Government of India, Legislative Department:

"The law regulating cinematograph exhibitions in British India which is contained in the 'Cinematograph Act, 1918,' as amended by subsequent legislation, does not provide specifically for the exercise of supervision over the character of the pictures shown to children, but it requires films to be certified before exhibition by an authority constituted by the local government of the province concerned."

Bombay.—Films which are considered unsuitable for education to juveniles are certified on the condition that their exhibition is restricted to adults.

Burma.—Steps are taken to exclude minors from admission to the exhibition of unsuitable films.

ITALY.—Law dated December 10th, 1925, No. 2277, on Maternity and Child Welfare:

Article 22.—"The Cinematograph Censorship Commission shall decide what cinematograph performances are suitable for children and young persons of either sex . . .".

Royal Decree No. 718 of April 15th, 1926, sanctioning the regulations in execution of Law No. 2277 of December 10th, 1925, for the Protection and Assistance of Mothers and Children.

Article 162.—The regulation governing admission, as enacted in Article 22, applies to children and young persons who have not attained the age of fifteen years.

For the purposes of Article 22, children and young persons shall be presumed to be under fifteen if they are under 1 m. 50 in height, unless proof to the contrary is furnished.

JAPAN.—Control exercised by the Ministry of the Interior:

"Each department is responsible for the supervision of morals in cinematograph establishments. A number of departments have adopted special regulations regarding the admission of children to cinematograph theatres and have fixed the conditions of admission as follows:

"1. Children under fourteen not accompanied by their guardians or similar persons are not admitted;

"2. Children under fourteen are not admitted after 9 at night, and children present at a cinematograph performance are warned ten minutes beforehand to leave the cinema at 9 o'clock."

Control exercised by the Ministry of Education:

"Six departments out of 47 have imposed special regulations as to the conditions of admission to cinematograph theatres of children attending elementary and secondary schools; in other departments, however, this special supervision is left to the school authorities. Forty-three elementary schools out of about 25,000 and 52 secondary schools out of about 2,000 absolutely forbid their pupils to enter cinemas. Sixty elementary schools and 50 secondary schools forbid their pupils to visit cinemas but allow certain exceptions. The others have issued no special regulations on this subject."

LATVIA.—Extracts from the Regulations for cinemas published in the *Valdibas Vestnesis* (No. 11, of January 14th, 1924):

Article 8. "Persons under sixteen years of age shall not be admitted to cinematograph exhibitions unless the films have been previously censored by the Ministry of Education."

LUXEMBOURG (Grand-Duchy of).[1]—Law of June 13th, 1922, providing for the supervision of public cinema halls and entertainments:

Article 1.—"No minor, of either sex, who has not reached the age of seventeen shall be allowed to enter

---

[1] The documentation concerning the Grand-Duchy of Luxembourg has not been supplied to the Secretariat of the League by the Grand-Ducal Government, but has been taken from the collection of laws published by the International Association for the Promotion of Child Welfare.

any cinema hall or theatre."

Article 2.—"The provisions of the preceding article shall not apply to cinema halls or theatres which only exhibit such films as have been licensed by a Commission the organization and the duties of which shall be laid down by an administrative regulation."

NETHERLANDS.—Law of May 14th, 1926, concerning the Campaign against the Moral and Social Dangers of Cinematograph Performances.

Article 4.—(1) The Municipal Council may, by a Regulation and subject to Our approval, make the granting of the permit referred to in Article 1 [1] subject to the conditions laid down in the Regulation.

(2) The above-mentioned conditions shall not apply in the case of cinematograph performances to which only persons over eighteen years of age are admitted, though the films to be shown and the posters may be supervised as usual.

Article 16.—(2) At public cinematograph performances where children not obviously over fourteen years of age are admitted or are allowed to be present, the only films which may be shown are those, the showing of which in the presence of children under fourteen

---

[1] *Article 1.*—(1). No public cinematograph performance may be organized without a written permit from the mayor or aldermen.
(2). Such permit shall not be required:
　(i) In the case of public cinematograph performances given in the educational establishments designated by Our Ministry of Education.
　(ii) In the case of public cinematograph performances at which the only films shown deal with scientific, industrial, agricultural or commercial subjects and which the Central Commission referred to in Article 15 has approved as such.

years of age has been approved by the Central Commission.

(3) At public cinematograph performances to which children under fourteen years of age are not admitted or are not allowed to be present, but where minors over fourteen years of age but not obviously of eighteen years of age, are admitted or allowed to be present, only those films may be shown, the showing of which to minors between fourteen and eighteen years of age has been approved by the Central Commission.

NEW ZEALAND.—Extract from a communication from the Prime Minister's Office:

"Before any cinematograph film is exhibited in New Zealand, it must first be passed by a Censor appointed by the Government. If he considers it desirable, the Censor may attach a condition to his certificate of approval that the film shall not be exhibited to persons under a certain age."

An Act to provide for the Censoring of Cinematograph Films, August 7th, 1916, No. 10, IV:

Article 4.—"Such approval may be given generally, or may be given subject to a condition that the film shall be exhibited only to any specified class or classes of persons."

NORWAY.—Law No. 4, of July 25th, 1913, including supplementary Act of June 3rd, 1921, concerning the public exhibition of films:

Appendix

Article 9.—"Children under the age of sixteen shall not be admitted to cinema entertainments at which films are shown which the experts have only approved for exhibition to adults. Children under the age of sixteen shall, moreover, not be admitted to entertainments which end later than 8 p. m. unless they are accompanied by their parents or guardians."

ROUMANIA.—The prohibition to attend the performance of films other than those of an instructive and educative nature only applies to pupils of secondary schools,[2] that is, up to the age of about eighteen or nineteen years.

SALVADOR.—Regulations concerning theatres, cinemas, etc.:

Article 25, amended by the Decree of February 7th, 1924—"Children under eight may not be present at performances given at night. Questions as to age shall be determined by the police, the Censors and the medical officer of the theatre, cinema or circus."

SPAIN.—Royal Decrees regulating cinematographic performances and public entertainments, dated November 27th, 1912, and December 31st, 1913, absolutely forbid children under ten years of age, if unattended, to enter any closed premises where a public entertainment is given, whether it be a cinema entertainment or what is commonly known as a variety show.

---

[2] The wearing of uniform on all occasions is compulsory for the children in the secondary schools, and the punishments, which are even visited on the parents, are very severe in cases of infraction of this order.

APPENDIX

The decrees in question add that "purveyors of public amusement may nevertheless be allowed to give, during the day, entertainments exclusively devoted to cinema exhibitions intended for children."

SWEDEN.—Royal Decree of June 22nd, 1911, concerning cinema exhibitions:

Article 3.—"Minors who have not turned fifteen shall not be allowed to be present at a cinema performance when films are exhibited other than those which, as hereinafter provided, shall have been judged suitable for minors; the same shall apply to the case of a minor who is not accompanied by a guardian as regards entertainments which end later than 8 p. m."

SWITZERLAND.—Extract from the report of the Federal Council to the Federal Assembly on the petition for the revision of Article 31 of the Federal Constitution (May 20th, 1925), submitted to the Federal Council by Dr. Zimmerli and other signatories:

"The general practice in the majority of the Cantons is to allow the admission of children to ordinary cinematographic performances, particularly if they are accompanied by their parents or guardians, or by grown-up persons; but this indulgence applies only to children up to a certain age. On the other hand, such children are allowed to attend spectacles or performances for young people which are organized in most cases by the school authorities, and which, in nearly all parts of the country, may not be exhibited unless they have been first seen and approved by the authorities.

"The age up to which children are prohibited from attending ordinary spectacles varies in different Cantons. In Friburg, Thurgau and Lower Unterwald, the prohibition is enforced up to the end of the school age. In Argau, children of communal and district schools are refused admission to cinemas. The great majority of the Cantons which favor this system Basle-Town, Soleure, Vaud, Ticino, Neuchatel, Valais, Glarus and St. Gall) fix the age-limit for admission to cinemas at sixteen. Some Cantons, namely, Lucerne, Uri, Schwyz, Zug and Zurich, have gone even further and have an age-limit of eighteen.

UNION OF SOUTH AFRICA.—It may be gathered from the documents furnished by the Provincial Secretaries of Natal and of the Orange Free State that the admission of minors to cinematograph representations is regulated in these two provinces.

UNITED STATES OF AMERICA.—Extract of a summary of legislation relating to the supervision or censorship of motion pictures, forwarded by the Secretary of State of the United States of America:

"*Censorship or State Regulation: Special Laws applying to Children only.*—In practically no place in the United *S*tates are regulations with reference to moving pictures made or administered primarily with reference to children, although the authorized censors in some localities report that they try to bear in mind the effect of the pictures on the morals of children and young people in the decisions they make.

"A few cities prohibit the attendance of children under certain ages at moving-picture shows during school hours and unless accompanied by adults at other times. In Paterson, minors may not attend theatres unless accompanied by parents or guardian; in Birmingham, children under 12 must be accompanied by an adult; in Los Angeles, children under 14 must be accompanied by an adult after 9 p. m.; in Detroit, children under 16 may not attend between 8:30 a. m. and 3:30 p. m., except during vacation days, nor after 8 p. m. unless accompanied by parent or guardian. It is probable that some other cities from which no information on this point was received have similar provisions. One city (Chicago) issues permits for certain pictures to be shown only to those twenty-one years of age and over.

URUGUAY.—Order making previous censorship compulsory: May 5th, 1922.

Article 1.—"Persons organizing public performances must obtain from the Child Welfare Commission authorization to admit children under fourteen years of age."

(b) *Complete Prohibition.*

DANZIG.—Law on the Cinematograph, December 1st, 1925:

Article 3, *Paragraph* 3.—"Children under six may not be admitted to cinema performances.

Appendix

GERMANY.—Law on Cinema Performances, dated May 12th, 1920:

Article 3, Paragraph 4.—"Children under six years may not be admitted to cinematographic performances."

HUNGARY.—Extract from the Regulations of the Royal Ministry of the Interior, chapter III:

Paragraph 20.—"Children under five years of age shall not in any circumstances be permitted to attend public cinematographic displays, even if accompanied by adults."

LATVIA.—Extract from the Cinematograph Regulation (published in the *Valdibas Vestnesis,* No. 11, of January 14th, 1924):

Article 8, Paragraph 2.—"Children under six years of age shall not be admitted to cinematograph exhibitions."

SALVADOR.—Regulations concerning theatres, cinemas, etc.:

Article 25 (amended by the Decree of February 7th, 1924).—"Children under three shall not be admitted to public entertainments."

APPENDIX.

In the following countries, the regulations require that notices should be conspicuously displayed outside buildings in which cinematographic representations are given, stating whether minors are or are not admitted.

BELGIUM.—A Law of September 1st, 1920, prohibiting minors who have not reached the age of sixteen attending cinema exhibitions:

Article 2, Paragraph 2.—"Such exhibitions are to be advertised as entertainments intended for families and children."

Appendix

HUNGARY.—Extracts from the Regulations of the Royal Ministry of the Interior, chapter III, page 7:

Paragraph 20.—"The proprietor of the cinema or his representative shall, when films are being exhibited which are considered unsuitable for young persons under eighteen years of age, cause to be displayed in an easily visible place, and also near the box-office, a notice bearing the words: 'Young persons under eighteen years of age are not admitted to this performance.' This notice must also appear on all placards or other advertisements relating to the cinema performance in question."

ITALY.—Law dated December 10th, 1925, No. 2277, on Maternity and Child Welfare:

Article 22.—"Where any film is not passed for exhibition to children, the management of the theatre must publish a notice to that effect on the posters of the film, and must see that the order is strictly observed."

Royal Decree No. 718 *of April* 15*th*, 1926, sanctioning the regulations in execution of Law No. 2277 of December 10th, 1925, for the Protection and Assistance of Mothers and Children.

Article 159.—Before granting the licenses required under Article 65 of the Public Safety Law, for the posting and distribution of printed or written advertisements for cinematograph performances, the competent authority shall satisfy itself that advertisements for performances from which children and young persons are to be excluded by the decision of the Censorship Commission, clearly and plainly advertise that fact in the following terms: "Children under fifteen years of age will not be admitted to this performance (Article 22 of Law No. 2277, of December 10th, 1925).

LUXEMBOURG (Grand-Duchy of).—Law of June 13th, 1922, providing for the supervision of public cinema halls and entertainments:

Article 2, Paragraph 2.—"Such exhibitions shall be advertised as entertainments intended for families and children."

Grand-Ducal Decree of June 16th, 1922, for the better enforcement of the Law of June 13th, 1922, providing for the supervision of public cinema halls and entertainments:

Article 7.—"The advertising, referred to by the afore-mentioned Law, of every public entertainment intended for families or minors of seventeen years of age shall consist of a notice, displayed at

Appendix

least twenty-four hours before the performance or entertainment shall take place, on the outer door of the building when the cinematograph entertainment or performance is to take place.

"The notice shall state that the performance or entertainment is intended for families and children, the subject of the entertainment or performance and the date of the license."

NETHERLANDS.—Law of May 14, 1926, concerning the Campaign against the Moral and Social Dangers of Cinematograph Performances.

Article 17.—(1) It will be desirable to set up in a conspicuous position at the entrance of the premises in which the performance is given, a notice indicating the age under which spectators cannot be admitted.

(2) If a film, as shown, has not been approved by the Central Commission for showing to minors of 18 years of age, it may not be publicly announced as a film which such minors may witness.

SWEDEN.—Royal Decree of June 22nd, 1911, concerning cinema exhibitions:

Article 3, Paragraph 2.—"It must be clearly stated on all notices whether the entertainment is intended for minors or not."

URUGUAY.—Decree for the Protection of Children, and provisions supplementary thereto, dated November 18th, 1921:

Article 3.—"The posters of performances must show clearly whether the performance is or is not suitable for minors."

B. Countries in which Admission does not appear to be subject to Regulation.

No special regulations regarding the admission of children to cinematograph performances appear to have been promulgated in the following countries:

CANADA	EGYPT
Provinces of Manitoba, New Brunswick and Prince Edward Island)	ESTHONIA
	FEDERATED MALAY STATES
	FRANCE
	GREAT BRITAIN
CUBA	MOROCCO

| APPENDIX |

TUNIS VENEZUELA
UNION OF SOUTH AFRICA
  Cape Province and
  Transvaal)

3. CONTROL OF FILMS.

A. STANDARDS ADOPTED IN VARIOUS COUNTRIES

In the following countries the official regulations for the control of films exhibited to minors require the fulfilment of certain conditions or, as the case may be, the avoidance of certain features.

AUSTRIA.—Extracts from the Decree of the Minister of the Interior dated September 18th, 1912:

> *Article 17.*—"Permission shall be refused if the performance is of a nature to constitute an offense, to disturb peace or public order or offend against the proprieties or public morals.
>
> "If the performance of the film, although not coming under the first paragraph, might be morally or intellectually injurious to minors, permission shall be refused to show the film at performances to which children or persons under sixteen are admitted."

CANADA.—Note from the Government of the Province of:

> *Alberta:* "The Censorship Board does not allow any scenes depicting white-slavery, seduction, malpractices, gruesome or distressing scenes, hanging, lynching, electrocution, insanity, delirium, gross drunkenness, exhibition of notorious characters, drug habit,

Appendix

counterfeiting, brutal treatment of persons or animals, coarse vulgarities, objectionable titles."

Saskatchewan.—(R. S. S., 1920, ch. 181, sec. 10):

"All films and slides intended for exhibition by the province shall first be inspected by the censor or censors, and such censor or censors shall examine and pass upon their fitness for public exhibition with a view to preventing the display of scenes of an immoral or obscene nature or which indicate or suggest lewdness or indecency or which may offer evil suggestions to the minds of young people or children or which the censor or censors may consider injurious to the public morals or for any other reason opposed to the public welfare."

CZECHOSLOVAKIA.—Note by the Czechoslovak Government:

"Permission to give public cinematographic performances open to children and persons under sixteen years of age may be refused if the films in question are likely to have a harmful effect on young people from a moral or intellectual point of view."

DANZIG.—Law on the Cinematograph, December 1st, 1925:

Article 3, Paragraph 1.—"In addition to the films prohibited under Article 1, paragraph 2,[1] it is for-

---

[1] *Article 1, Paragraph 2.*—"The exhibition of a film shall be permitted on application, but such permission may be refused if, on inspection of the film, its exhibition seems likely to endanger public safety or order, wound religious susceptibilities, exercise a depraving or corrupting influence, injure the good name of the Free City of Danzig, or pre-

bidden to show at performances attended by young persons anything of a nature to harm the moral, intellectual or physical development of young persons, or to over-stimulate their imagination."

DENMARK.—Extract from a report of September 18th, 1922, addressed to the Ministry of Justice by the censors of films:

"Films dealing with historical, geographical, zoological and generally social subjects of the kind taught at school are rarely prohibited for children, even if they contain scenes which are somewhat gruesome. If, however, the subject is of a more specialized nature, turning upon degeneracy, chronic alcoholism, venereal diseases, immorality, etc., to such an extent that these subjects may be said to characterize the film though not to call for its prohibition, the film may as a rule be shown to adults only, apart from special mitigating circumstances.

"Decisive factors in the question of subject are the artistic performance of the chief parts and the degree of *intensity* with which they are played. If the methods used are calculated to inflame or stimulate the imagination of children, who, unlike adults, lack the steadying influence of experience, the question of prohibiting the film must be seriously considered. Moreover, although as a rule the artistic treatment of an ordinary subject may help it over certain difficulties,

---

judice it in its relations with foreign States. Permission may not be refused for the sole reason that the film has a certain political, social, religious, moral or philosophical tendency."

the same factor may, if the artistic quality is mainly used in the interest of sensationalism, actually become an additional reason for prohibiting the exhibition of the film to children."

GERMANY.—Law on Cinema Performances dated May 12th, 1920:

Article 1, *Paragraph* 2.—"Permission to show films shall be refused if an inspection of the film shows that its exhibition would be liable to endanger public order or security, to outrage religious feeling, to have a degrading or demoralizing effect on the onlookers, or to diminish Germany's prestige or compromise her relations with foreign States. Permission should not be refused on account of its political, social, religious, ethical or philosophical tendencies as such. Permission may not be refused on grounds unconnected with the contents of the film."

Article 3, *Paragraph* 2.—"In addition to films excluded under Article 1, paragraph 2, no films may be shown before young persons if they are liable to have a detrimental effect on their moral, mental or physical development or unduly to excite their imagination."[1]

HUNGARY.—Extract from the Regulations of the Royal Ministry of the Interior (page 5):

Paragraph 13.—"Minors shall not be permitted to attend cinematograph displays the subject-matter or

---

[1] *Article* 11, *paragraph* 2 of the Law on Cinema Performances, May 12th, 1920.—"In the inspection of films which are to be shown to young people, the opinion of young persons between eighteen and twenty years of age appointed by the Children's Welfare Board should also be taken."

Appendix

method of presentation of which or of any parts of which are likely prejudicially to affect the character of adolescents or their mental or moral development or unduly to excite their imagination."

ITALY.—*Royal Decree No. 718 of April 15th,* 1926, sanctioning the regulations in execution of Law No. 2277 of December 10th, 1925, for the Protection and Assistance of Mothers and Children.

Article 157.—The general restrictions laid down by Article 3 of the Regulations of September 24th, 1923, No. 3287, shall remain in force, and children and young persons of both sexes shall accordingly be excluded from all cinematograph performances having a love or crime interest, or likely, in the opinion of the Censorship Commission, in any way either to excite the passions of the young or to corrupt their morals by force of suggestion.

The following classes of films shall be regarded as particularly suitable for exhibition to children and young persons: Films reproducing works of art or representing towns, scenery, historical scenes and national customs; facts of national history, scientific phenomena and experiments; agricultural work or industrial establishments and processes, or depicting subjects and scenes tending to exalt the civic and religious virtues, the sacredness of the home, family affections, maternal love, the spirit of sacrifice, and acts of heroism, or calculated to stimulate gaiety, kindness, energy and courage.

Appendix

JAPAN.—Control exercised by the Ministry of Education:

"The minister of Education, fully recognizing the beneficient influence which can be exercised by the cinematograph, has issued a decree regarding the examination of lantern slides and cinematograph films by the Special Committee dealing with popular education. This Committee passes films submitted to it for approval which it regards as being of educational value, registers the title of the film and the name of the applicant and publishes them in the *Official Journal* to enable the authorities to encourage the display of good films and to recommend them to the public."

LATVIA.—Extracts from the Cinematograph Regulations (published in the *Valdibas Vestnesis,* No. 11, January 14th, 1924):

Article 7, Paragraph 2.—"The exhibition of the film shall be prohibited if it is of a nature: (1) to disturb the public peace and order; (2) to offend religious sentiments; (3) to encourage brutality, or to have a harmful effect on the morals of the spectator, or to lower the prestige of the State, or to interfere with its good relations with other countries."

Article 8.—"In addition to the provisions in Article 7, the admission of minors is prohibited to exhibitions of films likely to produce a harmful effect on the moral development of youth or capable of over-stimulating youthful fancies."

Appendix

NORWAY.—Law No. 4, of July 25th, 1913, concerning the public exhibition of films, and supplementary Act of June 3rd, 1921:

Article 8.—"The experts shall not approve films for presentation to minors if they are of opinion that the exhibition of the same would have a pernicious effect on the minds of the children or on their conception of right and wrong."

ROUMANIA.—Note by the Roumanian Government:

"The Central Committee forbids the performance of films subversive of morals or public order. On the other hand, films of an educative or instructive character are recommended to school-children. The latter are forbidden to attend performances of any other films."

SALVADOR.—Circular letter to the Governors of fourteen Departments (October 21st, 1925):

"Only instructive and moral films may be shown at cinematograph performances given in the afternoons (at matinees), *i. e.*, the only performances which children are permitted to attend under the regulations. In no case may films be shown which are liable to implant evil sentiments in the minds of the young or encourage vicious propensities."

SPAIN.—Royal Decree of November 27th, 1912, and Royal Decree of December 31st, 1913, for the regulation of cinematographic representations and public entertainments:

APPENDIX

"In cinematograph representations intended exclusively for children and exhibited during the daytime, the films shall be of an instructive or educative character, such as reproductions of voyages, historical scenes, etc."

SWEDEN.—Royal Decree of June 22nd, 1911, concerning cinema exhibitions:

Article 6.—"As regards exhibitions to which minors under fifteen are admitted, no film likely to exercise a bad influence on the imagination of children or to prove detrimental to their mental development or to their health shall be passed for performance."

UNION OF SOUTH AFRICA.—*Orange Free State Province.*—Ordinance No. 3 of 1916 (assented to July 19th, 1916), to provide for the inspection of pictures and to prohibit the exhibition of objectionable pictures:

5.—"Objectionable pictures shall be deemed to be pictures representing:

. . . .

"(c) Scenes of debauchery, low habits of life or other scenes such as would injuriously affect the minds of young persons;

"(d) Successful crime or violence such as would injuriously affect the minds of young persons."

URUGUAY.—Decree concerning child welfare and supplementary provisions, dated November 18th, 1921:

Article 1.—"Only films coming within the following categories may be exhibited at cinematograph performances to which children are admitted:

APPENDIX

(*a*) Popular scientific films;
(*b*) Comic films;
(*c*) News films;
(*d*) Panoramic films;
(*e*) Comedies suitable for children, and in a general way films providing simple and harmless amusement.

"Films of a character likely to injure the child's development, as, for example, detective films, intensely dramatic films, films which have a painful effect on the child's imagination, films which encourage feelings of hostility towards other countries, etc., are prohibited at such performances."

APPENDIX

It should be pointed out that, in some countries, films of certain specified categories may be exhibited at cinematographic performances to which minors are admitted without being previously submitted to any censorship. We may quote the following cases:

BELGIUM.—Royal Decree relating to the organization and powers of the Cinema Film Control Commission (May 11th, 1922):

Article 13.—"The Cinema Film Control Commission is entitled to license, without proceeding to see the films, and on simple compliance with the formalities hereafter mentioned, the exhibition of films at entertainments which are organized without any idea of making a profit thereby, and given solely from an instructive or educational point of view."

Article 14.—"Instructive films and films exhibiting current events may be released without having been passed; they are not to be accompanied by any narrative nor need they be provided with the band specified by Article 10."

DANZIG.—Law on the Cinematograph, December 1st, 1925:

Article 6.—"Provided that there is no reason for prohibition in accordance with Articles 1 and 3, the local police shall authorize,

Appendix

in virtue of its office, on its own responsibility and without demanding a decision from the censor's office, films relating to current events and purely scenic films."

GERMANY.—Law on Cinema Performances dated May 12th, 1920:

Article 6.—"Films dealing with current events and films only representing scenery may be passed for exhibition in their districts by the local police authorities insofar as there is no reason for rejecting them on the grounds mentioned in Articles 1 and 3, and shall not be subject to examination by the Board of Censors."

LATVIA.—Note from the Latvian Government:

"Films of a technical character or films showing landscapes and topical subjects need not be previously shown to the censor."

NETHERLANDS.—Law of May 14, 1926, concerning the Campaign against the Moral and Social Dangers of Cinematograph Performances.

Article 16.—(4) Notwithstanding the above provisions, the holders of permits may, in urgent cases and according to rules which will be laid down by the Central Commission, show films of topical interest even before such films have been submitted to the Commission.

NORWAY.—An Act, No. 4, of July 25th, 1913, concerning the public exhibition of films, including supplementary Act of June 3rd, 1921. In accordance with this Act, previous approval is not required for the exhibition of films:

Article 6.—"Reproducing ordinary public events, provided the films are shown within fourteen days immediately following the event and provided the police have given permission for the exhibition";

or the exhibition of:

Article 10.—"Films in connection with education or lectures at educational establishments or in connection with education or lectures carried on by any person holding a position at an educational establishment."

SWEDEN.—Royal Decree of June 22nd, 1911, concerning cinema exhibitions:

Article 4.—"An exception shall be made in the case of films the subject of which has nothing to do with the military strength of Sweden, or have not been taken from an aircraft (viz., captive balloons, or otherwise, dirigibles and aeroplanes) above Swedish territory, and which faithfully reproduce events which have recently happened, provided that such films are shown not later than ten days at the most after the events filmed took place. Nevertheless, the permission of the police authorities shall be required for such exhibitions. (Amended by the Royal Decree of April 15th, 1921.) This exception applies to the exhibition of this class of films at all cinematographic performances."

Article 13.—"The provisions of the present Decree shall not apply to cases in which films which are not concerned with questions connected with the military strength of the country, and which have not been taken from an aircraft above Swedish territory, are exhibited after a speech or lecture in a school. Neither shall the provisions of the present Decree apply to any person who, on making application, has been dispensed by the King from the obligation to observe the provisions of the present Decree."— (Amended by the Royal Decree of April 15th, 1921.)

B. MEASURES ADOPTED TO ALLOW THE PROTECTION OF CHILDREN BY THE CONTROL AUTHORITIES OF CERTAIN COUNTRIES WHERE THE ADMISSION OF MINORS TO CINEMATOGRAPH REPRESENTATIONS DOES NOT APPEAR TO BE SUBJECT TO REGULATION.

In addition to the measures referred to earlier in the report, attention should be drawn to the following:

There are certain countries in which there exist no special regulations concerning the admission of children to cinematographic performances; from communications received, however, it appears that the general system of censorship of the films or of the cinematographic performances as a whole provides for certain measures to ensure that no films shall be shown in public likely to be detrimental to the mentality or morals of minors.

APPENDIX

ESTHONIA.—The Committee for the Censorship of Films is composed of five members, including *one representative of the Ministry of Education and one representative of the Schools Administration of the town of Reval.* The Committee is entitled to take decisions provided at least three of the members are present, including either the representative of the Ministry of Education or the representative of the Schools Administration.

FRANCE.—The first article of the Decree of July 25th, 1919, lays down that no cinematograph films, with the exception of topical films showing current facts or events, may be exhibited in public unless these films and their titles have been passed by *the Ministry of Education* or *of Fine Arts.*

GREAT BRITAIN.—From a Home Office Memorandum: The legal foundation of the censorship of films in Great Britain is to be found in the Cinematograph Act, 1909. Although the primary object of this Act was to secure the safety of the audience from special risks, in particular that of fire, attaching to the cinema, means have been found for the exercise under the Act of a sufficiently effective control over the character of the films exhibited. The Act—which applies to exhibitions for which inflammable films are employed—provides, *inter alia,* that a cinematograph exhibition shall (save in a few exceptional cases) be given only in premises licensed for the purpose, and subject to regulations made by the Secretary of State (or in Scotland the Secretary for Scotland) for ensuring safety. Responsibility for the granting of licenses—which

APPENDIX

may be refused, and are subject to annual renewal—lies in the hands of local licensing authorities—namely, County Councils (who may delegate their functions to other authorities, including Justices in Petty Sessions) or, in the County Boroughs, Borough Councils. The licensing authorities have discretion to grant licenses on such terms and conditions and under such restrictions as, subject to regulations of the Secretary of State, they may determine. By a series of decisions of the High Court it has become clearly established that the conditions which a licensing authority may attach to the grant of a license can properly relate to matters other than the safety of the audience, provided that they are reasonable and are administered by the authority in a judicial manner. Accordingly it is possible for each licensing authority to assume the functions of a censor, exercising, through the medium of conditions attached to its licenses, control over the character of the films shown in premises licensed by it.

JAPAN.—It will be remembered that the making of rules for the good conduct of cinematographic representations and for the admission of school-children is a matter within the sphere of each province; however:

"In virtue of a Ministerial Decree which came into force on July 1st, 1925, the Minister of the Interior is responsible for the censorship of films. In this Decree the Minister does not impose restrictions, with a view specially to the protection of children, in regard to the character of the films shown. However, a number of censorship measures are provided to safeguard spectators of tender years from the corrupting influence of certain pictures. Thus, the authorities refuse to pass, or only sanction subject to special conditions, any films which, for example, come under one of the following categories:

"1. Films likely to be harmful to the mental and moral development of the young and to their good education.

"2. Films likely to suggest unhealthy ideas to children or weaken the authority of teachers.

"3. Films representing, in an attractive light, scenes of cruelty or vice.

"4. Films demonstrating various criminal practices likely to suggest the idea of criminal acts, such as receiving of stolen goods, etc."

JAPANESE COLONIES.—(a) *Formosa.*— In the Island of Formosa the local authorities censor films before they are shown to the public. They only pass films which are not prejudicial to public order and national morals. They accordingly supervise the exhibition of films and prohibit performances when it is found that the films may exercise an evil influence on the minds and morals of children.

(b) *Kwangtung.*—In Kwangtung the supervision exercised over cinemas for the protection of children is based on a general regulation: "Rules for Cinematograph Performances and Cinemas" (No. 57 of the Governor's Decree promulgated on July 29th, 1922).

APPENDIX

APPENDIX: The note given below was sent to the school authorities on September 26th, 1923:

"*Note on the Exhibition of Films*.—If films shown in schools are badly chosen or if a large number of scholars are confined for a considerable time in small and badly ventilated rooms, the result is equally harmful from the educational and the hygienic point of view.

"The school authorities are requested to carry out scrupulously the following instructions:

1. Films must be examined and those of a definitely educational character selected;

"2. If the film takes more than an hour to show, there must be an interval of ten minutes for recreation, and during this interval all windows shall be opened and the rooms aired.

"3. To prevent overcrowding, the number present must be fixed beforehand according to the dimensions of the room.

"4. As far as possible, rooms must be ventilated even while films are being shown.

"5. Should it be impossible to open all the windows on account of the cold, every person present must leave the room during the interval for recreation; the room shall then be aired by opening all the windows, and the spectators will return ten minutes later."

(c) *Sakhalin*.—There are no special regulations for the purpose of protecting children in connection with the control of cinemas in Sakhalin. The chief of police are, however, instructed to censor films before they are publicly shown, and, if necessary, to suppress them or make cuts in them or to authorize them while at the same time prescribing an age below which children may not be admitted.

MOROCCO.—Cinematograph censorship has been established in the French zone since 1916. At the end of that year, a special committee was set up at Casablanca,

Appendix

which, in accordance with the regulations, is responsible for condemning wholly or in part films of which certain scenes or the whole contents are *"likely to exercise a pernicious influence on the young* or to be detrimental to public order and morality."

TUNIS.—The Municipal Decree of May 8th, 1916—the only existing act concerning the control of films exhibited in the cinema-halls of Tunis—prohibits the exhibition of pictures representing scenes of *brigandage or detective stories.*

APPENDIX.

GREAT BRITAIN.—From a Home Office Memorandum:

There has been in existence for many years an unofficial body. established and maintained by the cinematograph trade, known as the British Board of Film Censors. The submission of films to this body is voluntary and its decisions have in themselves no legal sanction, though, as will be shown later, they have been given such sanction by the action of the licensing authorities. Films submitted to the Board are viewed by experienced and highly qualified examiners on whose advice the Board may either reject a film altogether or may pass it for exhibition with or without alteration. In passing films it is the settled practice of the Board to classify them into two categories: a Universal or "U" Certificate is issued in respect of a film considered fit for exhibition to any audience, and a "Public" or "A" Certificate is issued for a film adjudged to be satisfactory for display to adults only and not to children. The Board, although maintained by the trade, has been able to preserve an entirely independent judgment, and its policy rarely fails to command the support of public opinion. As public opinion in England is sensitive in respect of the character of entertainments, it follows that the standard adopted by the Board is a high one. Independent testimony is afforded by the fact that few, if any, complaints have reached the Home Office in recent years. The Board publishes annual reports on its work.

In July, 1923, the Home Office, after consultation with represent-

Appendix

ative licensing authorities, recommended for universal adoption the following additional conditions:

1. No film—other than photographs of current events—which has not been passed for "universal" or "public" exhibition by the British Board of Film Censors shall be exhibited without the express consent of the Council.

2. No film—other than photographs of current events—which has not been passed for universal exhibition by the British Board of Film Censors shall be exhibited in the premises without the express consent of the Council during the time that any child under, or appearing to be under, the age of sixteen years is therein. Provided that this condition shall not apply in the case of any child who is accompanied by a parent or bona-fide adult guardian of such child.

The additional conditions of 1923 have since been adopted by a substantial number of licensing authorities; and even where independent authorities have preferred not expressly to adopt conditions in this form, it is common for them to conform in practice to the standard set by the Board. In this way the authority of the Board has been considerably strengthened and it has been possible to attain throughout the country an approximate uniformity based on the standard set by the Board.

Note.—It should be noted that this memorandum, so far as it relates to the functions of the licensing authorities, refers only to England and Wales.

UNITED STATES OF AMERICA.—Unofficial censorship: In the United States there are two bodies which unofficially censor cinematograph films, but neither makes any distinction between films which may be shown to children and films which are regarded as suitable only for adults.

1. *The National Board of Review.*—The National Board of Review was organized in 1909 by the People's Institute of New York City, under the name of the National Board of Censorship of Moving Pictures, to censor all pictures before being shown in New York City. Since that date, the name has been changed and the board's activities have grown to include an unofficial censorship of approximately 98 per cent of all pictures made in the United States. The board is composed of some 250 voluntary reviewers chosen from among the civic and social organizations in and near New York City. Five to 15 of these reviewers see each picture in the projection room of the producers and distributors

Appendix

before national distribution of the films. If the picture is satisfactory, the seal of the National Board and the statement "Passed and approved by the National Board of Review" is stamped on the films. The National Board withholds its approval if it thinks eliminations or changes are necessary.

2. *The Picture-Producing Companies.*—The Organization of Motion-Picture Producers and Distributors—a voluntary association—was formed in 1922 with a membership of nine companies, and, in April, 1925, had a membership of twenty-two companies, including the most important in the United States. Producers and distributors are opposed to legal censorship, and have undertaken, through this organization, to prevent the production of offensive films. In a resolution adopted February 26th, 1924, they agreed "to prevent the prevalent type of play from becoming the prevalent type of picture; to exercise every possible care that only books or plays which are of the right type are used for screen presentation; to avoid picturization of books or plays which can be produced only after such changes as to leave the producer subject to a charge of deception; to avoid using titles which are indicative of a kind of picture which could not be produced or by their suggestiveness seek to obtain attendance by deception—a thing equally reprehensible; and to prevent misleading, salacious or dishonest advertising."

To make this effective, it was agreed that when the scenario department of a company was offered the picture rights of a book or play which did not meet these provisions, it should decline to picturize the book or play and would notify the National Office of its rejection. If the rejection were confirmed by this office, a statement thereof would be forwarded to the other members.

Of the success of this scheme, Mr. Will Hays, president, says: "During the year just passed, the plan . . . has resulted in more than 100 books and plays—including some of the 'best sellers' and stage successes—being kept from the screen because our members believed them unsuitable for picturization. There have not been more than half a dozen disputed instances."

Advance information as to pictures.—Advance information as to the character of films has been one of the problems which parents have found difficult to solve. Under the laws of Maryland, New York and Virginia, the Boards of Censors are required to prepare lists of pictures suitable for children, to be available on request. The National Board of Review, through a National Committee for Better Films, has undertaken in this way to serve the whole country with information about all kinds of pictures. Its work includes the rating of pictures and the publication of bulletins giving synopses of pictures approved by it, classifying them as suitable for general audiences and family audiences, including boys and girls of high-school age; and for mature audiences. This Committee has branches and co-operating associations in many parts of the United States.

Lists of good pictures are also prepared by some local boards of censorship, and many committees of women's organizations and child-protective agencies have tried to disseminate information as to better pictures. Some of these committees report desire on the part of local exhibitors to co-operate in showing the better grade of pictures, but that this is rendered difficult because of the method of distributing known as block-booking, whereby an exhibitor accepts an entire block or blocks of pictures of a producer-distributor and does not make his own selection.

Reviews of important new productions are now regularly carried by the newspapers.

The National Picture Producers and Distributors are advocating special performances of specially chosen programmes for children, and, in this connection, have prepared a collection of 52 such programmes, including educational and historical films, dramas and comedies of a wholesome type, chosen for their attractiveness and value to youthful audiences.

SUB-ANNEX

The following documents are kept in the Archives of the Secretariat of the League of Nations and can be consulted there by the members and assessors of the Child Welfare Committee. (The documents marked # exist in English and French; the others exist only in the original language.)

BELGIUM.—A Law to prohibit minors who have not reached the age of sixteen attending cinema exhibitions (September 1st, 1920).#

Appendix

A Royal Ordinance relating to the Organization and Powers of the Cinema Film Control Commission (May 11th, 1922).#

CANADA.—*British Columbia.*—An Act to regulate theatres and cinematographs (Moving Pictures Act) 1914.

Regulations governing the operation of moving-picture theatres.

Manitoba.—An Act to amend and consolidate the law respecting the regulation and taxation of public amusements (Amusements Act) 1913.

New Brunswick.—Regulations for moving-picture machines, 1912.

Nova Scotia.—The Theatres, Cinematographs and Amusement Act Regulations thereunder (consolidated 1922).

Ontario.—An Act to regulate theatres and cinematographs (passed April 20th, 1912). An Act to amend the Theatres and Cinematographs Act (passed April 26th, 1918).

Quebec.—Chapter 174: An Act respecting exhibitions of moving pictures.#

Saskatchewan.—The Theatres and Cinematographs Act.

Censor Board Regulations and the Amusements Tax Act and Rules and Regulations thereunder (1916).

DANZIG.—Law on the Cinematograph, December 1st, 1925.

DENMARK.—Law concerning the operation of cinematographic theatres, dated March 17th, 1922.

Appendix

Proclamation concerning the censorship of cinematograph films throughout the country (Ministry of Justice, July 5th, 1913).

ESTHONIA.—Compulsory Regulation No. 9, issued by the Ministry of the Interior, dated May 8th, 1925 (Official Journal, No. 77-78).#

FRANCE.—Decree of July 25th, 1919, by the President of the Republic.#

FRENCH PROTECTORATE.—*Tunis.*—Municipal Decree of May 8th, 1916.#

GERMANY.—Law on cinema performances, dated May 12th, 1920.#

Law, dated July 31st, 1925, modifying the Law on the employment of child labour in industrial enterprises, dated March 30th, 1903.#

GREAT BRITAIN.—Cinematograph Act of 1909: regulations made thereunder by the Secretary of State for the Home Department.

HUNGARY.—Extract from Regulation No. 255,000/1924/B/N, of the Ministry of the Interior.#

ITALY.—Regulations for the Government censorship of cinematographic films, with subsequent amendments. Royal Decrees Nos. 3287 (September 24th, 1923) and 1682 (September 18th, 1924). Law dated December 10th, 1925, No. 2277 on Maternity and Child Welfare. *Royal Decree No. 718 of April 15th,* 1926, sanctioning the regulations in execution of Law No. 2277 of December 10th, 1925, for the Protection and Assistance of Mothers and Children.#

Appendix

JAPAN.—Control exercised by the Ministry of the Interior: Extract from the regulations [1] on the censorship of films:

1. Decree of the Ministry of the Interior, No. 10 (promulgated on May 26th, 1925).

2. Extract from the regulations regarding the control of theatrical and cinematograph performances in the Department of Tokushima.

3. Extract from the regulations of the Department of Ehime.

4. Extract from the regulations of the Department of Hiogo.

5. Extract from the Order of the Tokio prefect of police.

Control exercised by the Ministry of Education: Decree and regulations[1] regarding the censorship of films and lantern slides by the Ministry of Education (promulgated on October 10th, 1912); By-laws regarding the admission to cinemas of pupils attending elementary and secondary schools:

1. Regulations in the Department of Miye.

2. Instructions issued by the Prefect of Gifu to under-prefects, mayors and chiefs of police.

3. Extract from the Regulations of the Department of Yamagata.

4. Conditions of admission of pupils at the ordinary normal school to cinemas in the Department of Akita.

---
[1] These texts exist in French only.

Appendix

5. Conditions of admission of pupils at the ordinary normal school to cinemas in the Department of Fukui.

6. Conditions of admission of pupils at the ordinary normal school to cinemas in the Department of Shimane.

JAPANESE COLONIES.—*Formosa.*—Collection of regulations [1] regarding the censorship of cinematograph films:

1. Regulations for the censorship of cinematograph films (Decree No. 12 of the Department of Taihoku, promulgated in August, 1925).

2. Order regarding the control of theatrical and cinematograph performances (transmitted in March, 1916, to prefects by the Chief of the Formosa Police).

3. Orders regarding the censorship of cinematograph films (transmitted in January, 1918, to prefects by the Formosa Chief of Police).

LATVIA.—Extracts from the regulations for cinemas published in the *Valdibas Vestnesis,* No. 11, of January 14th, 1924.#

LUXEMBURG (Grand-Duchy of).—Law of June 13th, 1922, providing for the supervision of public cinematograph halls and entertainments.

Grand-Ducal Decree of June 16th, 1922.

NETHERLANDS.—Law of May 14th, 1926, concerning the Campaign against the Moral and Social Dangers of Cinematograph Performances.#

NEW ZEALAND.—An Act to provide for the censoring of cinematographic films, August 7th, 1916.

Appendix

NORWAY.—Act No. 4, of July 25th, 1913, concerning the Public Exhibition of Films, including supplementary Act of June 3rd, 1921 (secs. 8 and 9).#

Royal Decree of September 12th, 1913 (completed by the Royal Decree of November 6th, 1920, and July 2nd, 1921), by which the Ministry of Justice and Police is authorized, pursuant to the Act of July 25th, 1913, to give dispensation from the provisions of Articles 1 and 6 of said Act and by which the Rules and Regulations for the State Film Control are established.#

SALVADOR.—Circular letter to the Governors of fourteen Departments of October 21st, 1925.#

Regulations governing theatres, cinematographs, circuses and other public entertainments.

Decree of the Ministry of the Interior, published in the *Diario Official,* No. 33, of February 8th, 1924.

SPAIN.—A Royal Decree for the Regulation of Cinematographic Representation and Public Entertainments (November 27th, 1912).#

A Royal Decree dealing with the provisions set forth November 27th, 1912, relating to cinematograph exhibitions and public performances, December 31st, 1913.#

SWEDEN.—Royal Decree of June 22nd, 1911, concerning Cinema Exhibitions.#

A Royal Decree of June 22nd, 1911, amended on December 31st, 1913; on October 23rd, 1914; on November 9th, 1917; and on April 15th, 1921, concerning the Control of Cinema Films.#

Appendix

UNION OF SOUTH AFRICA.—*Cape Colony.*—The Cape Ordinance No. 21 of 1917 entitled Cinema Films Ordinance, 1917, and the regulations framed thereunder.[1]

Orange Free State.—The Orange Free State Ordinance No. 3 of 1916 entitled Inspection of Pictures Ordinance 1916, and the regulations framed thereunder.[1]

Transvaal.—Ordinance No. 1 of 1920, entitled the Public Entertainments Ordinance 1920.

UNITED STATES OF AMERICA.—*Connecticut.*—Public Acts 1925, Chap. 177, p. 3946, H. B. No. 1079: "An Act providing for the imposition of a tax on films from which motion pictures are to be exhibited within the State," approved June 14th, 1925.

Florida.—"An Act to Regulate the Exhibition of Motion Pictures in the State of Florida, providing for the appointment of members of the National Board of Review, and providing penalties for the violation of this Act," approved June 14th, 1921.

Kansas.—Chapter 308, concerning "motion-picture films or reels, and the censoring of same for public exhibition," approved March 9th, 1917, published in Official State Paper of March 31st, 1917.

Maryland.—"Maryland State Board of Motion-Picture Censors," 1922 Act, Chapter 390, approved April 13th, 1922. Rules adopted by the Maryland State Board of Motion-Picture Censors in pursuance of Section 16 of the 1922 Act, Chapter 390.

---
[1] This text exists in English and Dutch.

Appendix

New York.—"Motion Picture Commission of the State of New York," Chapter 715: "An Act to regulate the exhibition of motion pictures, creating a commission therefor, and making an appropriation therefor," became a law on May 14th, 1921, with the approval of the Governor; passed, three-fifths being present.

Ohio.—Laws regulating the censorship and exhibition of motion pictures in Ohio, as amended, effective August 27th, 1915.

Pennsylvania.—"Pennsylvania State Board of Censors (of Motion Pictures): Rules and Standards," No. 239: "An Act relating to motion-picture films, reels or stereopticon views or slides, providing a system of examination, approval and regulation thereof, and of the banners, posters and other like advertising matter used in connection therewith; creating the Board of Censors; and providing penalties for the violation of this Act."

Virginia.—"Virginia State Board of Censors: Censorship Law, 1923;" Chapter 257: "An Act to regulate motion-picture films and reels; providing a system of examination, approval and regulation thereof, and of the banners, posters and other like advertising matter used in connection therewith; creating the board of censors; and providing penalties for the violation of this Act;" approved March 15th, 1922 (as amended by Act of Assembly 1923, approved March 21st, 1923).

URUGUAY.—Decree concerning child welfare, and supplementary provisions, November 18th, 1921.#

APPENDIX

Order making previous censorship compulsory, May 5th, 1922.#

VENZUELA.—Decree of the Federal District Government establishing the Board for the Preliminary Censorship of Cinematograph Films, published in *Municipal Gazette,* No. 3,136, August 16th, 1924.

C. P. E. 62.

ANNEX 5a.

THE EFFECT OF THE CINEMATOGRAPH ON THE MENTAL AND PHYSICAL WELL-BEING OF CHILDREN.

Report prepared by the Secretariat of the League of Red Cross Societies and submitted to the Committee On March 27th, 1926

The question of the effect of the cinematograph on children is of special interest to the Red Cross; first, because the Junior Red Cross aims at improving the minds and morals of school-children and is fully aware of the dangers of the cinematograph; secondly, because the League of Red Cross Societies has for a long time past devoted special attention to health propaganda by means of films and has thus been able to acquire considerable experience of the advantages of educational cinema shows. The extension of the Junior Red Cross to school circles has enabled us to collect numerous opinions, leaving on one side questions of legislation which we knew were being dealt with by the Social Section of the League of Nations, and confining our-

Appendix

selves to soliciting the views of educationists, psychologists and hygienists. In this way we have collected very valuable information, although we have not yet received replies from all the countries to which we addressed inquiries. If necessary, we could later complete this documentation, and we shall be glad to place the original texts at the disposal of the Social Section of the League of Nations.

Meanwhile we have endeavored to classify the material received under the following headings:

(*a*) The part played by the cinematograph in the life of the child of today.

(*b*) Instances of typical abuses.

(*c*) Suggested ways and means of mitigating the harmful effect of the cinematograph on children.

(*d*) Proposals for the improvement of the cinematograph of today.

(a) *The Part played by the Cinematograph in the Life of the Child of Today.*

We have simultaneously received replies concerning the part played by the cinema in general and the sensational film in particular, expressing in a general way approval of the former and unreserved condemnation of the latter.

It is clear that these problems are quite distinct. There can be no question of dispensing today with the enormous pedagogic advantages of the educational film.

"The cinema," says Mme. Janvier (Belgium), "plays a predominating part in the life of the child of today. It is the greatest reward to which he can aspire, and it can be a powerful influence for good. Attendance at the cinema

APPENDIX

is to be warmly recommended when it contributes to popular instruction and education of which it is undoubtedly a valuable auxiliary. It is wrong to suppose that only the sensational romance can draw crowds to the cinema." She then quotes an observation made by Mme. Georgette Leblanc in industrial shipping circles at Le Havre: "These poor folk go to the cinemas even when trash is shown, but people are turned away when there is a good educational film."

The report of the French Junior Red Cross tends to the same conclusions. "At all ages," says this document, "the great majority of school-children give their preference to instructive films, and to films dealing with events of the day (cars with caterpillar wheels, travel or historical films); at all ages, too, comic films come last in the order of preference."

Other replies also give the impression that children are encouraged to go to cinema shows by artificial circumstances, such as the lack of supervision, unsatisfactory family life, excessive advertisement, etc., but that the intrinsic appeal of the sensational film to children is perhaps less considerable than is sometimes supposed.

"The film," says Dr. Lampe, of Berlin, "attracts the child because animated reproduction corresponds to his mode of thought, which responds to all that is in movement and is ignorant of the process of abstract logic. Children think by associations of ideas that are principally visual."

It may therefore be supposed that children are attracted rather by the cinematograph process than by the contents

APPENDIX

of the film, which often bore or disgust them—a fact which does not preclude the nervous shock or demoralizing impression produced by the traditional film melodrama.

Mme. Droscher, of Berlin, Director of the Pestallozzi-Froebel Institution, believes that the attraction of the cinema is losing ground owing to the counter-attraction of wireless telephony. The comparison she makes with the educational cinema, the use of which is growing more and more widespread, is in favor of the latter. The methods of the pedagogic institution directed by the author also appear to her to develop the taste of children. Mme. Droscher believes that one of the results of the rise in the cost of living has recently been to diminish the attendance at the cinemas. When children go there they prefer "stories of foreign lands," "things that really happened," "nature films and the life of animals," "anything but love-stories." In one class, two or three children expressed a preference for comic films, but the majority thought they were "silly." It should not be forgotten that the present German law forbids young people from 6 to 18 years to attend the sensational film. A child cannot go to the sensational film without breaking the law. Abuses are therefore less frequent.

The "Erziehungsrat" Society of Vienna recognizes that children are more attracted by the film than by the magic-lantern.

The same view is put forward in great detail in the report of the Committee of Inquiry on the Cinema of the National Council of Public Morals, drawn up by Sir James Marchant, London, George Allen & Unwin, 1925. This

APPENDIX

enquiry, says the author (page 88), may be defined as a vigorous effort to fight the cinema on its own ground. The effort was unavailing, for, as the report shows, the cinema has undoubted advantages from the educational point of view (this remark, of course, does not apply to the cinema-theatre).

Mr. Bennett, of the Cinematograph Committee of the Federation of New South Wales Teachers, considers that the cinema is one of the most important factors in forming the character of school-children in our modern towns. Auditory impressions are tending to be replaced by visual impressions.

The most illuminating reply on the part played by the cinema in the life of children today has been given us by the Polish Red Cross in an extremely full article by Dr. Bogdanowicz, which supplies the following statistics compiled from the replies of 1,056 boys and 418 girls at secondary schools, and 824 children in the lower forms, to a questionnaire on the frequentation of the cinema and its effects. Of the secondary school children, 98 per cent of the boys and 89 per cent of the girls go to the cinema. Of the pupils attending the supplementary courses—children of the working classes aged between 13 and 20 years—80 per cent of the boys and 56 per cent of the girls go to the cinema. In the lower forms, 51 per cent of the boys and 39 per cent of the girls go at least once a week to the cinema. An interesting question put to the boys and girls of the secondary schools was the order of their preference for the

APPENDIX

theatre, the circus, sports and the cinema. In all the forms the preference was in the order given.

This confirms the fact that children are attracted more by the process of the cinema than by what it displays. Nevertheless, to many children who are very fond of the cinema the danger consists of its *power of persuasion* taken in conjunction with the weakening of the critical sense by the emotion of the moment.

Dr. Bogdanowicz divides films into three categories: adventure films, modern dramas and comic films. The first category seems to be particularly appreciated by very young boys or by older but rather undeveloped children, who have a passion for criminal and detective stories, full of fighting, murders, etc., in which the imagination is stirred by scenes of torture, pursuit or struggles against armed force. Girls show a preference for more sentimental themes; for example: "the lives of princes," "the lives of counts," "the furniture of drawing rooms," "the tragedy of a soul," etc. All these films naturally exercise a bad influence.

The enquiry undertaken by 40 Australian teachers, which is interesting in more than one respect, gives very valuable figures concerning regular visits to the cinema. One of the most careful enquiries shows that 54 per cent of the children visit the cinema once a week and 46 per cent less regularly. The preference of children for good, instructive films is very marked.

In all these replies no voice is raised against the cinema as a technical invention and as an educational medium. It

APPENDIX

cannot be abolished today, as it seems to give scope for the natural instinct of children towards visual observation of movement and as it can thus certainly help them to assimilate fresh knowledge. On the other hand, all are unanimous in condemning the ordinary sensational film, which is infinitely below the level of popular taste. The latter, indeed, often condemns it, but, being forced to take what it finds, it is attracted by the cheapness of the amusement offered.

Summing up these judgments, we can say that the life of the child today is being invaded by the cinema and unfortunately by a cinema almost entirely unadapted to its needs. Numerous replies given by children show that their preference is not for the sensational films considered by certain producers to be the most remunerative. The film, which might interest and captivate children and the general public in so many different ways, has violently abused its power of pushing sensation to the extreme by visual representation, of pushing it to the point of exasperation through the medium of the picture and of thus giving rise to criminal suggestions even under the cloak of morality. It is for this reason that the censorship of pictures must be established on quite a different basis from the censorship of the press.

Dr. Gaupp, of Tubingen, sufficiently stigmatizes the character of the majority of popular adventure films. He quotes the statistics of Konradt, who, in 250 films successively viewed, found no less than 97 murders, 51 cases of adultery, 19 seductions, 22 abductions and 45 suicides.

Appendix

The principal protagonists of these films were classified as follows: 176 thieves, 25 prostitutes, 35 drunkards, etc.

The part played by the cinema in the life of the child today should clearly not be to make him live for several hours a week in such surroundings; its sole function should be, on the contrary, to assist him by visual methods to assimilate certain parts of his educational programme.

(b) *Instances of Typical Abuses.*

We shall only quote as typical abuses the new facts elicited by our enquiry tending to show the pernicious influence of the cinema on children; certain ill effects of the adventure film or melodramatic film are already too well known, but in this case repetition may be of value.

According to the enquiry undertaken by the French Junior Red Cross in girls' classes, all the pupils—even those who say they like the cinema—recognize its immediate drawbacks: unhealthy atmosphere of the hall, fatigue of the eyes and of the head, loss of sleep and, above all, sleep troubled by dreams and nightmares due to the strong impression made by dramatic films. Some of them are afraid of these dreams: "The films frighten me," "the cinema is sad," "these films are not for children of our age" (11 years). This influence on the nervous system is particularly noticeable among girls of ten to thirteen. The pupils who attend the supplementary courses are less impressionable because they understand better, but they are not at all fond of exciting films in which much play is made with the revolver. A very small number—only two or three in each class—show a marked liking for romantic

APPENDIX

situations which, when they are about twelve years old, are liable to warp their judgment, for they say that "these stories are real life," "it is the sort of thing that can happen." The historical films make a very strong impression and are taken absolutely for gospel truth.

The report of Mme. Janvier, a member of the Board of Film Censors, forwarded by the Belgian Red Cross, quotes an instance of sudden lunacy produced in a child after seeing a film full of bloodshed. Another child brought up on the best principles forced the door of a library at home and took a forbidden book. He admitted that this act of burglary had been suggested to him by the exploits of the heroes of comic films. The child was only fourteen years of age and was therefore only admitted to censored shows. Another boy of fifteen indulged in an escapade, suggested, on his own admission, by a cowboy film. In the case of girls, the matter is still more serious. The sentimental and romantic side of their nature drives them to launch out into adventures of which they often become the victims. The Belgian report gives numerous examples of escapades of this kind—simulation of rape, adventures leading to prostitution, etc.[1]

More categorical still and at the same time more general is the report submitted to the Belgian Red Cross by M. Paul Wets, Judge of the Children's Court at Brussels. "The children's judges of the country," he says, "are unanimously of the opinion that the harmful influence of

---
[1] See particularly Rouvier: "Cinematographic neurosis," *Oeuvre nationale de l'enfance*, March, 1924, Fifth Year, p. 350.

APPENDIX

the cinema on Belgian youth is one of the principal causes of crime among children." He asserts that the bad influence of the cinema on minors is proved by the character of the statements they make when questioned in court, which reflect details taken straight from the cinematograph films they have witnessed. M. Wets remarks that the criminal psychology of children is very different from that of adults. Children generally bring no element of passion into the offenses they commit but act under the direct influence of the films they have seen and follow, as it were, mechanically the examples they have been set.

The cinema is a wonderful instrument of education, but if the teaching is bad the result is easy to anticipate. M. Wets also confirms the fact that the cumulative effect of such influences on the mind sometimes even leads to lunacy.

As regards the moral influence, numerous replies from the Australian Red Cross emphasize the demoralizing effects of the sensational film, the falseness of the impression given, the debasement of taste, the deterioration of style and of a taste for reading, the introduction into the child's mind of unhealthy associations and of emotions and situations which otherwise would never spontaneously enter his imagination.

Lastly, according to one of the school teachers of the Junior Red Cross, the appreciation of human values is falsified; cinema stars become more important persons than the ideal of the hero and the great man. According to another teacher, children must become more superficial and more *blase*. Another teacher quotes a large number of

APPENDIX

instances of anti-social acts imitated from the cinema. One child, for example, deliberately broke all the windows in a kitchen, remarking: "Jackie Coogan did it" (this indirectly touches a point which is not dealt with in this enquiry—the moral and physical effect of the cinematograph trade on the child-actor. Our information on this question is still incomplete).

Such are the effects of the sensational film from the point of view of character and morals.

Moral and Intellectual Effects.—Numerous judgments corroborate the following opinion expressed by the Chief of the Committee of the Junior Red Cross at Scone, in Australia, which emphasizes the base feelings aroused in children by the cinema by creating a craving for artificial excitement harmful to the nerves and prejudicial to reading and to work in general.

The Director of the Junior Red Cross at Melbourne writes: "Rapid and fleeting impressions become a habit for the child, whose nerves are strained to excess, and who *loses the habit of concentration. Education suffers.* The child's mind is prematurely developed, and he is no longer content with the amusements of his age; his imagination wanders on the lines suggested by the scenes witnessed at the cinema. A child who visits the cinema is always precociously theatrical."

Mme. Janvier (Belgium) says: "The cinema destroys in children the sense of color, proportion and distance."

Effects on Physical Health (Ocular and Nervous Fatigue).—Dr. Gordon L. Berry, Secretary of the American

Appendix

National Committee for the Campaign against Blindness, definitely reaches the conclusion that there is a relation between the weakening of sight and too frequent visits to the cinema. Children who frequent the cinema often display symptoms of ocular tension, headaches and short-sightedness.

According to Mme. Janvier, the number of children obliged to wear spectacles has considerably increased in Belgium since the introduction of the cinema.

According to Dr. Bogdanowicz (Poland), one-third of the children complain of pains in the eyes during or after the performance, which is the result not only of the defective sight of the children but of the too-rapid movement of the pictures, of their sudden changes and of bad focussing. From 30 to 50 per cent of the children complain of headaches, giddiness, fatigue and depression, particularly frequent among girls, but often found in both sexes, particularly at the age of puberty. It is to be noted that the strongest reactions are provoked by adventure films, the effect is less with dramatic films and then scientific films. This gradation well demonstrates the psychic nature of the reaction.

Nearly all the Australian teachers consulted also observe the harmful effect on the child's sight.

Harmful Conditions of Display.—According to Mme. Janvier, the darkness of the halls creates an unhealthy and dangerous atmosphere and is liable to develop bad habits in nervous children.

APPENDIX

Mr. Cocksley (Australia) also says: "Darkness reinforces *criminal and erotic emotionalism.* Many young people only go to the cinema on account of the erotic excitement produced by the darkness, which still further dulls their critical sense of the film shown." All the schoolteachers also draw attention to the loss of sleep caused by visiting evening performances. The resulting fatigue exercises an extremely unfavorable influence on the nourishment and general condition of the child and on his aptitude for school work.

Furthermore, the habit of the cinema turns children away from sports, open-air exercise and direct contact with nature.

(c) *Suggested Ways and Means of Mitigating the the Harmful Effect of the Cinematograph on Children*

All the suggestions received in answer to our enquiry presuppose a censorship, obviously operating before the release of the film.

On the other hand, an opposite view is taken by Dr. Marie Delcour, Member of the Advisory Committee of the Junior Red Cross in Belgium. "It would appear," she says, "that censorship is always ineffectual. If we exclude children below a certain age from the cinema, we are giving the condemned film a free advertisement among older children; and it will be admitted that what is dangerous at 15 is highly likely to be still dangerous at 17."

All the other writers admit that censorship prevents at least part of the damage done by the cinema.

Appendix

Generally speaking, the recommendations of our correspondents may all be reduced to the following:

(1) The age at which children may be admitted to the cinema should be raised rather than lowered. We have often met with the proposition, which has already been put into effect in certain legislations, that, with the exception of special children's performances, the cinema should be totally forbidden to children under 18.

If legislation to this effect were universally introduced, the automatic corollary would be the abolition of half-price admission for children, which is in many countries one of the reasons for the excessive patronizing of the cinema.

(2) In Australia, Austria, Germany and Belgium, there is a tendency to ask for the appointment of educationists as members of all censorship committees. In view of the influence of the cinema on adolescents, there should be a much stricter censorship than there now is over all crime and love scenes, *regard being paid to the psychological power of suggestion and the suspension of the critical faculty* by the representation of living action. The total prohibition of the exhibition on the screen of any scene of crime, or of certain sensational scenes, might be contemplated; and I judge from the general trend of the replies received that any educationists who might be consulted would probably approve of the regulations quoted in the document drawn up by the Secretariat of the Advisory

APPENDIX

Commission, which are in force in Alberta (Canada).[1]

(3) It has been suggested in many quarters that the censorship should also apply to photographs, figures, posters and letterpress displayed outside the cinema-theatres for purposes of advertisement.

(4) Judge Wets (Belgium) thinks that it is not enough to establish censorship committees with the sole duty of deciding as to the value of the film and authorizing its performance. The supervision of theatres and cinemas is primarily a matter for the police; in his view, a special administrative branch of the police should be formed for child welfare, and the duties of that branch would include the supervision of theatres and cinemas.

(5) It would be for this supervisory branch, rather than for the censorship committee, to obtain the issue of prohibitions against insufficient lighting in the main halls of all cinema-theatres in order to reduce the cinematographic neurosis as far as possible and to facilitate the maintenance of order in the halls. From the technical point of view, this arrangement presents no difficulties, in view of the power of modern apparatus. Indeed, Sir James Marchant, in his book "The Cinema and Education," mentions new systems by which moving pictures can be shown in daylight or in a diffused light. Preference will be given to these systems in the case of the school cinema.

---

[1] "In the Province of Alberta the Censorship Committee prohibits the exhibition of scenes dealing with the white slave traffic, seduction and immorality, and gruesome and painful subjects, such as hanging, lynching, electrocution, mania, delirium, visible intoxication; it further forbids the representation of immoral persons, drug-fiends, coiners and persons indulging in cruelty to others or to animals; coarse expressions and indecent titles are also prohibited."

Appendix

The supervisory branch would also enforce the regulations concerning ventilation and eyesight protection; it would see that the proper distances (minimum 6 metres) separate the seats from the screen, would study the question of maximum distance, and would take steps to deal with the technical defects such as flickering, and scratched or worn films, liable to damage the spectators' eyesight.

(d) *Proposal for Improving the Modern Cinematograph.*

On this point also opinions are unanimous. In view of the attractions which the *cinematograph process* has for the child, the elimination of bad films and the total prohibition of the cinema-theatre to children would be rendered easier if the film were given a large part in school curricula, and if amusement performances were organized in which the duty of a censorship committee would not be limited to rejecting harmful films but would involve the *positive responsibility* of selecting films likely to have a good influence on the child.

"At the same time," says Mme. Janvier, "as the educative film cannot stand up unaided against its formidable competitors, it must be protected, fostered, and even subsidized by qualified educationists." Mme. Janvier suggests clean and wholesome films, providing genuine fun, and diversified from time to time with scenes from history, travels, stories, fairy-tales, and so forth. She cites such authorities as Professor Collette, of Paris, the "apostle of the cinema," M. Sluys, Director of the Brussels Training College, etc.

Appendix

The German experts Walter Gunther and Mme. Harbou Lang also ask for assistance from Ministries of Education or provincial centers in distributing films to school authorities.

The Polish Red Cross specially recommends for children scientific films dealing with nature, history, geography, hygiene, etc., and would also allow certain dramatic and comic films but objects to the travestying of classical literature on the screen.

Dr. Lemke, representing the Danzig Red Cross, prefers films providing changes of scene (geographical and historical films), and also calls attention to the consistent success of films dealing with sport and hygiene.

Dr. Marie Delcour suggests that small grants should be made for educative and descriptive performances; these grants might equally well take the form of effective and gratuitous publicity in certain educational circles such as the Junior Red Cross. To attract the children to these films, raffles might be got up for books to be given as prizes.

In the opinion of the "Erziehungsrat" Society of Vienna, bad films can only be eliminated by the creation of a good school cinema showing films dealing with national history, exploration, geography, the history of other nations, trade, industry, international relations, natural history, etc.

M. Edouard Golias, Adviser to the "Urania" Popular Education Society of Vienna, finds that special children's performances are not a success; the children generally refuse to go, because they prefer adults' performances. The

APPENDIX

reason is that a sufficiently clear distinction has not yet been made between films suitable to different ages. Fairy-tales and films making little demand on the imagination should be kept for quite small children, while for the elder children a programme more suited to their state of development should be arranged. It is also desirable that associations formed for the benefit of children should set on foot a movement to warn them against the abuses and dangers of the cinema theatre.

Australian teachers are anxious that films shown to children should be limited, as regards subject, to geography, history, industry, natural history, historical scenes, lives of great men, travel and exploration, and scenes of national life, *e.g.*, in certain countries, life and work on a farm.

Other teachers are in favor of films depicting the life of children and young people in other countries, and slow-motion studies of various sports and crafts.

Some of the teachers have already observed an increase in the children's knowledge of geography due to the cinema.

Many teachers ask for better apparatus, preferably light and portable, for school use, and would like to see organizations for distributing good school films.

If the cinema were thus introduced in schools, it would, of course, do away with all films which have an undesirable moral atmosphere. At the same time, it should not be allowed to have any of the disadvantages of the cinema-theatre. The children's eyesight should be protected by seating them neither too close nor too far from the screen;

the apparatus should not produce flicker, attention should be paid to the wear and tear of films, so as to prevent spots and scratches, which are bad for the eyesight; children with weak eyes should wear yellow glasses, preference should be given to apparatus which will work in a diffused light or even in daylight; not more than an hour a week, on an average, should be devoted to cinema performances; teachers, child-welfare societies and children's societies themselves should be encouraged to make a stand against sensational dramatic films and to promote the exhibition of historical, geographical, informative and educative films. The question now arises of national or international relations between the industrial or private undertakings concerned in the production of films of the kinds mentioned. It is generally known that the International Institute of Intellectual Co-operation is interesting itself in this question; in particular, by collating all available information as to the production of films. The Advisory Commission for the Protection and Welfare of Children and Young People would undoubtedly be well advised to inform the Institute of the importance which it attaches to the question in connection with the moral and physical welfare of children and to ask it to establish relations between the various circles interested in the production of such films as may effectively remedy the present situation. The union of all those interested in the circulation of good films could hardly fail to exercise a favorable influence on the cinematograph industry.

The League of Red Cross Societies has a direct interest

Appendix

in this question, since it is adding every year to the collection of films (at present 150) which it lends to its members, mainly for popular hygiene propaganda, and many of which are used for school demonstrations.

Further, the Secretariat of the League of Red Cross Societies has recently collaborated in the production of popular hygiene films, and the Junior Red Cross has quite lately decided upon a valuable supplement to inter-school correspondence in the form of new films, taken quite independently, depicting the life, habits and activities of schoolchildren in different countries.

This enterprise can do nothing but good in promoting school education and international understanding.

(Signed) Dr. F. HUMBERT.

Paris, March 24th, 1926.

Our thanks are due for the information on which this report is based:

To the *German* Red Cross for various documents and printed matter and for the reviews and notes by Mme. von Harbou Lang, Professor Lampe, Fraulein L. Droescher, and M. Walter Gunther;

To the *American* Red Cross for a very full list of organizations and publications dealing with the question;

To the *Australian* Red Cross for the 40 reports from directors of Junior Red Cross Societies and from schools;

To the *Austrian* Red Cross for reports from M. Edouard Golias, Adviser on Popular Education to the Urania Development Society; M. Jaksch, Educational Adviser and

APPENDIX

Director of School Entertainments to the Urania Society; and the "Erziehungsrat" Society of Vienna;

To the *Belgian* Red Cross for reports from Mme. J. Janvier, social worker and member of the Film Control Commission; M. Paul Wets, Magistrate of the Children's Court of the Brussels Arrondissement; Dr. Marie Delcour, member of the Advisory Committee of the Junior Red Cross; and Mme. Houtain, social worker, attached to the Mental Health Center;

To the *British* Red Cross for forwarding important documents;

To the *Danzig* Red Cross for reports from M. Dumkow and Rector Lemke;

To the *French Junior* Red Cross for a first-hand investigation in the middle, upper and continuation classes;

To the *French National Committee for the Prevention of Tuberculosis*;

To the *Polish* Red Cross for reports from Mme. Degen Slosarska, Director of the Junior Red Cross Society of Wloclawek; Mme. Bieniewska; and Mme. Radolinska de Kalisz; and the translations of articles by Dr. J. Bogdanowicz.

APPENDIX 3

Resolutions of International Motion Picture Congress, Held Under the Auspices of the International Committee on Intellectual Cooperation, Paris, 1926.

RESOLUTIONS

INTERNATIONAL MOTION-PICTURE CONGRESS

The first International Motion-Picture Conference was held in the International Institute from September 27th to October 3rd, 1926.

It was organised by the French National Committee on Intellectual Cooperation at the suggestion of the International Committee on Intellectual Cooperation of the League of Nations (July 28th, 1924).

The Institute undertook the technical organisation of the Congress.

Four hundred and thirty-five delegates, representing thirty-one counties were present at the Congress.

Sixteen governments sent official delegates to the Congress. Thirteen international organisations, such as the I. L. O., the Red Cross, the International Confederation of Intellectual Workers, the Save the Children Fund, etc., took part in the Congress.

(The International Institute of Intellectual Cooperation published these important Resolutions in pamphlet form for information without accepting any resposibility for their contents.)

Appendix

FIRST COMMISSION

Study of means of improving motion-picture production, from the intellectual and artistic point of view.
Study of the means of improving motion-picture production, from a moral point of view.
Respecting of national themes. Films taken from history, literature, etc.

1º The International Motion-Picture Congress recommends authors, scenario-writers, publishers, and in general, all persons interested in the artistic and industrial aspects of film production:

a) To avoid carefully scenarios liable to arouse a spirit of animosity between nations and tending to perpetuate the idea of war;

b) To avoid presenting foreign nations or races in a degrading or ridiculous light on the screen;

c) To show the characteristics and qualities of a foreign people in such a way as to arouse sentiments of interest and sympathy in their favour, and to utilise the resources of the cinema to the fullest possible extent to bring about international peace and universal progress;

2º The International Motion-Picture Congress recommends authors, scenario-writers, publishers the world over:

a) To treat historic truth with scrupulous exactitude, and above all to avoid tempering historical films with a romantic interest likely to reflect unfavorably upon the people with whom the historical tale deals;

APPENDIX

b) To collaborate closely, when working upon historical films, with nationals of the country in question, whose advice will go far to prevent errors;

3⁰ The Congress further resolves that literary works in being adapted for the screen suffer no changes in the spirit, characterisation or actual setting of the original;

4⁰ In order to maintain the original value of films, the Congress resolves that the speed at which films are shown be uniformly regulated;

5⁰ The Congress recommends film publishers the world over:

a) In the case of every foreign film, to mention on the screen and on the programme, the name of the author, the scenario-writer, the firm producing the film and the country in which it is produced;

b) To respect scrupulously the thought of the author, the producer and in general of all those connected with the creation of the film;

6⁰ The Congress resolves that the League of Nations be requested to recommend the various governments to encourage by means analogous to those employed for other arts, and eventually to support financially films of recognised artistic value which would have no chance of success commercially;

7⁰ The Congress resolves:

1⁰ That the exhibition and international exchange of educational films tending to improve the mental, moral or physical condition of youth be encouraged by every possible means;

APPENDIX

2⁰ That each country enact the hygiene and safety measures necessary for the prevention of fire, etc.;

8⁰ The Congress notes with regret the steady monopolisation of the film industry which is gradually controlling the distribution of films the world over. It considers that for the sake of the intellectual and artistic development of the film-industry it is necessary to keep it free from the spirit that usually pervades the industries controlled by trusts;

9⁰ The Congress resolves that all who contribute to the making of films, authors, producers, manufacturers, and in general all the technical and intellectual collaborators the world over, be invited to aid in creating and in increasing the use of new technical and intellectual means, in order to make the film industry as independent as possible of the other arts;

10⁰ The Congress resolves that in all countries authors, publishers and producers shall continually endeavour to do all in their power to improve their work from the intellectual, artistic and moral point of view;

11⁰ The Congress invites industrial magnates, film-producers and benevolent patrons of arts and letters to organise competitions with annual prizes in which members of universities and artists of all kinds may take part, and present films, or parts of films, conceived by them. This may reveal hitherto unknown talents without which there can be but little artistic development of the film industry;

12⁰ The Congress resolves that efforts be made to effect

a better synchronisation of the explanatory notes to the different parts of the film;

13° Whereas the film could be the source not only of the amusement but also of the culture of the masses, and could therefore serve to bring about a better understanding between the different nations of the world and whereas, by the intermediary of the film, East and West might be brought into contact with one another, since the film is a means of explaining the history, customs and traditions of the different peoples of the world, this Congress recommends that Western films shall portray in a simple, romantic, ethical and entertaining manner the history, culture, science, and powerful industrial development of the Western nations—the heritage of humanity—and that the film should likewise serve to reveal the ancient culture, and all the wonders of the East.

RESOLUTIONS OF THE SECOND COMMISSION

National libraries of cinema films. An International Library. Means of ensuring the preservation and distribution of the best films.

Motion picture in rural districts. (Entertainment.)

The Congress recommends:

1° That a National public Film-library be established in each country, that film producers be compelled by appropriate legislation to file in this Film-library a card with a descriptive summary of each film produced; that as many films as possible, especially original negatives, should be collected;

Appendix

2⁰ That an uniform plan for the classification of films and the arrangement and contents of the files be adopted in each country;

3⁰ That an International Film-library should be established under the auspices of the League of Nations to centralise the National Catalogues and organise exchanges between one country and another;

4⁰ That the National Film-libraries and their local offices be required to supply details to the International Film-library of all films which they may acquire or produce;

5⁰ That film producers in every country should, as soon as possible, conclude an agreement concerning the standardisation of film dimensions.

RESOLUTIONS OF THE THIRD COMMISSION
Educational films.
Scientific films.
Films for technical instruction.
Films for social education (hygiene, etc.).
Agricultural films (Educational).
Study of the means of encouraging the distribution of the educational films. (Abolition of import duties, etc.).
Local and international libraries for educational films.
International exchange of educational films.

The Congress hereby recommends:

1⁰ That Governments and public health bodies and institutions for physical and mental welfare should take effective measures to obtain instruction in hygiene in

APPENDIX

schools, particularly by means of the cinema, that every moral and financial encouragement be given to producers to make good films dealing with the prevention of contagious diseases, child-welfare and pedagogy;

2⁰ That the international interchange of educational and social-welfare films should be facilitated as far as possible and relieved of all custom-duties; that the international Institute of Intellectual Co-operation should be approached with regard to the question of remitting custom-duties on such films and that a Committee should be set up for the purpose of regulating the conditions of international exchanges;

3⁰ That such a system may lead to the regular international exchange of social-welfare films with a view to attain scientific and technical perfection;

4⁰ That a research bureau, composed of producers, technical experts and educational authorities be established at the International Cinema Office to conduct investigations as to the best films on social hygiene; that at least until such a bureau is established, films of this nature should not be exhibited until they have been approved by associations, qualified to judge from the scientific, medical and pedagogical points of view, or by committees especially organised for this purpose by the proper minister in each country;

5⁰ That close co-operation be established between scholars, producers, technicians and propagandists in order to produce the best results possible for teaching hygiene through the Cinema;

APPENDIX

6⁰ That cinema-theatre managers exhibit social-hygiene films without charge;

7⁰ That the moving picture be used in a regular and methodical manner for agricultural instruction and the recreation of the rural population;

8⁰ That the valuable work carried on by governments in this field be increased and that a central office for films dealing with agricultural life be established in every state under the control of the public authorities but preserving an unofficial character and financial autonomy to accept all material assistance available;

9⁰ That apart from instructive and technical films, collections of ordinary films created for amusement only, which have passed the censor, should be made; national and international files of these films should be kept;

10⁰ That these films should be shown with the most up-to-date apparatus and with high-power lights by means of so-called "professional" projections mounted on motor-carriages;

11⁰ That the building of amusement places, where films can be shown at various functions, educational and otherwise, should be encouraged. Films might thus be shown during concerts, radiophone programmes, balls, amateur theatrical performances, physical culture, lecture, etc.;

12⁰ Concerning national and international libraries of cinema-films with particular reference to educational films, this Congress recommends:

a) That film-libraries should be organised in each

country and regular relations be maintained between the various regional film-libraries;

b) That regional film-libraries should give their attention to collect films dealing with their special area;

c) That an international film-library consisting of the best educational films of all countries should be established on practical lines;

d) That these films should be chosen in each country by the proper authorities and approved of by the Committee of the International Film-library.

e) That all such films should be accompanied by an explanatory text in the languages of the countries contributing to the international film-library and co-operating with it;

f) That a list be compiled of the best films of each country, especially of those dealing with cultural subjects, social hygiene, international reconciliation, and subjects of international interest;

g) That the international educational film-library be one of the international sections of the International Film-Office and occupy the same building.

13° That agricultural film-libraries with distributing offices for their films be established in the different countries. That the League of Nations be requested, in view of the great advantages resulting from the exhibition of agricultural films; to recommend that they should be shown in agricultural educational establishments and in rural primary schools;

14° That an International Film-library for educational films be established at the International Institute of Intellectual Co-operation of the League of Nations without delay, consisting of very competent specialists and technicians, for the purpose of compiling and maintaining a catalogue of all the educational films actually in existence;

15° That this office begins its work by establishing a universal terminology for the cinematograph;

16° Whereas the entire production of educational films should be the object of a preliminary scientific investigation, for the purpose of establishing the necessary uniformity between educational films and modern methods of education, this Congress recommends:

That this new pedagogical method of educating through the cinema and especially the standardisation of films be studied by a competent body in each country;

17° That in the preparation of educational and scientific films psychologists co-operate closely with film technicians;

18° That for the preservation of films in good condition a mixed committee, representing manufacturers, technicians and educational experts, be established in the regional offices, for the purpose of:

a) Organising the staff to distribute the films;

b) Delivering certificates of proficiency to this staff;

c) Examining the films and apparatus periodically;

19° That the League of Nations recommends, as favouring the wider application of the cinema to education, that all governments pass appropriate legislative measures, based on common principles, to remove all import and export duties from educational films of all kinds and from hygiene-films, certified as such by official authorities, when the sale, renting or exchange of such films takes place between organisations or individuals recognised by the competent authorities of the particular state;

20° That an international catalogue of scientific films containing the following information furnished by the owners of the films be established: length of film, date made, name of author, name of the publisher, short description written by the author (maximum 20 lines), sources from which the film was made.

This catalogue should be compiled according to the decimal system of classification in use at Brussels and on a card index;

21° That national committees should be established in all countries to classify films as follows:

a) Scientic research films;

b) Films to be used in university-work;

c) Secondary-school films;

d) Films of general instruction;

22° The Congress moves that an international inquiry be undertaken on the different efforts made to increase the valuable work of the cinema in working-class centres.

That an inquiry be made to discover the best means of increasing and improving this work by international co-operation.

That an International Labour Office undertake the inquiry, for which it has already gathered the primary essentials, in connection with the International Institute of Intellectual Co-operation, the government, public bodies and associations;

APPENDIX

23⁰ That the producers of films should make documentary and scientific films as interesting as possible; that public administration encourage either by granting subsidies or facilitating distribution, or by the purchase of collections, the production of those films which for the moment is, and which for some time probably will be less remunerative than the production of amusement-films;

That the organisations for popular education by means of the cinema, compose cinema-programmes of proper length, and of sufficient variety, so that the worker may find in them the relaxation which he needs and at the same time the culture which he demands;

24⁰ The Congress moves that in each community there should be a room either in the school, or the townhall, where popular cinematograph performances may be given under hygienic and safe conditions and with all technical equipment necessary for the success of such performances. That governments and public authorities should come to the aid of municipal authorities when necessary, in order to erect these centres of popular instruction which will in general tend to raise the intellectual standard not only of small communities but of the nation and of the whole humanity,

25⁰ That all the facilities of distribution which are granted to the educational film, either within a country's frontiers or beyond, should be extended to the film for popular education; that all the organisation and equipment (catalogues, film-libraries, etc.) available for the former should be equally well adapted to the needs of the latter; that, if an International Cinema Office is estab-

APPENDIX

lished in Paris, the interests of popular education by means of the cinema should be attended to by a representative in the executive body, in the meetings, and in the permanent Secretariat;

26° That due authorisation be given by various professors to their students to do reasearch work for their theses with the aid of the cinematograph.

27° That a press campaign be undertaken by the International Cinema Office to persuade the public that the cinema ought to hold an important place in the social and intellectual life of a nation;

28° That in all Normal schools a course in cinematographic work should be established to train teachers to use the cinema in teaching;

29° That there should be established an International Association of Cinematographic Educational Press, comprising the directors of publications specialised in this matter;

30° That the International Confederation of Students should endeavour to form University Committees of professors and students, and national committees in each country, with a view to encourage the production of scientific films; that the International Bureau and national bodies should co-ordinate the efforts of producers by indicating the scientific films which are required, and obviating useless duplication; that state and public organisations and the different faculties should create a fund for subsidising secondary and university educational films; that scholarships should be founded, to be allotted for research work on the cinematograph;

APPENDIX

31⁰ Whereas the cinematograph could and should fulfil an important function in teaching children the first principles of social hygiene; and whereas the Assembly of the League of Nations on September 26, 1924, passed a resolution according to which the child should be the first to be protected against social scourges, of which one of the most appalling is alcohol, this Congress hereby recommends:

That anti-alcoholic-propaganda films, especially made for purposes of primary education, be placed at the disposal of the masters of each school by the public authorities;

32⁰ That the International Cinematograph - Office should give detailed instructions for the selection of titles and explanatory notices for pictures in order to facilitate and increase their international distribution;

33⁰ That the exhibitions of great educational films in public halls should be encouraged, and that teachers in co-operation with managers of motion-picture theatres should organise special performances for school children, which would ensure an appreciable increase in receipts and be at the same time an excellent means of propaganda.

That these performances specially reserved for school children should be free from all taxes;

34⁰ That the role of the bodies seeking to centralise educational films should be limited, and that in no case they should be called on to produce films likely to compete with private bodies, the latter being always obliged to make intellectual and financial efforts deserving of legitimate remuneration;

APPENDIX

35⁰ That subsidies in aid of instruction through the medium of the cinematograph should be included in the budgets of the different countries, taking into consideration the proceeds accruing from the cinema tax and on the understanding that no new burdens are, in consequence laid on the cinematographic industry.

RESOLUTIONS OF THE FOURTH COMMISSION
The legal status of the motion picture.
Author's rights. Artistic property with regard to the film.
Conditions of work.

The following are the conclusions reached from the study of authors' rights in film productions by the 4th Committee:

A) With reference to the law actually in force it was decided:

1⁰ That the authors of a cinematographic production are those who have conferred upon this production its original artistic form, in the case of dramatic films, the author of the scenario, the producer, the actors and in some cases the scene-painters and photographers;

2⁰ That according to the common law, the above mentioned authors are collectively entitled to all authors' rights in their common creation, share and share alike, unless otherwise stipulated by the parties;

3⁰ That the financial backer of a film, who very often has to be called upon because of the heavy expenses involved in its production, in general acquires authors' rights by contract with the actual authors and in all cases where actors and producers are in receipt of salaries;

4⁰ That although the authors are free to alienate their authors' rights, either in the manner specified in three or in other ways, their personal rights are inalienable.

5⁰ That, by virtue of this right, the aforementioned authors have the power of insisting that their names shall be mentioned in the film, and of resisting any modification, or mutilation of their work which distorts their original conception of the subject.

B) Concerning the future international regulation of authors' rights the committee deems it necessary:

1⁰ That an international convention should be concluded as soon as possible to define in a general way the rights of authors in relation to the cinema;

2⁰ That this conception should not, like the Berne convention, envisage only the protection of foreign works, but should be based on principals applicable to foreigners and nationals alike;

3⁰ That to obtain, or at least to facilitate, the adhesion of all states and particularly of film-producing countries (which is indispensable), all statutes of the future convention should refer exclusively to cinematographic productions; and that these statutes should be drafted with the pliancy of form and moderation that is necessary if they are to be generally if not universally, accepted;

4⁰ That, subject to the findings of the enquiry eventually to be undertaken by the League of Nations, the future convention should comprise:

a) The definition of authors' rights in relation to cinematographic productions;

b) A clause defining the authors of cinematographic productions in conformity to the existing law, and comprising the persons mentioned above under A, n⁰ 1;

c) A clause regulating, in the simplest possible manner, the necessary procedure to assure an author's rights in a film;

d) Another clause fixing the duration of the right;

e) A clause establishing the presumption of the loss of that right in all cases of salaried engagement, except when otherwise stipulated by contract;

f) A statute confirming the personal right of authors of cinematographic work, rights which should be defined, in accordance with existing principles, as destined to safeguard all their moral interests, and as giving them, in particular, power to insist on mention of their names in the films, and to prevent alterations in their work which have the effect of distorting their conception;

g) Lastly, a statute for the purpose of settling disputes which may arise in the application of the convention, and, for this end, authorising the Permanent Court of International Justice to decide questions concerning the interpretation of the convention, appointing, as an arbitration body, a committee composed of representatives of film-producing countries, to which interested parties might apply directly.

The following resolutions, submitted by the 4th Committee, have been adopted:

1⁰ That an enquiry should be undertaken:

a) Into the existence, and, in the event of an affirmative result, into the exact nature of the professional diseases of cinematographical artists and technical workers;

b) Into the scientific, technical and legal means taken in the different countries for avoiding these professional diseases, or at least for diminishing their injurious effect;

c) Into the scientific, technical, or legal measures which might he generalised and embodied in an international convention;

And that the International Labour Office should undertake this enquiry with the support of the governments, scholars, technical workers of every kind, organisers, employers and organisation of employees;

2⁰ The Congress recommends that the question of the employment of children of either sex under 15 years of age to take part in cinematographic pictures should be submitted for study to the International Labour Office with a view to a future international convention;

3⁰ The Congress further recommends, that the public exhibition of films should be no longer subject to particular regulations apart from the necessary measures to ensure a decent standard of morality;

4⁰ That Customs' formalities concerning the distribution of films and of materials intended for the making of films should be simplified, and that this question should be submitted for study to the Transport Committee of the League of Nations;

5⁰ That a permanent and autonomous Committee should be set up, entrusted with investigation, from the international point of view, both of the international status of cinematographic art and industry, and of the moral as well as material rights of those interested in the industry.

The results of this enquiry will be forwarded directly to the competent bodies of the League of Nations, in the first place to the International Institute of Intellectual Co-operation, to the International Institute of Private Law in Rome, and to the United International Bureaux of Industrial, Literary and Artistic Property, at Berne.

RESOLUTIONS OF THE FIFTH COMMISSION

Enrollment and selection of artists and technicians of the motion-picture industry. Motion-picture schools.
Syndicates, trade-unions and federations.
Pensions, annuities and rest-houses.

The Congress recommends:

1º That private cinema schools should be registered and inspected;

2º That in all film-producing countries courses in film work, under official auspices, should be inaugurated, on the same plane as any other artistic course;

3º That an artistic and technical cinema-manual should be published and brought within the reach of all film artists and technicians;

4º That an International Union of Cinema-artists should be formed, along the lines of the International Theatrical Union, created after the Berlin Congress, unless an International Cinema-Section should be formed

APPENDIX

in the latter Union, and that its title be changed to the International Union of Theatrical and Cinema Artists;

5⁰ That special Professional Associations should be formed as soon as possible in each country;

6⁰ That a Permanent International Committee should be founded composed of the representatives of all the cinema-associations; that it should work for, encourage and bring about the union, in one Universal Cinema-Association, of all branches of the cinema industry;

7⁰ That Mutual-Insurance Societies should be formed in all countries where they do not already exist, and that an effective system of liaison should be established between these different societies;

8⁰ That in each country schools under the control of the official authorities should train and qualify operators in photography and projection. These schools should confer an official certificate to which international recognition might be given by the International Cinema Bureau;

9⁰ That an International Federation of Cinematograph Operators and Technicians should be formed, to further the development of the artistic side of the cinematographic industry.

RESOLUTIONS OF THE SIXTH COMMISSION
Motion-picture corporative press.

The Congress recommends:

1⁰ That articles in the Cinematographic Press should never be reproduced by other journals without a reference to the author, and to the journal in which they were originally published;

2⁰ That producers of films or those who rent them should not utilise for publicity purposes, without the consent of the author, any criticisms appearing in the press, nor quote extracts from them which might misrepresent the spirit of the original article;

3⁰ That the archivists and librarians of the entire world should appeal for the general use of "cine-type" in order to obtain authentic reproduction of all perishable works;

4⁰ That the "fakes" and devices employed by producers which, while protecting the lives of the artists at the same time create for the public the illusion of reality, should not be disclosed in the press, especially in that intended for the general public;

5⁰ That as soon as possible an International Federation of the Cinematographic Press should be founded, uniting the national associations of all countries to protect the professional interests of journalists, and in the interest of the cinematographic art.

RESOLUTIONS OF THE SEVENTH COMMISSION
Relations between the Cinema and other arts.
Music.
The Plastic Arts.
The Decorative Arts.

The Congress recommends:
1⁰ That the great film-producing countries of the entire

world should henceforward enter in closer relations with the schools of decorative art existing in each country; that they should appoint instructors in the technique of cinematographic art in these schools, who will give courses, for architects, decorators, painters, etc.; anxious to learn the artistic technique peculiar to the cinema, so that they may adapt their creative efforts to the needs of the cinema. Moreover, just as some producing firms have already established schools for training cinema-artists, others could, if they are of sufficient importance, inaugurate courses on their own premises, which artists who wish to learn the technique of the cinema might attend;

2⁰ That the respective Governments should take a keen interest in the establishment of courses in decorative art, applied to the cinema, and should more or less supervise them;

3⁰ That to facilitate and promote the aesthetic progress of the cinema, producers should endeavour more and more to avail themselves of all forms of expression, form and colour, so that the cinematograph which is above all an art expressing forms in movement, may be profitably employed for exhibiting colours in movement;

4⁰ That the International Institute of Intellectual Co-operation should endeavour to secure the foundation of a Nobel Prize for the Cinematograph.

RESOLUTIONS OF THE EIGHTH COMMISSION
Study of the organisation and function of an International

Bureau of the motion-picture connected with the League of Nations.

First Resolution

Whereas it is the sentiment of the Congress that a permanent body is necessary for the execution of the decisions of various congresses, and for protecting in general the interests of the cinema-industry, and whereas it is the sentiment of this Congress that such a Committee should be entrusted with the following tasks:

A statistical survey of the cinema industry from the points of view of production, markets and public taste (amount of production, number of films exported and imported, prices, capacity and attendance of cinema-theatres, government regulations, etc.):

Investigation of the legal problems of the cinema, such as authors' rights, proprietary rights, etc. (problems concerning the relations between employers and employees fall within the jurisdiction of the International Labour Office.)

Investigation of problems involved in an international agreement for the exhibition of films (international censorship, custom-duties, treatment of subjects of national interest, etc.)

Investigation of technical problems capable of an international solution (standardisation-processes for preserving films, professional training, etc.)

International stimuli to develop cinematographic art (prizes, scholarships, International Cinema Museum, establishment of film-libraries, catalogues, etc.).

APPENDIX

Investigation of methods of improving education in all grades by the employment of the moving-picture.

Conciliatory intervention with a view to the amicable settlement of certain disputes.

Preparation for subsequent Congresses.

This Congress hereby resolves that a provisional international committee be appointed immediately with an office in the League of Nations and be entrusted with the tasks of:

1. Carrying out the resolutions of the Congress;
2. Preparing for the next Congress;
3. Examining eventually the question of an international cinema-organisation.

That the President of this Committee be a national of the country in which the next Congress is to be held.

And it is further resolved that a permanent Committee composed of the following members be founded:

	MM.
Austria................	Pr. Carl HUEBL.
Belgium...............	FOLLEBOUCKT.
England..............	DOVENER
France...............	AUBERT. BREZILLON. RIVOIRE. BURGUET
Germany.............	BAUSBACK. GRUNE. ROSENTHAL. MELAMERSON.

Appendix

Holland...............	HAMBURGER.
Hungary...............	KOVACT.
Italy..................	DE FEO.
Sweden................	MAGNUSSON.
Switzerland...........	DR. IMHOF.

M. Julien LUCHAIRE, Director of the International Institute of Intellectual Co-operation.

M. Louis GALLIE, Secretary General of the International Confederation of Intellectual Workers.

The President of the International Federation of the Cinematographic Press.

A representative of the International Labour Office.

A representative of the International Federation of Students.

A representative of the International Literary and Artistic Association.

And finally, it is resolved that the Committee should co-operate with other members, in order to assure the representation of different countries and interests, particularly of associations of authors, producers, technical workers, artists, members of the teaching professions and social workers.

Second Resolution

The Congress,

taking cognizance of the proposal of the German delegation concerning the next International Cinematograph Congress,

Appendix

hereby resolves to hold that session at Berlin and instructs the German delegation to make the necessary preparations, and to co-operate for that purpose with the provisional International Committee.

APPENDIX 4

Censorship Regulations.

The following censorship regulations appear in the 1926 *Film Year Book*:

MARYLAND STATE BOARD OF CENSORS' STANDARDS,
211 N. Calvert St., Baltimore, Md.

Personnel: Dr. George Heller, Chairman, 1937 Gough St.; Asa G. Sharp, Vice-Chairman, Knollwood, Md.; Marie W. Pressman, Secretary, Wyman Park Apts., Baltimore.

Improper exhibition of feminine underwear.

Bedroom and bathroom scenes of suggestive and indecent character.

Offensive vulgarity and indecent gestures.

Women promiscuously taking up men.

Indelicate sexual situations.

Nude figures.

Indecorous dancing.

Attempted criminal assaults upon women.

Excessive drunkenness, especially in women.

Overpassionate love scenes.

Discussion of the consummation of marriage.

Cruelty and abuse of children.

Crime condoned.

Impropriety in dress.

Appendix

Men and women living together without marriage and in adultery.

Prostitution and procuration of women.

Excessive use of firearms.

Disrespect for the law, third degree scenes.

Doubtful characters exalted to heroes.

Maternity scenes, women in labor.

Infidelity on part of husband justifying adultery on part of wife.

Sacrifice of woman's honor held as laudable.

Justification of the deliberate adoption of a life of immorality.

Disorderly houses.

Use of opium and other habit-forming drugs (instructive details).

Counterfeiting.

White slave stories.

Drugging and chloroforming victims for criminal purposes.

Gruesome murders, actual stabbing and shooting of persons.

Seductions and attempted seductions treated without due restraint.

Burning and branding of persons.

Profanity in titles.

Salacious titles and captions.

Advocacy of the doctrine of free love.

Scenes indicating that a criminal assault has been perpetrated on a woman.

Suicide compacts, suicide scenes.

APPENDIX

Executions and lynchings and burlesque hangings.

Deeds of violence, lighting and throwing bombs, **arson**, especially to conceal crimes, train wrecking.

Modus operandi of criminals.

Birth control, malpractice.

Suggestions of incest.

Morbid presentations of insanity.

Prolonged and harrowing death scenes.

Venereal disease inherited or acquired.

Irreverent treatment of religious observances and beliefs.

Inflammatory scenes and titles calculated to stir up racial hatred or antagonistic relations between labor and capital.

NEW YORK STANDARDS

Chief offices, Candler Bldg., W. 42nd St., New York City.

J. H. Walrach, Chairman; Mrs. Elizabeth W. Colbert and Arthur Levy.

Albany—Wm. E. Leonard, the State Capitol.

Buffalo—Mrs. Orpha Stucki, 32 Argyle Park.

A statement issued by the Motion Picture Commission of the State of New York says that it "has not established any fixed rules or standards for the judging of pictures except those prescribed by the statute creating the Commission."

No motion picture will be licensed or a permit granted for its exhibition within the State of New York, which may be classified, or any part thereof, as obscene, indecent, immoral, inhuman, sacrilegious, or which is of such a character that its exhibition would tend to corrupt morals or incite to crime.

"The Commission has deemed it wise not to attempt to formulate fixed standards or rules for the reviewing of pictures, but rather to examine such picture on its merits to determine whether the film, or any portion of it, violates any provisions of the statute."

NEW YORK

In January the New York Board reported for the work of the preceding year, and showed the following eliminations:

Films with cuts	627
Films without cuts	2,241
Features condemned in toto	34
Total number eliminations	3,780

The eliminations are classed as follows:

Scenes eliminated	3,214
Titles eliminated	566
Reels examined	9,063

The following is a statement of the grounds upon which the eliminations were made. In some cases, eliminations were made on more than one ground:

Indecent	624
Inhuman	924
Tending to incite to crime	1,318
Immoral or tending to corrupt morals	816
Sacrilegious	66

APPENDIX

Obscene..................................... 32

The films from which eliminations were made may be classified as follows:

Dramas...................................... 328
Comedies.................................... 115
Comedy dramas.............................. 61
Serials....................................... 101
News... 11
Educational.................................. 3
Cartoons..................................... 1
Miscellaneous................................ 7

OHIO STATE BOARD OF CENSORS
233 S. High St., Columbus

The Ohio State Board of Censors is composed of three women, under the direction of Vernon M. Rigel, Director of Education, Columbus. Assistants: Mrs. Mary B. Williams, Miss Susannah M. Warfield, 1184 Bryden Road.

All scenes which are obscene, salacious, indecent, immoral, or teach false ethics, such as the following, should be eliminated:

a) Sex.

1. Productions which emphasize and exaggerate sex appeal or depict scenes therein exploiting interest in sex in an immoral or suggestive form or manner.

2. Those based upon white slavery or commercialized vice or scenes showing the procurement of women or any of the activities attendant upon this traffic.

APPENDIX

3. Those thematically making prominent an illicit love affair which tends to make virtue odious and vice attractive.

4. Scenes which exhibit nakedness or persons scantily and suggestively dressed, particularly suggestive bedroom and bathroom scenes and scenes of inciting dances.

5. Scenes which unnecessarily prolong expressions or demonstrations of passionate love.

6. Stories or scenes which are vulgar and portray improper gestures, postures and attitudes.

7. Scenes which tend to give the idea that sexual vice accompanied by luxury makes vice excusable.

b) *Vice, Crime and Violence.*

1. Theme predominantly concerned with the underworld or vice or crime, and like scenes; unless the scenes are a part of an essential conflict between good and evil.

2. Stories which make crime, drunkenness and gambling, and like scenes which show the use of narcotics and other unnatural practices dangerous to social morality, attractive.

3. Stories and scenes which may instruct the immature and susceptible in methods of committing crime or by cumulative processes emphasize crime and the commission of crime.

4. Stories or scenes which unduly emphasize bloodshed and violence without justification in the structure of the body.

5. Scenes which tend to produce approval of business institutions or conditions that naturally tend to degrade and deprave mankind.

APPENDIX

6. Productions whose tendency is to incite sympathy for those engaged in parasitical or criminal activities.

7. Productions that teach fatalism or the futility of individual resistance of adversity.

8. Expiation of crime by some act of physical bravery.

9. Crime must not be made attractive and the punishment must be clear.

10. Plays which exhibit prominently movie stars who have committed crimes or whose good names are in question, judged by generally accepted moral standards.

c) Respect for Social Institutions.

1. Scenes which ridicule or deprecate public officials, officers of the law, and the United States Army, the United States Navy or other governmental authority, or which tend to weaken the authority of the law.

2. Scenes which offend the religious belief of any person, creed or sect or ridicules ministers, priests, rabbis or recognized leaders of any religious sect, and also which are disrespectful to objects or symbols used in connection with any religion.

3. National, racial and class hatred should not be fostered.

d) Subtitles.

1. Titles and subtitles should not be salacious.

The Ohio Board of Censors does not publish a list of rejections made over any given period.

PENNSYLVANIA STATE BOARD OF CENSORS' STANDARDS, 1222 Vine St., Philadelphia

The members of the Board are: Harry L. Knapp,

APPENDIX

Chairman; Mrs. Edward C. Niver, Vice-chairman; Henry Starr Richardson, Secretary, and Joseph A. Berrier, executive clerk. Branch offices are located at Telegraph Bldg., Harrisburg, and Vandergritt Bldg., Pittsburgh.

The Board will not approve the following:

1. What is immoral, indecent, obscene, salacious, objectionably vulgar or contains improper suggestions or incentive; what is unduly gruesome, morbid, shocking, sordid or debased; what is decadent or unwholesome; cruelty to animals, abnormal brutality.

2. What reflects upon National fame, patriotism, self-respect, or adversely affects international relations; attacks or ridicules public institutions or organizations, or constituted authority in law enforcement or performance of duty; what may produce riots, mob violence, defiance of proper exercise of authority or suggests action tending to same.

3. What reflects upon, is prejudicial to, or ridicules particular races, creeds, religious beliefs, priests or ministers thereof; irreverent use of religious symbols, the name of the Deity, or Jesus; blasphemy, profanity, excepting when the latter may be essential to scene or characterization.

4. Glorification of crime, criminals or criminal acts, and all that makes crime, criminals or criminal acts alluring, heroic or sympathetic; depictions informative as to commission of crime or evasion of detection; what through the power of suggestion would induce commission of crime or improper acts, or set up false standards of conduct or living.

APPENDIX

5. Views showing the use of habit-forming drugs or narcotics; information as to the sale and distribution of same.

During the past fiscal year the Pennsylvania Censor Board rejected 22 subjects, representing 116 reels, and approved 10,608 subjects, embracing 16,720 reels. There were 23,704 eliminations made, covering 3,034 subjects and 15,282 reels. The Board collected $97,210 from all sources and expended $61,169.

Pennsylvania Non-Theatrical Regulations

The following regulations were adopted in 1922 by the Pennsylvania State Department of Labor and Industry concerning the showings of non-theatrical firms:

1. No permit will be issued for any auditoriums for the use of flammable film where an enclosing, standard-fireproof booth is not provided for the projection machine.

2. No permit will be issued for any auditorium located at, above or below the first floor of a building where it is intended to use flammable film.

3. No permit will be issued for any auditorium located above the second floor of a building.

4. No permit will be issued for any auditorium for the use of any balcony for any purpose other than to accommodate the projection machine, booth and accessory equipment.

5. No permit will be issued for an auditorium without an enclosing, standard fireproof booth, where the machine to be used has not been approved by the Industrial Board for the use intended.

6. No permit will be issued for any auditorium where

Appendix

the machine operator has not first applied for and received the permit required by the Industrial Board Rulings.

7. To obtain a permit for any auditorium, floor plans or sketches, in duplicate, showing aisles, seating arrangements, and all exit facilities, with all dimensions plainly marked and drawn to scale, must be submitted to the office of the Chief Inspector, Department of Labor and Industry.

FOREIGN CENSORSHIP REGULATIONS

British Board of Film Censors, London, England

Indecorous, ambiguous and irreverent titles and subtitles.

Cruelty to animals.

Drunken scenes carried to excess.

The modus operandi of criminals.

Cruelty to young infants, and excessive cruelty to and torture of adults, especially women.

Profuse bleeding.

Unnecessary exhibition of women's underclothing.

Nude figures.

Offensive vulgarity and impropriety in conduct and dress.

Indecorous dancing.

Excessively passionate love scenes.

Improper bathing scenes.

Scenes tending to disparage public characters and institutions.

APPENDIX

Realistic horrors of warfare.

Scenes and incidents in war calculated to afford information to the enemy.

Scenes in which the king and officers in uniform are seen in an odious light.

Executions.

Gruesome murders and strangulation scenes.

Vitriol throwing.

The use of drugs, e. g. opium, morphine, cocaine, etc.

Subjects dealing with the white slave traffic.

Subjects dealing with the deliberate seduction of girls.

"First night" scenes.

Indelicate sexual situations.

Situations accentuating delicate marital relations.

Views of men and women in bed together.

Illicit sexual relationships.

Prostitution and procuration.

Disparagement of the institution of marriage.

Misrepresentation of police methods.

Surgical operations.

Commitment of crime by children.

Criminal poisoning by dissemination of germs.

Practice of the third degree by the police.

Branding men and animals.

Women fighting with knives.

Exaltation of doubtful characters as heroes.

Making the sacrifice of a woman's virtue laudable.

Infidelity on part of a husband justifying adultery of a wife.

Confinement and puerperal pains.

Appendix

Views of dead bodies.
Subjects in which sympathy is enlisted for criminals.
Animals gnawing men, women and children.
Realistic scenes of epilepsy.
Insistence upon the inferiority of colored races.
Advocacy of the doctrine of free love.
Salacious wit.
The perpetration of criminal assaults on women.
Scenes depicting the effect of venereal diseases, inherited or acquired.
Incidents suggestive of incestuous relations.
Themes and references to "race suicide."
Scenes laid in disorderly houses.
Materialization of the conventional figure of Christ.

During the year, however, President T. P. O'Connor issued a bulletin to the trade with reference to "crime" films, which, in part, said:

"In March, 1917, I addressed a letter to the trade dealing with the question of 'crime' films. In view of a recrudescence of films coming within this category, I think it well to recapitulate the principles then laid down, which are as follows:

"*a*) No serial dealing with 'crime' will be examined except as a whole.

"*b*) No film in which 'crime is the dominant feature, and not merely an episode in a story, will receive a certificate.

"*c*) No film will be passed in which the methods of "crime" are shown or illustrated.

APPENDIX

"*d*) No 'crime' film will be passed, even in cases where, at the end of the film, retribution is supposed to have fallen on the criminal, or where actual crime is treated from the comic point of view.

"This question of 'crime' as a main theme for films has been further accentuated of late by a tendency to present stories in which sympathy is enlisted for the criminals, and in which they are made out to be either the victims of unavoidable circumstances or of early environment, and as such, to be held more or less irresponsible for their social delinquencies. There is also an almost invariable tendency in such films to hold up the recognized authority of the law either to odium or ridicule, a procedure of which the constant repetition cannot be considered to be in the best interests of society.

For these reasons, the Board will have to refrain from issuing its certificate for films of this character, and think it advisable to give this public note of warning in the hope that it may have some effect upon producers, both in this country and abroad."

FRANCE

"The Journal Officiel" of May 24, 1925 (page 4841), publishes a decree of the Ministry of Public Instruction and Fine Arts making further amendments to the decree of December 11, 1924, which laid down certain regulations for the taking of motion pictures in public buildings and grounds.

The original decree required that no motion pictures

APPENDIX

should be taken in such places without authorization from the Ministry of Public Instruction and Fine Arts. The amendment is now made that authorization will only be given where the scenario contains scenes presenting an actual historic character. Such a character will be considered as presented either when the scenes actually form a part of the plot for which authorization to film is asked; or in an imaginary plot in which historic characters have actually figured in the places shown.

The second part of the new decree requires that inspectors shall be appointed for the purpose of seeing that no damage is done to the building or grounds during the filming. These inspectors are to be paid by the film company concerned.

French censors will not allow:

Licentious or immoral titles or subtitles;

Scenes of capital punishment;

Scenes showing burglary in general, but particularly in banks, postoffices or private houses;

Murder scenes must be reduced to a minimum;

As a rule, no immoral or violent scenes;

No opium smoking, no displeasing Mexicans, Chinese or negroes;

No violent strikes;

No unpatriotic manifestations;

No scenes likely to hurt the feelings of foreigners;

No jokes on religious subjects;

No scenes showing ill treatment of children and animals.

APPENDIX

In "The Morals of the Movie," Dr. Oberholtzer, formerly secretary of the Pennsylvania State Board of Censors, says (p. 107) : "Since 1916 France has had a commission of five members to examine and control the exhibition of film. Unless it be accompanied by a certificate which they have issued, no picture may be shown in any theatre of the country. So long ago as in 1913 the prefects of the departments were authorized to prohibit "les representations, par les cinematographes, des crimes, executions, capitales et d'une facon generale de toutes scenes a charactere immoral et scandaleux."

INDIA

Bombay

From Wilbur Keblinger, American Consul

Laws and Regulations

The Bombay Board of Film Censors was created by the Bombay Presidency Government in July, 1920, under authority of the Government of India, "Cinematograph" Act 1918 (II of 1918) as amended by the Cinematograph (Amendment) Act.

Films Examined

Since the creation of the Board and up to June 23, 1925, 4,164 films have been examined. Of this number 15 have failed of certification and 135 have been passed after certain deletions have been made.

Co-operation of Indian Boards

There are four Censor Boards in India and these Boards exchange information as to the number of pictures examined, their names and whether they have been certified or delected.

Suggestions of Bombay Board to Inspectors, General Principles

1. No generally and rigidly applicable rules of censorship can be laid down.

2. It is essential to be consistent but impossible to aim at strictly logical decisions.

3. Each film must be judged on its own merits.

4. Nothing should be approved which in the Inspector's honest opinion is calculated to demoralize an audience of any section of it.

5. The following kind of films are liable to objection. Those which:

a) Extenuate crime; or which familiarize young people with crime, so as to make them conclude that theft, robbery, and crimes of violence are normal incidents of ordinary life and not greatly to be reprobated; or which exhibit the actual poses and make the methods of crime the chief methods by which thieves carry out their purposes; and make the methods of crime the chief theme; or in which crime is the dominant feature of a serial and not merely an episode in the story.

b) Undermine the teachings of morality, by showing vice in an attractive form even though retribution follows; or casting a halo of glory or success around the heads of the vicious; or suggesting that a person is morally justified in succumbing to temptation in order to escape from bad circumstances or uncongenial work or bringing into contempt the institution of marriage; of suggesting abnormal sexual relations or lowering the sacredness of the family ties.

c) Exhibit indecorous dress or absolute nudity of the living (except infants and small children) or nude statues of figures in suggestive positions.

d) Bring into contempt public characters acting as such, e. g. soldiers wearing His Majesty's uniforms, ministers of religion, ministers of the crown, ambassadors and official representatives of foreign nations, judges, the police, civil servants of government, etc.

e) Are calculated to wound the susceptibility of foreign nations or of members of any religion.

f) Are calculated or possibly intended to foment social unrest and discontent, i.e. not scenes merely depicting realistically the hard conditions under which people live, but depicting the violence that results in an actual conflict between capital and labor.

g) Are calculated to promote disaffection or resistance to Government or to promote a breach of law and order.

6. Inspectors should consider the impression likely to be made on the average audience in India, which includes a not inconsiderable proportion of illiterate people or those of immature judgment.

7. Inspectors should remember that a film may be in itself innocent yet dangerous because of the bad reputation of the book it reproduces, and that a book may be harmless but a film of it dangerous.

8. Inspectors should distinguish between errors of

conduct caused by love, even guilty love, and those that result from the pursuit of lust.

9. Objections to films may be removed by the Board either: (1) by modification or removal of titles or subtitles or of the film narrative or description; or (2) by cutting out portions of films, or (3) by both.

10. Two inspectors or the secretary and one inspector should be present at the inspection of a film.

The objections of the Bombay Board to certain scenes, etc., practically follow those of the British Board of Censors of London.

Suggestions for India Censors

Censorship suggestions to American trade for India, made by Consul General A. W. Weddell, Calcutta:

There are three boards of censorship in India—at Bombay, Calcutta and Rangoon—which represent the educational, religious, political and commercial organizations of those cities. The charge for censoring a picture is 5 rupees per 100 feet, and the picture is usually viewed by one paid official before its public exhibition.

From interviews with the various operators in Calcutta, the following suggestions are made as to producing and exporting American films to India: (1) A reduction in price by the manufacturers for exhibition rights in India, (2) more caution as to the nature of the film sent to India, (3) more attention to detail in films depicting India for the distribution of films and general management of the trade.

APPENDIX

ITALY

La Gazetta Ufficiala de Rome of December 6 last has published a Royal Decree of September 24, 1923, approving of the regulations of Supervision of Cinematographic Films.

We reproduce herewith some points of these regulations:

No film can be projected in the Kingdom without first having been examined by the competent Service of the Home Department. In order that the film may be submitted to this examination, it is previously necessary to present to the Home Department a recapitulation of the scenario, same has to be accompanied by an application in duplicate, drawn up on stamped paper and addressed to the Central Bureau of Cinematographic Supervision (Home Department). However, the presentation of this recapitulation is not compulsory for films of actualities and instruction bearing on one of the following subjects:

a) Sports, monuments, works of art, towns and scenery.

b) Morals and habits of the populations, natural history, phenomena and scientific experiments.

c) Agricultural works, agricultural methods, installations and industrial experiments.

The "nulla osta" of the projection cannot be granted if the subject of the film is immoral, contrary to the prestige of the nation, the good international relations, the dignity of public installations or authorities, officials and agents of the public forces or army or if same contain acts of cruelty or repulsive scenes also in regard to animals, delinquences or exciting suicides, surgical operations or hypnotic phenomena, and in general all those scenes based on subjects apt to induce to misdemeanor or disturb the public order.

The request for "nulla osta" has therefore to be addressed to the Home Department, accompanied by the film in question and has to be drawn up in duplicate one specimen on stamped paper, drawn up in accordance with the example reproduced at the end of this article. This request has to be made for the account and in the name of the importer by the person who legally represents him.

Foreign firms have to install a branch office in the Kingdom and appoint a legal representative and to submit themselves to the stipulations of articles 230, etc., of the Commercial Code. The fulfillment of these obligations has to be proved by the production of a certificate issued by a public notary or by the Court's Chancery. The two specimens of the request have to be identical and have to contain:

a) The indication of the firm for whom the demand is made, its seat, also the name and domicile of their representative in Italy.

b) The indication of the title, the manufacturer's name and the exact length of the film.

c) A detailed description of the title, the subtitles and of the explanatory text, in the order of the projection, so that in projecting the film the text corresponds exactly with the scenes it refers to.

d) A declaration certifying that the film is for the first time submitted to the Censor.

Appendix

The titles and subtitles both on the film and on the copies of the request have to be drawn up in the Italian language. They can also be written in a foreign language, but in this case only on the condition that they are accompanied by an accurate and exact translation in the Italian language.

The tax for the revision of the contents, the subject and that pertaining to each meter of the declared length of the film has to be directly paid in to the Registration Bureau (Manomorta econcessioni governative) in Rome; or either by postal order to the same Bureau. The Receiver issues in each case a special receipt which has to be fixed on the request hereunder.

If it is found that the length of the film exceeds that of the length given on the declaration, the revision is suspended until the person interested has proved that he has deposited the supplementary tax.

In case that the ministerial or prefectoral "nulla osta" is refused or if same is only granted on special conditions, the person interested can within a period of thirty days appeal to the Home Department. Unless he sends a written statement declaring that he renounces the right thus granted to him until settlement of the litigation has been made or after the term for the presentation of the appeal has expired.

JAPAN

Rough translation of Decree No. 10, Department of Home Affairs, Tokyo. National Film Censorship Regula-

APPENDIX

tions to go into effect July 1, 1925. As announced in Official Gazette of May 26:

1. All films to be exhibited to the public are subject to censorship.

2. Appplicants are required to present two copies of the story of each film to the Department of Home Affairs, except films containing pictures of current events, such as news reels, which may be exhibited by permission of prefectural governors.

3. Government will stamp or seal each film and story, (translation) passed.

4. The period for which censorship will be effective is three years.

5. The censor (inspector) is authorized to take action limiting the period of effectiveness or the districts where films are to be shown as considered necessary.

6. Censors are authorized, in case they find films injurious to the public order, customs or health, to prohibit showing of films or restrict such exhibition, even though previously authorized.

7. If owners of films desire to change titles of films they must secure permission to do so.

8. Charges for censorship will be 5 sen per 3 meters of original film and 2 sen per 3 meters for copies or duplicates of the same film, which are submitted within three months after passing of original, and 2 sen for any required reinspection of the same film within 6 months of having been passed.

For such films as news reels, etc.:

APPENDIX

Charges for inspection by prefectural authorities (Governors of Prefectures) will be 1 sen per three meters.

All above charges will be waived in cases where the authorities consider it advisable, i.e. when it would be considered a public service to do so.

9. Government officials of the Censorship Bureau and police shall be free to enter motion picture theatres or places of exhibition at any time and to request to see the story translations or explanations of films.

10. In case owners of films spoil the official seal or lose the story books or seals thereon, they can request new seals by stating reasons.

11. Penalties:

Persons will be subject to arrest or imprisonment or fines of amounts up to Yen 100 for violation of the following regulations:

a) Violation of Article 1 above.

b) In case of false representation in the documents required under Articles 2 and 10.

c) Violation of Articles 5 and 6.

12. Persons will be subjected to fines for violation of the following provisions:

a) Article 6.

b) Article 7.

c) Article 9.

13. These penal regulations will be applied to statutory agent in case the persons are incompetent or minors.

14. These penal regulations will also be applied to persons who exhibit the films to the public in case the

violation was made not by him, but by his representative, members of his family or other of his employees.

15. These penal regulations will also be applied, in case of corporations, or their representatives.

Supplementary provisions:

This regulation is effective from July 1, 1925.

For those films inspected by former local regulation prior to the enforcement of the present provisions, the application of the present regulation is exempted for one year and six months following the enforcement.

APPENDIX 5

French Cinema Decree, February 18, 1928

Shortly after February 18, 1928, the *Film Daily* printed the following:

Text of the new official French decree which places the exhibition of all motion pictures in the hands of the Ministry of Public Instruction and Fine Arts, as translated from the Journal Officiel de la Republique Francaise:

Government Administration of Cinema Operation and Film Control.

The President of the French Republic,

On the recommendation of the President of the Council, Minister of Finance, the Minister of Public Instruction and Fine Arts and the Minister of the Interior,

In view of the opinion of the Keeper of the Seals and Minister of Justice, dated February 4, 1928, and the opinion of the Minister of Commerce and the Minister of the Interior, dated January 30, 1928;

In view of the laws of August 16 and 24, 1790, part XI, and April 3, 1884, article 97;

In view of the law of Pluviose 28 of the year VIII, article 16, and the decision of the consuls on Messidor 12 of the year VIII, article 12;

In view of the decrees of June 8, 1806, and January 6, 1864;

In view of the decree of July 25, 1919;

Appendix

In view of articles 49 and 50 of the law of December 31, 1921;

With the approval of the Council of States:

Decrees

Article 1. The opening and operation of motion picture theaters is permissable on condition that every person desiring to operate a cinema theater will submit a statement at least 15 days prior to the opening thereof to the Prefecture of Police, if in Paris, and to the Prefecture and Mayor of the commune of the department, if located in the provinces.

Article 2. This statement shall contain the following information:

a) The location of the theater.

b) The conditions under which it will be operated, especially as regards the provisions made for assuring the safety of the audience.

c) The full name, profession, domicile, place of birth and nationality of the proprietors, directors and operators.

d) If the theater is owned by a company, or is to be operated by a company, the members of its Board of Directors and a certified copy of its by-laws.

Receipt of this statement shall be acknowledged promptly.

The prefectural administration shall send a copy of this statement to the Minister of Public Instruction and Fine Arts.

Changes in the ownership, management or operation of cinema theaters must be reported under the same conditions as the first statement.

APPENDIX

Article 3.—The concessionaries and operators of cinema theaters must comply with all ordinances, decrees and regulations respecting public order, safety and sanitation.

The laws regarding the policing and closing of theaters shall be applicable to cinemas and the established fee for the benefit of the poor and the hospitals shall continue to be levied.

Article 4. The public projection of moving picture films shall be subjected to the control of the Minister of Public Instruction and Fine Arts.

With the exceptions determined by a ministerial decree to be issued based on the opinion of the Commission organized by virtue of Article 5 of this decree, no moving picture film may be shown to the public unless this film, including its titles and subtitles, has obtained the visa of the Minister of Public Instruction and Fine Arts.

This visa can be granted only on the proper recommendation of the Commission referred to in the preceding paragraph. This visa must appear in every film exhibited.

Every foreign film submitted for a visa must be presented in the exact and integral version as it was or is projected in the country of origin, and with an exact and integral reproduction of the title and subtitles, of which a French translation must be furnished.

Article 5. A Commission composed of 32 members, appointed by the Minister, shall be formed at the Ministry of Public Instruction and Fine Arts for the control of films.

This Commission will include: The Director General of Fine Arts, one of the Assistant Directors or Bureau

APPENDIX

Chiefs of the Department of Fine Arts, three representatives of the Ministry of Public Instruction and Fine Arts, four representatives of the Ministry of the Interior, one representative of the Ministry of Agriculture, one representative of the Ministry of Foreign Affairs, one representative of the Ministry of Colonies, one representative of the Ministry of Justice, one representative of the Ministry of Commerce, one representative of of the Ministry of War, one representative of the Ministry of Marine, two representatives of French producers of films, two representatives of French authors of films, two French directors of motion picture theaters and two French motion picture artists and eight persons chosen on account of their special competence.

The members of the Commission, other than those who are members by right of their official positions, are appointed for three years. They may be renominated.

The Director General of Fine Arts is President of the Commission. Two Vice-Presidents are appointed by the Minister of Public Instruction and Fine Arts.

Article 6. The Commission, after having examined the films, shall draw up a list of those approved for a visa.

In thus listing the films, the Commission shall take into consideration the whole of the national interests involved, and more particularly the interest in the conservation of national customs and traditions, and, also, in the case of foreign films, the facilities for the release of French films in the various countries of origin.

Article 7. The Minister of Public Instruction and Fine Arts shall appoint annually ten members of the

Commission, three of them representatives of the Ministry of the Interor, to form a permanent section headed by one of the vice-presidents of the Commission chosen by the Minister. The said Commission may delegate its powers to this permanent section as regards the examination of films and their eventual inclusion in the list provided for in the preceding article.

The Commission and its permanent section may permit authors and editors interested to submit written or oral observations.

Article 8. The members of the Commission and its permanent section shall be paid by means of "chits" given to each person present at a meeting, the value and the method of payment of which are fixed by a decree countersigned by the Minister of Public Instruction and Fine Arts and the Minister of Finances.

The fees for the censorship and visa of the films, including those for verifying the translations of the titles and subtitles, fixed according to the tariff established by law, shall be paid by the persons interested.

Article 9. The provisions of this decree do not limit local police measures that may be taken for the enforcement of the provisions of article 97 of the law of April 5, 1884, and, at Paris, of the law of August 16 and 24, 1790.

Article 10. This decree shall become effective beginning with March 1, 1928. It is applicable to Algeria.

Article 11. The President of the Council, Minister of Finance, the Minister of Public Instruction and Fine Arts, the Minister of the Interior, the Keeper of the Seals, Minister of Justice, the Minister of Foreign Affairs, the

Appendix

Minister of War, the Minister of the Marine, the Minister of Commerce and Industry, the Minister of Agriculture, the Minister of Colonies, are each charged, insofar as they are concerned, with the enforcement of this decree, which shall be published in the Journal Official of the French Republic and inserted in the Bulletin des Lois.

Done at Paris, February 18, 1928.

GASTON DOUMERGE.

By the President of the Republic:
The President of the Council, Minister of Finance,
RAYMOND POINCARE.
The Minister of Public Instruction and Fine Arts,
EDOUARD HERRIOT.
The Minister of the Interior,
ALBERT SARRAUT.
The Keeper of the Seals, Minister of Justice,
LOUIS BARTHOU.
The Minister of Foreign Affairs,
ARISTIDE BRIAND.
The Minister of War,
PAUL PAINLEVE.
The Minister of Marine,
GEORGE LEYGUES.
The Minister of Commerce and Industry,
MAURICE BOKANOWSKY.
The Minister of Agriculture,
HENRI QUEUILLE.
The Minister of the Colonies,
LEON PERRIER.

APPENDIX 6

Brief American statistical data on the motion picture industry.

According to the figures current in the industry in America, box office receipts in America and Canada are said to be about $750,000,000 a year. Of this sum $185,000,000 is said to be received by the distributors as film rentals. The cost of distribution is about 40% which on these figures equals $74,000,000 and leaves only $111,000,000 for the producers whose production costs are said to be about $93,000,000. The industry's tax returns in America for the year 1926 disclosed an unexplained production loss in excess of $16,000,000 and in 1925 a similar loss of over $11,000,000.

The foreign income of distributors in America, exclusive of Canada which is estimated at 4% of the American distributors' gross receipts, is said to be about $80,000,000 yearly. This sum is said to come from the countries of the world in the following percentages:

	Per Cent		Per Cent
Great Britain	40	Egypt, Syria and Palestine	½
France	3	South Africa	1
Belgium	2	Panama and Central America	¼
Switzerland	1	Mexico	2
Holland	1	Cuba	1¼
Spain and Portugal	2	West Indies	½
Italy	2½	Brazil	2½
Germany	10	Argentine, Uruguay, Paraguay, Bolivia and Ecuador	6
Czecho-Slovakia	1	China	½
Hungary	¾	India, Burma and Ceylon	1
Poland	1	Japan	4
Austria	¾	Philippines	¾
Baltic States	¼	Australia, New Zealand, Dutch East Indies and Straits Settlements	8
Jugo-Slavia, Roumania, Bulgaria, Turkey and Greece	1		
Scandinavia and Finland	6		

The 1928 *Film Year Book,* page 3, states that the yearly production budget is $175,000,000 and that there are 350,000 active workers in the industry, about one-third of this total being engaged in exhibition, including over 24,000 projectionists and production employees numbering 75,000.

Appendix

It is believed that these estimates, apart from the number of projectionists engaged in the industry, are highly inflated and in consequence not reliable.

It has been the common and almost universal practice to describe the motion picture industry as the fourth largest in the United States. This statement also is wholly without foundation.

The Biennial Census of Manufacturers, 1925, published by the Department of Commerce, which appeared in August, 1928, lists at pages 21 and 24 to 27 approximately 98 of the leading American industries.

The first 15 of these industries, with motor vehicles at the head of the list, have products valued at $1,000,000,000 or over.

The motion picture industry does not appear even in the list of the leading 98 industries of America.

The following figures with reference to the motion picture industry taken from page 1295 of the Census shows the largely inflated nature of the supposed statistical data in circulation throughout the industry.

Motion Pictures, Not Including Projection in Theatres.

Number of establishments	132
Total persons engaged in industry	11,565
Proprietors and firm members	47
Salaried officers and employees	5,945
Wage earners (average number)	5,573
Salaries	$35,950,778
Wages	13,065,756
Paid for contract work	5,368,593

APPENDIX

Cost of materials........................ 33,258,368
Value of products....................... 93,636,348
Value added by manufacture............... 60,377,980

THE PUBLIC AND MOTION PICTURE INDUSTRY
By William Marston Seabury

The following are some of the comments on this important and widely read book:

"There can be no question of the descriptive worth of his book." —*The Times (London) Literary Supp*lement.

" * * * already recognized as a 'standard work' * * * "
—*Daily Express (London.)*

" * * * an illuminating book * * * He has formulated proposals that demand careful consideration."
—*Lord Riddell in John O'London's Weekly.*

"A striking condemnation of the business methods of the American film 'Kings.' " —*Evening Express (Liverpool.)*

"In a very lucid exposition of the economic position of the film industry, Mr. Seabury * * * shows that America also is confronted with an undesirable monopoly."
—*Glasgow (Scotland) Herald.*

" * * * he speaks with authority." —*Manchester Guardian.*

" * * * by far the most profound analysis of the problems of the screen we have yet had." —*The Referee (London.)*

"A scathing denunciation of the business methods of the four or five American film 'kings.. "
—*The Westminster.. Gazette.*

" * * * a brilliant summary of the history of the business in America. —*London Evening News.*

"A valuable book, especially because it was written and published in America."—*Dr. R. Otto, in The Film Kurier (Berlin.)*

"Mr. Seabury's book contains much food for thought."
—*Evening Transcript (Boston, Mass.).*

"A fascinating survey of the movie world."
—*George Currie in the Weekly Book Review of the Brooklyn Eagle.*

"The book is crowded full of interesting facts."
—*St. Louis Globe Democrat.*

" * * * unquestionably the most significant book yet written on the problem of motion pictures * * * Mr. Seabury has produced a notable work which will prove an invaluable contribution toward the ultimate solution of the question."
—*Educational Screen (Chicago.)*

"This book is the only true explanation of the structure and practice of the motion picture business."
—*Frank J. Rembusch, president of the Motion Picture Theatre Owners of Indiana.*

INDEX

A

Advance Theatrical Company, 35
Advisory Committees of the League, 173
Alsace, 120
American Irish Vigilance Committee, 80
Angell, Norman, 48, 50, 51, 52
Annals of The American Academy of Political and Social Science, 21, 40
Anti Trust Laws (U.S.A.), 189
Anti War Treaties of August 27, 1928, 110, 111, 113
Arbitration Boards, 34, 36
Assembly of the League of Nations, 171
Associated First National Pictures, 200
Association of Motion Picture Producers, Inc., of California, 200
Atlantic Monthly, 58
Australia, 30, 67
Australian Red Cross, 32
Austria, 32, 142, 157

B

Baldwin, Stanley, 26
Banergi, Sir Albion, 55
Basle Congress, 162
Bausbeck, Dr., 160
Beith, Ian Hay, 87
Belgium, 32, 67, 71, 157
Belgium Film Censorship, 185
Belgium Red Cross, 31
Berlin, 74
Berlin Congress, 159
Berliner Tageblatt, 68
Better Films Movement, 147
Birkenhead, Lord, 96, 97, 102
Bismarck, Prince Otto V., 46, 47
Bogdonowicz, Dr., 30
Bombay, 91
Borah, Senator, 104
Brazil, 32, 67, 78, 79, 143, 219
Briand, M. Aristide, 62, 111
British Board of Film Censors, 99, 100, 185, 392
British Empire, 172
British Films, 22, 26
British Cinematograph Films Bill, 23, 29, 168, 206
British International Company, 94
British War Council, 87
Brussels, 31
Budget of League of Nations, 175
Butler, D. Nicholas Murray, 22, 104, 112, 228

C

Calcutta, 91
Canada, 60, 172
Catechism on Motion Pictures in Interstate Commerce by William Sheafe Chase, D.D., 198
Cavell, Edith, 68, 95, 96, 98, 103, 104, 105, 106, 107, 115
Cavell, Edith, Hospital, 106
Cecil, Lord Robert, 208

419

INDEX

Censorship, 184
Censorship Regulations, 183-190, 383-407
Chamberlain, Sir Austen, 98, 102, 208
Chase, Rev. Canon William Sheafe, D.D., 22, 198
Chesterton G. K., 56, 57
Child Welfare Committee of the League of Nations, 143, 144, 147, 151, 162, 173, 176, 219
Chile, 172
China, 22, 92, 172, 211, 215
Cippico, Count, 163
Claudel, M. Paul, 61, 62, 63
Columbia, 172
Commercial reconstruction, 218
Commercial & Financial Chronicle, 36.
Committee on Arts and Letters, 165, 166
Committee on Economics, 176, 178
Committee on Intellectual Cooperation, 148, 150, 158, 166, 170, 173, 176, 209
Committee on the Judiciary (U. S. Senate), 35
Committee on the Traffic in Women and Children, 173
Committee on Transit and Communications, 176, 178
Connick, H. D. H., 40
Cornelissen, Fred, 159
Council of League of Nations, 144, 171, 172
Covenant of the League, 173, 174
Crowd, The, A Study of the Public Mind, by Gustav LeBon, 49
Cuba, 32, 172
Cunliffe-Lister, Sir Philip, 28

D

deCasseres, Benjamin, 40, 49, 50
Delhi, India, 90
deMille, Cecil B., Pictures Corporation, 200
Demosthenes, 118
Denmark, 32, 71
Department of Commerce (U.S.A.), 33, 109
Department of Justice (U.S.A.), 34, 35, 101, 109
de Rivera, General Primo, 78
de Reynold, M., 162
Deulig, 75
Diest, 88
Dominican Republic, 32
Duranty, Walter 82
Dutch East Indies, 67

E

Eastman, Max, 81
Echo, 75
Economic Committee of League of Nations, 36, 151
Economic Conference of League of Nations, 131, 137
Economic Convention, 137, 138 139, 140.
Economic Organization of the Soviet Union, 81
Economic reconstruction, 218
Economic Treaty of November 8, 1927, 135, 136, 143
Educational Cinema Institute at Rome, 163, 164
Educational Film Exchanges, 200
Educational Screen, 40
Egypt, 67, 88
Eighth Commission of International Cinema Congress, 157
Eliot, Charles W., 121, 123
Emelka, 75
Ems, 46, 47
England, 26, 55, 56, 65, 71, 100, 150, 157, 167, 191, 231
Eskay Harris Feature Film Co., 34
Euripides, 118
Executive control, 126, 127

INDEX

F

Famous Players Lasky Corporation, 33, 35, 66, 109, 160, 200
Fanshawe Maurice, 175, 176, 180 211, 212, 213, 214, 215
Far East 22, 28, 29, 84, 85, 230
Fay, H. van V., 36
F. B. O. Pictures Corporation, 200
Federal censorship, 80
Federal regulation, 117
Federal Trade Commission, 33, 34, 35, 88, 109, 169
Film Arbitration Boards, 34, 36
Film Boards of Trade, 34, 35, 36
Film Daily, 23, 55, 63, 75, 77, 81, 82, 90, 92, 148, 149, 150, 153, 154, 159
Film import inspectors, 191
Film inspection, 180, 194, 195, 197, 218, 225, 226, 227, 229
Film Year Book 1926, 184, 185, 186
Finland, 172
First National Pictures, Inc., 35, 109, 200
Foch, Marshal, 67
Foreign, Censorship Regulations, 392
Foreign Relations Committee (U. S. Senate), 213
"Formula," 147
Fourth Commission of International Cinema Congress, 155, 220
Fox Film Corporation, 33, 34, 200
Fox, William, 21
Fox, William, Vaudeville Corporation, 200
France, 47, 58, 61, 62, 63, 64, 65, 66, 67, 70, 77, 78, 93, 115, 116, 131, 132, 134, 142, 154, 157, 172, 192, 209, 214
Franco-Prussian War, 46
French Association of Motion Picture Exhibitors, 63, 64
French Cinema Decree of February 18, 1928, 131, 134, 135, 136, 137, 141, 178, 203, 206, 407
French film censorship 186, 395
French government, 63
French Minister of Education, 137
French National Committee of Intellectual Cooperation, 149
French pictures, 132, 135, 140

G

Gallie, M. Louis, 159
Galsworthy, John, 165
General Film Company, 58
Geneva 1926, by H. Wilson Harris, 175, 208, 212
Geneva League Council, 74
Gerard, James W., 102 107
German Imperial General Staff, 76
Germany, 32, 58, 65, 68, 69, 74, 75, 76, 77, 87, 88, 91, 104, 119, 142, 150, 154, 157, 172, 192
Goldwyn Pictures Corporation, 200
Gouraud, General, 67
Government control, 117
Government film monopoly, (Italy), 94, 95
Grant, A. J., 46
Great Britain, 29, 58, 195, 214, 230,
Greenwood, A., 167, 168

H

Hague Convention of 1912, 212, 213
Hardy, Jack, 81
Harris, H. Wilson, 175, 208, 212
Harvard Graduate School of Business Administration, 54
Havre, 61
Hays Association, 34, 107, 153
Hays, Will H., 149
Health Organization, 176

INDEX

Henderson's *Federal Trade Commisson*, 169
Herriot, M., 206
Herriot Commission, 57
Herron, Maj. F. L., 149, 150
Hindenberg, President von, 68, 71, 73
Hodkinson, W. W., 35
Holland, 67, 71, 157, 172, 214
Hollywood, 57, 58, 61, 65, 66, 78, 83, 86, 91
Hoover, Herbert, 27
House of Commons, 100
Hugenberg, Alfred, 73, 75
Hughes, Charles Evans, 23
Humbert, Dr. F., 29, 143
Hungarian government, 60
Hungary, 32, 157

I

India, 90, 142, 210, 214
Indian film censorship, 186, 397
Indies, 84
Industrial Property Convention, 33
International cinema accord, 178, 189
International Alliance, 128
International Chamber of Commerce, 206, 207
International Committee of Intellectual Cooperation, 161, 162, 164
International control, 128, 204
International Convention, 131
International Economic Conference, 33, 36
International Federation of the Cinematographic Press, 157
International Federation of Students, 157
International Federaton of Trade Unions, 90
International Institute of Intellectual Cooperation, 156, 159, 177, 210
International Institute of Private Law in Rome, 156

International Labor Office, 157, 174, 176, 178, 205
International Literary and Artistic Association, 157
International Motion Picture Congress at Paris, 29, 133, 147, 149, 150, 151, 152, 153, 154, 155, 156, 158, 159, 161, 170, 176, 191, 206, 219, 357
International Office for Educational and Social Welfare Films, 162
International Opium Convention, 212
International Trade Agreements, 219
Irish race, 79, 80
Irish World, 80
Italian film censorship, 186
Italy, 71, 78, 92, 93, 94, 95, 142, 157, 163, 192, 401

J

Japan, 171, 214
Japanese film censorship, 186, 403
Joffre, Marshal, 67
Jugoslavia, 211

K

Kaiser, ex-, 71, 73
Kahn, Otto, 102, 103
Kellogg, Dr. Vernon, 165
Kendell, Herr von, 91
Kent, Sidney R., 54
Kenworthy, Lieut.-Comdr. J. M., 112, 113
Klein, Dr. Julius, 28
Kollontai, Madame, 83
Krows, Arthur Edwin, 21, 40

L

Laemmle, 21
Latin America, 77, 232
League, The, by Sir Austen Chamberlain, 208

INDEX

League Conference for the Suppression of the Traffic in Obscene Publications, 145
League of Nations, 144, 171, 172
LeBon, Gustav, 49, 51
Lecky, William Edward Hartpole, 47
Legislative control, 126, 127
Loew, Marcus, 21
Lohmann, Capt., 75
London Daily Telegraph, 97
London Times, 84, 95, 101
Loos, Anita, 83
Lowry, Col. Edward J., 153
Luchaire, M. Julien, 21, 28, 147, 157
Ludendorff, 73

M

MacCormack, D. W., 211
MacCormack, John, 86
MacDonald, Ramsaye, 23
Mackensen, 71
Madras, 91
Malaya, 86
Manitoba, 144, 219
Martin, Everett Dean, 45
Maryland Board of Censors, 184, 383
Marx, Chancellor, 74
Mayer, Louis B., 33
Mayor of New York, 103
Mencken, H. L., 21, 104, 105
Metro-Goldwyn-Mayer Distributing Corporation, 35, 66, 75, 76, 77, 88, 109, 160, 200
Mexico, 77
Midi (Paris), 111
Milton, John, 118
Minister of Public Instruction and Fine Arts (France), 131
Mitchell, Peter Chalmers, 44, 45, 46
Moskowitz, Charles C., 107
Moslems, 90
Motion pictures as a new public utility, 190, 217
Motion Picture Producers and Distributors of America, Inc., 34, 36, 58, 107, 108, 147, 150, 200
Motion Pictures Today, 22, 27, 40, 50, 78, 79, 107
Munsterberg, 119, 122, 123
Mussolini, Premier, 92, 93, 94, 95

N

National Association of Motion Picture Industry, 198, 200
National Board of Review, 127, 147, 198
National Committee for Better Films, 147
National Committees of Proposed International Cinema Committee, 223, 232
National tariffs, 134
National and international film inspection, 143, 144, 145
Nearing, Scott, 81
New York City, 60
New York Evening Sun, 22, 84, 166
New York Herald Tribune, 65
New York State Censorship Commission, 101, 385
New York Times, 23, 24, 26, 28, 32, 57, 60, 61, 65, 66, 67, 68, 69, 70, 71, 72, 73, 74, 75, 79, 83, 84, 86, 89, 90, 91, 93, 95, 97, 98, 99, 100, 101, 102, 104, 106, 107, 111, 132, 136, 149, 206, 211
New York World, 21, 170
New Zealand 67
Non-permanent members of the Council of League of Nations, 172
North America, 27
Norway, 60, 71, 143, 219

O

Obscene films, 145
O'Connor, T. P., 99

INDEX

Ohio State Board of Censors, 184, 387
Open Conspiracy, The, by H. G. Wells, 112
Opium Committee of the League, 210
Opium Conference, 212, 215
Observatore Romano, 23, 210

P

Pan American Conference, 78, 79
Paramount Famous Lasky Corporation, 35, 109, 136, 200
Paris Agreement of the International Union for Protection of Industrial Property, 32
Parliament, 100
Parliamentary Debates, 23, 26, 28, 29
Pathe Consortium, 61
Pathe Exchange, Inc., 200
Peace and America, The, by Hugo Munsterberg, 119
Peekskill Theatre, Inc., 35
Pennsylvania Board of Censors, 185, 389
Permanent Court of International Justice, 112
Permanent International Organization, 156, 157, 160
Permanent members of the Council of the League, 172
Persia, 211, 215
Persian Commission, 211
Petain, Marshal, 67
Phoebus Films, 75
Poland, 74, 172
Polish Red Cross, 29
Porter, Stephen G., 213
Portugal, 32, 214
Preamble of the Covenant of League of Nations, 170
Press, The, by Sir Alfred Robbins, 118

Proposed international accord, 184, 193, 194, 204
Proposed cinema alliance, 116, 191, 204
Proposed Cinema Committee of League of Nations, 146, 155, 159, 169, 177, 178, 179, 180, 181, 188, 190, 191, 192, 194, 203, 205, 216, 217, 218, 219, 220, 223, 231
Proposed International Committee of Film Experts, 152
Proposed film inspection law, 195, 196
Public and Motion Picture Industry, The, 22, 23, 25, 26, 34, 40, 133, 135, 147, 190
Public Mind, Its Disorders; Its Exploitation, by Norman Angell, 48, 50, 52
Pushkin, Alexander, 82

Q

Quotas of pictures, 224

R

Ramsaye, Terry, 20, 21, 40, 190
Rangoon, 91
Rathenau, 71
Real Situation in Russia, The, Leon Trotsky, 81
Reapportionment of world trade, 133, 193, 204, 224
Reconstruction, by Maurice Fanshawe, 175, 176, 180, 211, 214
Redesdale, Lord, 46
Resolution of Committee on Child Welfare pertaining to the cinema, 177
Resolutions of International Motion Picture Congress, 357-382
Resolutions of National Association of Motion Picture Industry, adopted 1921, 198
Robbins, Sir Alfred, 118

INDEX

Rocco, M., 162
Ross, Alsworth, 29
Roumania, 54, 172
Russia, 80, 81, 83
Russian Revolution, 82

S

Salvador, 172
Sand, Dr. Rene, 161
Scandinavian countries, 192
Schenck, Nicholas M., 107
Secretariat of the League, 172
Secretary of the Treasury (U.S.A.), 101
Selwyn, Arch, 102, 106
Serbia, 32
Serruys, M. D., 36, 134
Shaw, George Bernard, 37, 38, 50, 100, 105
Sheehan, Winfield, 71
Sherwood, George H., 60
Siam, 214
Simmons, Senator, 36
Snowden, Rt. Hon. Philip, 167, 168
Socrates, 118
Sophocles, 48
South America, 27
Soviet Kino, 84
Spain, 32, 65, 71, 77
Spanish government, 60
Spanish Premiere, 77
The Spokesman, 80
Steed, Wickham, 62
Story of the Films, The, 28, 54
State Department (U.S.A.), 109
Stresemann, Foreign Minister, 74, 99
Sweden, 32, 71, 87, 143, 157, 219
Switzerland, 32, 67, 157

T

Taegliche, Rundschau, 76, 99
Tage, 76

Tageblatt, 68, 69
Tariff systems, 141
Technical organizatons of the League, 173
Temperley, Harold, 46
Tolstoy, 82
Trade Conference of October 1927, 200
Transvaal, 143, 219
Treaties, Tariff Systems and Contractual Methods, by M. D. Serruys, 134
Triangle Film Corporation, 33
Trotsky, Leon, 81
Trust Laws and Unfair Competition, 33
Turkey, 91, 143, 211, 215, 219

U

Ufa, 66, 69, 71, 73, 75, 76, 94, 160
Union of South Africa, 143, 219
United Artists Corporation, 200
United International Bureaux of Industrial, Literary and Artistic Property at Berne, 156
United States, 58, 64, 131, 137, 211
U. S. Tariff Act of 1922, 101
Universal Film Manufacturing Company, 200
Untermeyer, Samuel, 117
Upper Silesia, 74, 89

V

Valentino, Rudolf, 75
Variety, 60, 77, 81, 92, 132
Vilallonga, M. Jose de, 159
Vitagraph Company of America, 33, 200
Vossiche, Zeitung, 89

W

Walsh, Senator, 34
Warner Brothers Picture Company, 200

Index

Wells, A. G., 21, 112
West Coast Theatres, Inc., 35, 109
Wets, Paul, 31
Wilson, Hugh E., 131, 137
Wilson, President Woodrow, 35, 36, 37, 169
World War, 48

Y

Young, Allyn A., 36

Z

Zukor, Adolph, 21, 107, 136, 137

ASPECTS OF FILM

An Arno Press Collection

Adler, Mortimer J. **Art and Prudence.** 1937
Conant, Michael. **Anti-Trust in the Motion Picture Industry.** 1960
Croy, Homer. **How Motion Pictures Are Made.** 1918
Drinkwater, John. **The Life and Adventures of Carl Laemmle.** 1931
Hacker, Leonard. **Cinematic Design.** 1931
Hepworth, T[homas] C[raddock]. **The Book of the Lantern.** 1899
Johnston, Alva. **The Great Goldwyn.** 1937
Klingender, F.D. and Stuart Legg. **Money Behind the Screen.** 1937
Limbacher, James L. **Four Aspects of the Film.** 1969
Manvell, Roger, ed. **The Cinema 1950.** 1950
Manvell, Roger, ed. **The Cinema 1951.** 1951
Manvell, Roger, ed. **The Cinema 1952.** 1952
Marchant, James, ed. **The Cinema in Education.** 1925
Mayer, J.P. **British Cinemas and Their Audiences.** 1948
Sabaneev, Leonid. **Music for the Films.** 1935
Seabury, William Marston. **Motion Picture Problems.** 1929
Seldes, Gilbert. **The Movies Come from America.** 1937
U.S. House of Representatives, Committee on Education. **Motion Picture Commission: Hearings.** 1914
U.S. House of Representatives, Committee on Education. **Federal Motion Picture Commission: Hearings.** 1916
U.S. Senate, Temporary National Economic Committee. **Investigation of Concentration of Economic Power.** 1941
Weinberg, Herman G. **Josef von Sternberg.** 1967